Data Quality

THE ACCURACY DIMENSION

Acquisitions Editor	Lothlórien Homet
Publishing Services Manager	Edward Wade
Editorial Assistant	Corina Derman
Project Management	Elisabeth Beller
Cover Design	Frances Baca
Cover Image	EyeWire of Getty Images
Text Design	Frances Baca
Technical Illustration	Dartmouth Publishing, Inc.
Composition	Nancy Logan
Copyeditor	Daril Bentley
Proofreader	Jennifer McClain
Indexer	Steve Rath
Interior Printer	The Maple-Vail Book Manufacturing Group
Cover Printer	Phoenix Color Corporation

Designations used by companies to distinguish their products are often claimed as trademarks or registered trademarks. In all instances in which Morgan Kaufmann Publishers is aware of a claim, the product names appear in initial capital or all capital letters. Readers, however, should contact the appropriate companies for more complete information regarding trademarks and registration.

Morgan Kaufmann Publishers
An Imprint of Elsevier
340 Pine Street, Sixth Floor
San Francisco, CA 94104-3205
www.mkp.com

07   5   4   3

Permissions may be sought directly from Elsevier's Science and Technology Rights Department in Oxford, UK. Phone: (44) 1865 843830, Fax: (44) 1865 853333, e-mail: permissions@elsevier.co.uk. You may also complete your request on-line via the Elsevier homepage: http://www.elsevier.com by selecting "Customer Support" and then "Obtaining Permissions".

Library of Congress Control Number: 2002112508

ISBN-13: 978-1-55860-891-7
ISBN-10: 1-55860-891-5

This book is printed on acid-free paper.

Data Quality

THE ACCURACY DIMENSION

Jack E. Olson

*Understanding the concepts of
accurate data is fundamental to
improving the ways we collect
and use data.*

MORGAN KAUFMANN PUBLISHERS

An Imprint of Elsevier

AMSTERDAM   BOSTON   LONDON   NEW YORK
OXFORD   PARIS   SAN DIEGO   SAN FRANCISCO
SINGAPORE   SYDNEY   TOKYO

to Jean

FOREWORD
Colin White
President, Intelligent Business Strategies

Over the past thirty years I have helped organizations in many different countries design and deploy a wide range of IT applications. Throughout this time, the topic of data accuracy and quality has been ever present during both the development and the operation of these applications. In many instances, however, even though the IT development group and business managers recognized the need for improved data quality, time pressures to get the project in production prevented teams from addressing the data quality issue in more than a superficial manner.

Lack of attention to data quality and accuracy in enterprise systems can have downstream ramifications. I remember working with an overseas bank on a data warehousing system a few years ago. The bank was struggling with delivering consistent business intelligence to the bank's business users. On one occasion, a business manager discovered that financial summary data in the data warehouse was wrong by many millions of dollars. I visited the bank several months later, and I was told that the reason for the error had still not been found. Trying to analyze a data quality problem caused by upstream applications is time consuming and expensive. The problem must be corrected at the source before the error is replicated to other applications.

Lack of accuracy in data not only erodes end-user confidence in IT applications, it can also have a significant financial impact on the business. As I write this, I am reading a report from the Data Warehousing Institute on data quality that estimates that poor-quality customer data costs U.S. businesses a staggering $611 billion a year in postage, printing, and staff overhead. The same report states that nearly 50% of the companies surveyed have no plans for managing or improving data quality. At the same time, almost half the survey respondents think the quality of their data is worse than everyone thinks.

These results clearly demonstrate a gap between perception and reality regarding the quality of data in many corporations. The report goes on to state that "although some companies understand the importance of high-quality data, most are oblivious to the true business impact of defective or substandard data." To solve this problem, companies need to become more educated about the importance of both data quality and techniques to improve it. This is especially important given that the world economy is becoming more and more information driven. Companies with access to timely and accurate information have a significant business advantage over their competitors.

I must admit that when I was approached to write the foreword for this book, I had some reservations. As a practitioner, I have found that books on data quality are often very theoretical and involve esoteric concepts that are difficult to relate to real-world applications. In truth, I have a suspicion this may be one reason why less attention is given to data quality than in fact it deserves. We need education that enables designers and developers to apply data quality concepts and techniques easily and rapidly to application development projects.

When I read this book I was pleasantly surprised, and my concerns in this regard vanished. The author, Jack Olson, has a background that enables him to address the topic of data quality and accuracy from a practical viewpoint. As he states in the preface, "Much of the literature on data quality discusses what I refer to as the outside-in approach. This book covers the inside-out approach. To make the inside-out approach work, you need good analytical tools and a talented and experienced staff of data analysts . . . . You also need a thorough understanding of what the term *inaccurate data* means." The bottom line for me is that the book presents techniques that you can immediately apply to your applications projects. I hope that you will find the book as useful as I did and that the ideas presented will help you improve the quality and accuracy of the data in your organization.

CONTENTS

Foreword vii
Preface xv

PART I

Understanding Data Accuracy 1

CHAPTER 1 The Data Quality Problem 3

1.1   Data Is a Precious Resource 3
1.2   Impact of Continuous Evolution of Information Systems 5
1.3   Acceptance of Inaccurate Data 8
1.4   The Blame for Poor-Quality Data 9
1.5   Awareness Levels 10
1.6   Impact of Poor-Quality Data 12
1.7   Requirements for Making Improvements 14
1.8   Expected Value Returned for Quality Program 15
1.9   Data Quality Assurance Technology 16
1.10 Closing Remarks 22

CHAPTER 2 Definition of Accurate Data 24

2.1   Data Quality Definitions 24
2.2   Principle of Unintended Uses 27
2.3   Data Accuracy Defined 29
2.4   Distribution of Inaccurate Data 32
2.5   Can Total Accuracy Be Achieved? 34
2.6   Finding Inaccurate Values 35
2.7   How Important Is It to Get Close? 40
2.8   Closing Remarks 41

CHAPTER 3 Sources of Inaccurate Data..........................43

3.1 Initial Data Entry 44
3.2 Data Accuracy Decay 50
3.3 Moving and Restructuring Data 52
3.4 Using Data 62
3.5 Scope of Problems.. 63
3.6 Closing Remarks.. 64

PART II

Implementing a Data Quality Assurance Program 65

CHAPTER 4 Data Quality Assurance 67

4.1 Goals of a Data Quality Assurance Program.................... 68
4.2 Structure of a Data Quality Assurance Program................ 69
4.3 Closing Remarks.. 78

CHAPTER 5 Data Quality Issues Management 80

5.1 Turning Facts into Issues 81
5.2 Assessing Impact 85
5.3 Investigating Causes 87
5.4 Developing Remedies 94
5.5 Implementing Remedies 99
5.6 Post-implementation Monitoring 99
5.7 Closing Remarks.. 101

CHAPTER 6 The Business Case for Accurate Data 103

6.1 The Value of Accurate Data 103
6.2 Costs Associated with Achieving Accurate Data................ 108
6.3 Building the Business Case 108
6.4 Closing Remarks.. 118

PART III

Data Profiling Technology............................... 119

CHAPTER 7 Data Profiling Overview 121

7.1   Goals of Data Profiling.................................. 122
7.2   General Model.. 123
7.3   Data Profiling Methodology............................. 130
7.4   Analytical Methods Used in Data Profiling 136
7.5   When Should Data Profiling Be Done? 140
7.6   Closing Remarks 141

CHAPTER 8 Column Property Analysis 143

8.1   Definitions... 143
8.2   The Process for Profiling Columns 152
8.3   Profiling Properties for Columns 155
8.4   Mapping with Other Columns 167
8.5   Value-Level Remedies................................... 169
8.6   Closing Remarks 171

CHAPTER 9 Structure Analysis............................ 173

9.1   Definitions... 173
9.2   Understanding the Structures Being Profiled............. 187
9.3   The Process for Structure Analysis 188
9.4   The Rules for Structure................................ 193
9.5   Mapping with Other Structures 210
9.6   Structure-Level Remedies............................... 212
9.7   Closing Remarks 213

CHAPTER 10 Simple Data Rule Analysis..................... 215

10.1   Definitions... 216
10.2   The Process for Analyzing Simple Data Rules 220
10.3   Profiling Rules for Single Business Objects 225
10.4   Mapping with Other Applications....................... 230
10.5   Simple Data Rule Remedies 232
10.6   Closing Remarks 235

CHAPTER 11 Complex Data Rule Analysis 237

11.1   Definitions... 237
11.2   The Process for Profiling Complex Data Rules........... 238

11.3 Profiling Complex Data Rules 240
11.4 Mapping with Other Applications 244
11.5 Multiple-Object Data Rule Remedies. 245
11.6 Closing Remarks 245

CHAPTER 12 Value Rule Analysis 246

12.1 Definitions 246
12.2 Process for Value Rule Analysis 247
12.3 Types of Value Rules 249
12.4 Remedies for Value Rule Violations 252
12.5 Closing Remarks 253

CHAPTER 13 Summary 255

13.1 Data Quality Is a Major Issue for Corporations. 255
13.2 Moving to a Position of High Data Quality Requires
        an Explicit Effort 256
13.3 Data Accuracy Is the Cornerstone for Data Quality Assurance 257

APPENDIX A Examples of Column Properties,
Data Structure, Data Rules, and Value Rules 260

A.1 Business Objects 260
A.2 Tables. 260
A.3 Column Properties 263
A.4 Structure Rules 266
A.5 Simple Data Rules 269
A.6 Complex Data Rules 270
A.7 Value Rules 271

APPENDIX B Content of a Data Profiling Repository 272

B.1 Schema Definition. 272
B.2 Business Objects 272
B.3 Domains 273
B.4 Data Source 273
B.5 Table Definitions. 274
B.6 Synonyms 276
B.7 Data Rules. 277
B.8 Value Rules 277
B.9 Issues 278

References 279

Books on Data Quality Issues 279
Books on Data Quality Technologies 279
Articles 281

Index 283

About the Author 294

PREFACE

This book is about *data accuracy*. Data accuracy is part of the larger topic of data quality. The quality of data is measured against a number of dimensions: accuracy, relevance, timeliness, completeness, trust, and accessibility. The accuracy dimension is the foundation measure of the quality of data. If the data is just not right, the other dimensions are of little importance.

The book has many goals. The first is to demonstrate and characterize the data quality problem that affects all large organizations. Hopefully it will increase awareness of problems and help motivate corporations to spend more dollars to address the problem. The next goal is to outline the functions of a data quality assurance group that would bring considerable valuable to any corporation. The third goal is to promote the use of data-intensive analytical techniques as a valuable tool for executing data quality assurance activities.

Data quality is getting more and more attention in corporations. Companies are discovering that their data is generally of poor quality. This, coupled with the fact that companies are trying to squeeze more and more value from their data, leads to the greater concern. This is costing them money and opportunities. Improving the quality of data produces valuable financial returns to those who diligently pursue it.

The technology for identifying quality problems and dealing with them has lagged behind technology advances in other areas. Because of the awakening of corporations to this problem, newer technologies are coming forward to help address this important topic. One of them is *data profiling:* the use of analytical techniques to discover the true content, structure, and quality of data.

This book discusses the use of data profiling technology as the central strategy for a data quality assurance program. It defines inaccurate data, demonstrates how data profiling is used to ferret out inaccurate data, and shows how this is put together in a larger data quality program to achieve meaningful results.

Data quality assurance groups fundamentally operate by identifying quality problems and then fabricating remedies. They can do the first part through either an outside-in approach or an inside-out approach. The outside-in approach looks within the business for evidence of negative impacts on the corporation that may be a derivative of data quality problems. The types of evidence sought are returned merchandise, modified orders, customer complaints, lost customers, delayed reports, and rejected reports. The outside-in approach then takes the problems to the data to determine if the data caused the problems, and the scope of the problems.

The inside-out approach starts with the data. Analytical techniques are used to find inaccurate data. The inaccurate data is then studied to determine impacts on the business that either have already occurred or that may occur in the future. This strategy then leads to remedies much like those of the outside-in approach.

Much of the literature on data quality discusses what I refer to as the outside-in approach. This book covers the inside-out approach. To make the inside-out approach work, you need good analytical tools and a talented and experienced staff of data analysts that understands the business and can dig problems out of the data. You also need a thorough understanding of what the term *inaccurate data* means.

This book is divided into three parts. The first part defines inaccurate data, shows the scope of problems that exist in the real world, and covers how data becomes inaccurate. The intent is to provide a thorough understanding of the basic concepts of data inaccuracies and how this fits into the larger data quality topic.

The second part covers how a data quality assurance program is constructed with the inside-out approach. It covers the methodology used, the skills needed, and the general business cases for justifying projects targeting corporate databases.

The third part focuses on the technology of data profiling. It describes the basic concept of the technology and shows how individual parts contribute to the overall result. It covers some of the techniques used to expose inaccurate data and gives examples from the real world.

This topic is applicable to all sorts of organizations. Corporations, government organizations, educational organizations, and large nonprofit organizations all have information system departments that build and maintain large databases. They all depend on these databases for executing their daily tasks and for making large and small decisions that can have huge impacts on the success or failure of their enterprises. The importance of these databases and the accuracy of the data in them is no different for any of them. Although I use the term *corporation* in this book, you can assume that what I am saying applies equally to all types of organizations.

The target data for this book is structured data captured in corporate databases. This is predominantly record-keeping data dealing with orders, invoices, expenditures, personnel, payroll, inventory, customer data, supplier data, and much more. Data enthusiasts frequently note that only 20% of the data in a corporation is stored in corporate databases. The other 80% of the data consists of reports, memos, letters, e-mails, diagrams, blueprints, and other noncoded, nonstructured information. Although this is true, the structured 20% in the databases generally constitutes the heart and soul of the company's operations. Its value is certainly greater than 20%.

The audience for this book includes several groups of people. The primary target is those practitioners who are directly involved in data quality assurance or improvement programs. This gives them a strong framework for defining and executing a program based on the inside-out strategy. Other data management professionals who will be interacting with the data quality staff on a regular basis should also know this material. This includes data analysts, business analysts, database administrators, data administrators, data stewards, data architects, and data modelers.

Directly related to this group are the information management managers and executives who support this effort. The book specifically provides information on the scope of the quality problem and the potential for gaining back some of the value lost that should be of direct interest to IT management, chief information officer, chief technology officer, and chief knowledge officer executives and their staffs. It should also appeal to managers in data consumption areas who are heavily involved as part of the information process.

This book provides considerable benefit to application developers, system designers, and others who help build and maintain the information systems we use. Understanding the concepts of accurate data will likely result in better-designed systems that produce better data.

This book is also applicable to students of computer science. They should gain an appreciation of the topic of data quality in their studies in order to better prepare them to assume roles in industry for creating and maintaining information systems. Knowledge of this topic is becoming more valuable all the time, and those information systems professionals who are schooled in the concepts will be more valuable than those who are not. Data quality is becoming more commonplace as part of the curriculum of computer science. This book could serve as a textbook or a reference book for those studies.

Data quality problems are not relegated exclusively to large corporations with formal information system departments and professional data management staff. Inaccuracies occur in databases of all sizes. Although most small companies and some mid-range companies do not have formal organizations, they all have data that drives their operations and on which they base important business decisions. The general concepts in this book would be valuable to this audience as well. Although the employees of these companies would not normally immerse themselves in this topic, the consulting and software development firms that support their applications and operations would be better off if they understood these concepts and incorporated them into their practices.

Acknowledgments

Most of my knowledge on this topic has come from working in the field of data management. I have been involved in the design and development of commercial software for database or data management for most of my career. As such, I have been in countless IT shops and talked with countless application developers, database administrators, data analysts, business analysts, IT directors, chief information officers, chief technology officers, and chief executive officers about data management issues. Most of these conversations consisted of them telling me what was wrong with products I developed or what problems I have not yet solved. All of this has helped shape my thinking about what is important.

I have also read many books on the topic of data management over the years. I have read books by, interacted with, and absorbed as much as I could from the gurus of data quality. Those I have particular admiration for are Richard Wang, Ph.D., from Massachusetts Institute of Technology and co-director for the Total Data Quality Management program at M.I.T.; Larry English, president of Information Impact; Thomas Redman, Ph.D., president of Navesink Consulting Group; Peter Aiken, Ph.D., from Virginia Commonwealth University; and David Loshin, president of Knowledge Integrity Incorporated. Anyone interested in the field of data quality needs to become familiar with the work of these experts.

Those closer to me that have helped bring this book to completion through their professional interaction with me at Evoke Software include Lacy Edwards, Art DeMaio, Harry Carter, Jim Lovingood, Bill Rose, Maureen Ellis, Ed Lindsey, Chris Bland, John Howe, Bill Bagnell, Shawn Wikle, Andy Galewsky, Larry Noe, and Jeffrey Millman. They have all, in some way, contributed to the content, and I thank them for the many hours of conversations on this topic. If I have left someone's name out that has helped me understand this topic, please forgive me. There are so many that I could not list them all, let alone remember them all.

PART I

Understanding Data Accuracy

Data quality is gaining visibility daily as an important element in data management. More and more companies are discovering that data quality issues are causing large losses in money, time, and missed opportunities. The cost of poor quality is usually hidden and not obvious to those not looking for it.

Data management technology has focused on the containers we put data in. We have made huge strides in developing robust database management software, transaction monitors, data replication services, security support, and backup and recovery services. These are all technologies that support the efficient gathering, storage, and protection of data. We have also created an extensive technology for accessing data. Data warehouse, data mart, data mining, and decision support technologies have all seen explosive growth, along with a great deal of sophistication.

With all of this, we have not done much about the actual data itself. Data quality technology has lagged behind these other areas. The robustness of the other technologies has brought about rapid growth in the amount of data we collect and the uses we put it to.

The lack of managing the content is now beginning to emerge as a major problem. Companies all over the globe are instituting data quality improvement programs. They are looking for education and tools to help them begin to get the content to the same level of robustness as the containers that hold it.

The first three chapters position data accuracy within the larger topic of data quality. They define the scope and severity of the data quality problems facing corporations. Data accuracy is rigorously defined. The causes of data inaccuracies are classified and discussed in order to show the breadth of challenges any program needs to address if there is any chance of making a meaningful contribution.

CHAPTER 1

The Data Quality Problem

Accurate data is a fundamental requirement of good information systems. And yet most information systems contain significant amounts of inaccurate data, and most enterprises lack enough of a basic understanding of the concepts of information quality to recognize or change the situation. Accurate data is an important dimension of information quality—the most important dimension.

The lack of accurate data costs organizations dearly in correction activities, lost customers, missed opportunities, and incorrect decisions. Most corporations are very much unaware of the magnitude of the costs. Most corporations are unaware of the extent of inaccurate data in their systems. Most corporations are content in their belief that their data is good enough, although they have no basis for that belief. They are missing an opportunity to improve their overall efficiency and effectiveness and to bring more dollars to the bottom line.

Accurate data does not come free. It requires careful attention to the design of systems, constant monitoring of data collection, and aggressive actions to correct problems that generate or propagate inaccurate data. To have highly accurate data you need a formal data quality assurance program with a specific component dedicated to accurate data. Ignoring the topic or having a passive program with little teeth in it only continues to deny your corporation the full value of high-quality data.

1.1 Data Is a Precious Resource

Data is the fuel we use to make decisions. It records the history of enterprise activities. It is used to drive processes of all sorts. It is used to make important decisions. We maintain and use data as individuals. We maintain and use data as corporations, governmental organizations, educational institutions, and virtually any other organization.

Many large organizations are nothing but data processing engines. Insurance companies, banks, financial services companies, and the IRS are all organizations that live in a sea of data. Most of what they do is process data.

Think about companies that process credit card transactions. What products do they produce and sell? Just information products. They process tons of data every day. Take their information systems away and there is nothing left.

Other organizations may appear to be less involved with information systems because their products or activities are not information specific. However, looking under the covers you see that most of their activities and decisions are driven or guided by information systems.

Manufacturing organizations produce and ship products. However, data drives the processes of material acquisition, manufacturing work flow, shipping, and billing. Most of these companies would come to a resounding halt if their information systems stopped working. To be a profitable manufacturing company today you need highly tuned information systems for just-in-time parts delivery, effective purchasing systems for adjusting what you produce to ever-changing demand, highly accurate cost accounting systems, applications for the care and feeding of customers, and much more. Those with poor information systems fall behind competitively, and many fall out of business.

The most successful companies are not always those with the best products. Companies must recognize that they must sell what is profitable and drop products that are not. Profitability requires knowledge of the supply chain; knowledge of past, present, and future buying patterns; marketing costs; and sales costs. Consolidation of data from many different systems is required to make the right profit decisions.

Retail operations depend completely on information systems to keep them profitable. They must have the latest technology for highly efficient supply chain management. If not, their competitors will lower prices and force the inefficient information processors out of business. Many are now moving to customer relationship management systems in order to gain an even better competitive position.

Data is becoming more precious all the time. Enterprises are using data more and more to help them make important decisions. These can be daily, routine decisions or long-term strategic decisions. New trends in data warehousing, data mining, decision support, and customer relationship management systems all highlight the ever-expanding role data plays in our organizations.

➤ *Data gets more valuable all the time, as additional ways are found to employ it to make our organizations more successful.*

1.2 Impact of Continuous Evolution of Information Systems

From about 1950 through today, there has been a clear evolution in the use of computer-generated data from simple historical record keeping to ever more active roles. This trend does not show signs of slowing down. Data is generated by more people, is used in the execution of more tasks by more people, and is used in corporate decision making more than ever before.

➤ *The more technology we develop, the more users demand from it.*

When we look at the past 50 years, the degree to which information systems have played a role has been in a state of constant change. Every IT department has had a significant amount of their resources devoted to the task of implementing new or replacement systems. As each new system is deployed, it is often already obsolete, as another replacement technology shows up while they were building it. This drives them to again replace the just-finished system. This process of "continuous evolution" has never stopped, and probably will not for a number of years into the future.

The constant need to remodel systems as fast as they are developed has been driven by enormously fast technology innovation in hardware, communications, and software. No organization has been able to keep up with the rapid pace of technological change. All organizations have been chasing the technology curve in the hope of eventually reaching a stable point, where new systems can survive for awhile. They will not reach stability for a long time in the future, as much more technology is being born as this is written.

The need to change is also fueled by the rapid change in the nature of the companies themselves. Mergers and acquisitions drive very rapid and important changes as companies try to merge information systems. Changes in product lines or changes in markets served drive many hastily implemented changes into information systems. For example, the decision to "go global" can wreak havoc on currency, date, address, and other data elements already in place. Business change impacts are the ones that generally are done the quickest, with the least amount of planning, and that usually derive the worst results.

External changes also cause hastily implemented patches to existing systems: tax law changes, accounting changes such as those experienced in recent years, the Y2K problem, the EURO conversion, and on and on. This rapid evolution has meant that systems have been developed hastily and changed aggressively. This is done with few useful standards for development and control. The software industry has never developed effective standards similar to those the hardware and construction industries enjoy (through blueprints), nor does it have the luxury of time to think through everything it does before committing to systems. The result is that many, if not all, of our systems are very rough edged. These rough edges particularly show through in the quality of the data and the information derived from the data.

A lot of this rapid change happened in order to push information systems into more of the tasks of the enterprise and to involve more people in the process. The Internet promises to involve all people and all tasks in the scope of information systems. At some time in the future, all companies will have an information system backbone through which almost all activity will be affected. As a result, information systems become bigger, more complex, and, hopefully, more important every time a new technology is thrown in. The data becomes more and more important.

Just about everything in organizations has been "databased." There are personnel databases, production databases, billing and collection databases, sales management databases, customer databases, marketing databases, supply chain databases, accounting databases, financial management databases, and on and on. Whenever anyone wants to know something, they instinctively run to a PC to query a database. It is difficult to imagine that less than 25 years ago there were no PCs and data was not collected on many of the corporate objects and activities of today.

I participated in an audit for a large energy company a few years ago that inventoried over 5,000 databases and tens of thousands of distinct data elements in their corporate information systems. Most corporations do not know how much data they are actually handling on a daily basis.

Not only has most corporation information been put into databases, but it has been replicated into data warehouses, data marts, operational data stores, and business objects. As new ways are discovered to use data, there is a tendency to create duplication of the primary data in order to satisfy the new need. The most dramatic example today is the wave of customer relationship management (hereafter, CRM) projects proliferating throughout the IT world.

Replication often includes aggregating data, combining data from multiple sources, putting data into data structures that are different from the original structure, and adding time period information. Often the original data cannot be recognized or found in the aggregations. As a result, errors detected in the aggregations often cannot be traced back to primary instances of data containing the errors.

In addition to replicating, there are attempts to integrate the data of multiple databases inside interactive processes. Some of this integration includes reaching across company boundaries into databases of suppliers, customers, and others, examples of which are shown in Figure 1.1.

Adding the demands of replication and integration on top of operational systems adds greatly to the complexity of information systems and places huge burdens on the content of the primary operational systems. Data quality problems get magnified through all of these channels. Figure 1.2 indicates aspects of integration, operation, and replication.

THE *claim that systems are in a state of continuous evolution seems to be belied by the resilience of legacy systems built years ago that seem to resist all attempts to replace them. In reality, these systems are the worst offenders of evolution because they change all the time, at a high cost, and usually extend themselves through replication and integration. In fact, many new requirements can only be satisfied through replication or integration extensions.*

Because of the inherent inflexibility of such systems, these extensions *are much more complex and often turn out to be badly implemented. This is a classic case of pushing the problems downhill and not addressing root problems.*

If corporations want quality systems, they will need to eventually replace the old technologies with new ones. Retrofitting older systems to new requirements and new standards of quality is almost impossible to achieve with quality results.

Target System	Reason for Connecting
• Supplier	• Searching database for a critical part
• Customer	• Determining amounts to ship for just-in-time delivery
• Local law agency	• FBI accessing local databases for investigative info
• Business to business	• Accepting orders
• Business to business	• Placing orders
• Research organizations	• Making research available on portal

FIGURE I.I Examples of cross-company systems.

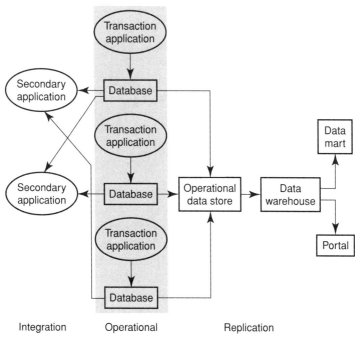

FIGURE 1.2 Demands on operational databases.

Along with the increasing complexity of systems comes an increase in the impact of inaccurate data. In the primary systems, a wrong value may have little or no impact. It may cause a glitch in processing of an order, resultingin some small annoyance to fix. However, as this wrong value is propagated to higher-level decision support systems, it may trigger an incorrect reordering of a product or give a decision maker the wrong information to base expanding a manufacturing line on. The latter consequences can be much larger than the original.

Although a single wrong value is not likely to cause such drastic results, the cumulative effect of multiple wrong values in that same attribute can collectively deliver very wrong results. Processes that generate wrong values rarely generate only one inaccurate instance.

1.3 Acceptance of Inaccurate Data

Databases have risen to the level of being one of the most, if not the most, important corporate asset, and yet corporations tolerate enormous inaccuracies in their databases. Their data quality is not managed as rigorously as are most other assets and activities. Few companies have a data quality assurance program, and many that do have such a program provide too little support to make it effective.

The fact of modern business is that the databases that drive them are of poor to miserable quality, and little is being done about it. Corporations are losing significant amounts of money and missing important opportunities all the time because they operate on information derived from inaccurate data. The cost of poor-quality data is estimated by some data quality experts as being from 15 to 25% of operating profit. In a recent survey of 599 companies conducted by PricewaterhouseCoopers, an estimate of poor data management is costing global businesses more than $1.4 billion per year in billing, accounting, and inventory snafus alone. Much of that cost is attributable to the accuracy component of data quality.

This situation is not restricted to businesses. Similar costs can be found in governmental or educational organizations as well. Poor data quality is sapping all organizations of money and opportunities. A fair characterization of the state of data quality awareness and responsiveness for the typical large organization is as follows:

- They are aware of problems with data.

- They consistently underestimate, by a large amount, the extent of the problem.

- They have no idea of the cost to the corporation of the problem.

- They have no idea of the potential value in fixing the problem.

If you can get commitment to a data quality assessment exercise, it almost always raises awareness levels very high. A typical response is "I had no idea the problem was that large." Assessment is the key to awareness, not reading books like this. Most people will believe that the other guy has a larger problem than they do and assume that this book is written for that other guy, not them. Everyone believes that the data quality problem they have is small and much less interesting to address than other initiatives. They are usually very wrong in their thinking. It takes data to change their minds.

1.4 The Blame for Poor-Quality Data

Everyone starts out blaming IT. However, data is created by people outside IT, and is used by people outside IT. IT is responsible for the quality of the systems that move the data and store it. However, they cannot be held completely responsible for the content. Much of the problem lies outside IT, through poorly articulated requirements, poor acceptance testing of systems, poor data creation processes, and much more.

Data quality problems are universal in nature. In just about any large organization the state of information and data quality is at the same low levels.

The fact that data quality is universally poor indicates that it is not the fault of individually poorly managed organizations but rather that *it is the natural result of the evolution of information system technology.* There are two major contributing factors. The first is the rapid system implementations and change that have made it very difficult to control quality. The second is that the methods, standards, techniques, and tools for controlling quality have evolved at a much slower pace than the systems they serve.

Virtually all organizations admit that data quality issues plague their progress. They are all aware of the situation at some level within the enterprise. Quality problems are not restricted to older systems either. Nor are they restricted to particular types of systems. For example, practitioners intuitively assume that systems built on a relational database foundation are of higher data quality than older systems built on less sophisticated data management technology. Under examination, this generally turns out not to be true.

Information technology evolution is at a point where the next most important technology that needs to evolve is methods for controlling the quality of data and the information derived from it. The systems we are building are too important not to address this important topic any later than now.

ALTHOUGH *data quality problems are universal, this should not excuse egregious examples of poor quality or cases in which awareness was high but no actions taken. In the absence of these, CEOs should not dwell on fault but instead spend their energies on improvement.*

Ten years from now, poor data quality will be a reason to find fault.

With the growing availability of knowledge, experts, books, methodologies, software tools, and corporate resolve, high-quality database systems will become the norm, and there will be no excuse for not having them. What we consider excusable today will be inexcusable then.

1.5 Awareness Levels

Almost everyone is aware that data from time to time causes a visible problem. However, visibility to the magnitude of the problems and to the impact on the corporation is generally low. There are several reasons for this.

Correction activities, rework, order reprocessing, handling returns, and dealing with customer complaints are all considered a normal part of corporate life. Many of the problems are not associated with information quality, even when that is the problem. The activities tend to grow in size with little fanfare or visibility. Since the people who carry out these activities are generally not isolated within a function, the cost and scope of such problems are generally not appreciated.

When decision makers reject IT data because "they just know it can't be right," they generally do not rush into the CEO's office and demand that the data coming from IT be improved. They usually just depend on their previous methods for making decisions and do not use the information from the databases. Many times data warehouse and decision support systems get built and then become not used for this reason. To make matters worse, decision makers sometimes generate alternative data collection and storage mini-systems to use instead of the mainline databases. These often tend to be as bad or worse in quality than the systems they reject.

IT management often does not want to raise a red flag regarding quality, since they know that they will get blamed for it. Their systems are collecting, storing, and disseminating information efficiently, and they are content with not surfacing the fact that the quality of the data flowing through these systems is bad.

Corporate management wants to believe that their IT departments are top notch and that their systems are first rate. They do not want to expose to their board or to the outside world the facts of inefficiencies or lost opportunities caused by inaccurate data.

If a company included in its annual report a statement that their information quality caused a loss equal to 20% of their operating profit, their stock price would plunge overnight. They do not want this information published, they do not want investors to know, and they do not want their competitors to know. The obvious psychology drives them to not want to know (or believe) it themselves.

Companies tend to hide news about information quality problems. You will never see a company voluntarily agree to a magazine article on how they discovered huge data quality problems and invested millions of dollars to fix them. Even though this is a great story for the corporation, and the results may save them many times the money they spent, the story makes them look like they lost control and were just getting back to where they should have been. It smacks of saying that they have been bad executives and managers and had to spend money to correct their inefficient ways.

I had a conversation with a government agency official in which they indicated that disclosure of data accuracy problems in a particular database would generate a political scandal of considerable proportions, even though the root cause of the quality problems had nothing to do with any of the elected officials. Needless to say, they went about fixing the problem as best they could, with no publicity at all about the project or their findings.

- Low awareness of the cost of data quality problems
- Low awareness of the potential value of improvements
- Tolerance for errors is high in primary systems
- Treatment of known issues as isolated problems instead of symptoms
- Coping; acceptance of poor quality
- Business case for improving quality is not as high as for alternatives
- Skepticism over ability to improve things and get returns

FIGURE 1.3   Reasons not much has been done about quality problems.

Data quality (and more specifically, data accuracy) problems can have liability consequences. As we move more into the Internet age, in which your company's data is used by other corporations to make decisions about purchasing and selling, costs associated with bad data will eventually be the target of litigation. Corporations surely do not want to trumpet any knowledge they have of quality problems in their databases and give ammunition to the legal staff of others.

The time to brag about spending large budgets to get and maintain highly accurate data and highly accurate information products has not yet arrived. However, the tide is turning on awareness. If you go into almost any IT organization, the data management specialists will all tell you that there are considerable problems with the accuracy of data. The business analysts will tell you that they have problems with data and information quality. As you move up the management chain, the willingness to assert the problems diminishes, usually ending with the executive level denying any quality problems at all. Figure 1.3 summarizes reasons for lack of initiative in regard to problems with information quality.

1.6 Impact of Poor-Quality Data

We usually cannot scope the extent of data quality problems without an assessment project. This is needed to really nail the impact on the organization and identify the areas of potential return. The numbers showing the potential savings are not lying around in a convenient account. They have to be dug out through a concerted effort involving several organizational entities. Some areas in which costs are created and opportunities lost through poor data quality are

- transaction rework costs

- costs incurred in implementing new systems

- delays in delivering data to decision makers

- lost customers through poor service

- lost production through supply chain problems

Examples of some of these, discussed in the sections that follow, will demonstrate the power of data quality problems to eat away at the financial health of an organization.

Transaction Rework Costs

Many organizations have entire departments that handle customer complaints on mishandled orders and shipments. When the wrong items are shipped and then returned, a specific, measurable cost occurs. There are many data errors that can occur in this area: wrong part numbers, wrong amounts, and incorrect shipping addresses, to name a few. Poorly designed order entry procedures and screens are generally the cause of this problem.

Costs Incurred in Implementing New Systems

One of the major problems in implementing data warehouses, consolidating databases, migrating to new systems, and integrating multiple systems is the presence of data errors and issues that block successful implementation. Issues with the quality of data can, and more than half the time do, increase the time and cost to implement data reuse projects by staggering amounts.

A recent report published by the Standish Group shows that 37% of such projects get cancelled, with another 50% completed but with at least a 20% cost and time overrun and often with incomplete or unsatisfactory results. This means that only 13% of projects are completed within a reasonable time and cost of their plans with acceptable outcomes. This is a terrible track record for implementing major projects. Failures are not isolated to a small group of companies or to specific industries. This poor record is found in almost all companies.

Delays in Delivering Data to Decision Makers

Many times you see organizations running reports at the end of time periods and then reworking the results based on their knowledge of wrong or suspicious values. When the data sources are plagued by quality problems, it generally requires manual massaging of information before it can be released for decision-making consumption. The wasted time of people doing this rework can be measured. The poor quality of decisions made cannot be measured. If it takes effort to clean up data before use, you can never be sure if the data is entirely correct after cleanup.

Lost Customers Through Poor Service

This is another category that can easily be spotted. Customers that are being lost because they consistently get orders shipped incorrectly, get their invoices wrong, get their payments entered incorrectly, or other aspects of poor service represent a large cost to the corporation.

Lost Production Through Supply Chain Problems

Whenever the supply chain system delivers the wrong parts or the wrong quantity of parts to the production line, there is either a stoppage of work or an oversupply that needs to be stored somewhere. In either case, money is lost to the company.

The general nature of all of these examples is that data quality issues have caused people to spend time and energy dealing with the problems associated with them. The cost in people and time can be considerable. However, over time corrective processes have become routine, and everyone has come to accept this as a normal cost of business. It is generally not visible to higher levels of management and not called out on accounting reports. As a result, an assessment team should be able to identify a great deal of cost in a short period of time.

1.7 Requirements for Making Improvements

Too often executives look at quality problems as isolated instances instead of symptoms. This is a natural reaction, considering that they do not want to believe they have problems in the first place. They tend to be reactive instead of proactive. Making large improvements in the accuracy of data and the quality of information from the data can only be accomplished through proactive activities.

Considering the broad scope of quality problems, this is not an area for quick fixes. The attitude that should be adopted is that of installing a new layer of technology over their information systems that will elevate their efficiency and value. It is the same as adding a CRM system to allow marketing to move to a new level of customer care, resulting in higher profits.

The scope of quality problems and the potential for financial gain dictate that a formal program be initiated to address this area. Such a program needs to have a large component dedicated to the topic of data accuracy. Without highly accurate data, information quality cannot be achieved.

To get value from the program, it must be viewed as a long-term and continuous activity. It is like adding security to your buildings. Once you achieve it, you do not stop pursuing it. In spite of the fact that data quality improvement programs are long term, it is important to repeat that significant returns are generally achievable in the short term.

Some of the problems will take a long time to fix. The primary place to fix problems is in the systems that initially gather the data. Rebuilding them to produce more accurate data may take years to accomplish. While long-term improvements are being made, short-term improvements can be made through filtering of input data, cleansing of data in databases, and in creating an awareness of the quality that consumers of the data can expect will significantly improve the use of the data.

A major theme of this book is that you need to train all of your data management team in the concepts of accurate data and to make accurate data a requirement of all projects they work on. This is in addition to having a core group of data quality experts who pursue their own agenda.

There will still be times when overhauling a system solely for the purpose of improving data accuracy is justified. However, most of the time the best way to improve the overall data accuracy of your information systems is to make it a primary requirement of all new projects. That way, you are getting double value for your development dollars.

1.8 Expected Value Returned for Quality Program

Experts have estimated the cost of poor information quality at from 15 to 25% of operating profits. This assumes that no concerted effort has already been made to improve quality. The actual achievable number is less. However, even if you could get only 60% of that back you would add 9 to 15% to the bottom line. This is a considerable amount. If you are a corporation, this is a lot of profit. If you are an education institution, this is a lot of money added for improving the campus or faculty. If you are a charitable organization, this is a lot more money going to recipients. If you are a governmental organization, this is more value for the tax dollar.

Although these numbers are considerable, they represent the value of concentrating on improving information quality for the organization as it currently exists. However, I suggest that better-quality information systems will reduce the cost of, and accelerate the completion of, steps in evolving the organization to newer business models. There has never been a time in my lifetime when companies were not in the process of implementing newer business or manufacturing systems that promised huge returns when completed.

Many of these changes were considered essential for survival. The latest example of this is the move to being Internet based.

Changing a corporation's business and operating systems to a base of high-quality data makes changes occur faster, at lower cost, and with better-quality outcomes. CRM projects are a good example. Moving to a customer-centric model, whereby information about customers drives sales and marketing activities, promises huge returns to corporations. However, we hear that over 60% of CRM implementations either are outright failures or experience long delays. Many of these problems are caused by inaccurate data, making it difficult, if not impossible, to complete the projects.

➤ *The major reason for improving the quality of data is to make the corporation more able to make business and operational changes.* This adds a degree of flexibility to the corporation, giving it the potential for huge paybacks over time. If your company is the first one to complete implementation of new technologies, the competitive edge you gain can be considerable.

1.9 Data Quality Assurance Technology

Although information quality has remained at low levels or even degraded over the years, there has been progress in the technology for improving it. Although information technology is not yet considered a formal technology, its parts are coming together and will be recognized as such in the near future. The essential elements of the technology are

- availability of experts and consultants

- educational materials

- methodologies

- software tools

These factors combined allow a corporation to establish a data quality assurance program and realize substantial gain. It is important that these factors become established as standard methods that incorporate the best practices. This will allow the entire IT industry to use the emerging technology effectively and for rapid transfer of knowledge between individuals and organizations.

This does not mean that the technology will not evolve, as everything is not yet known about this area. It means that changes to the set of tools should be judged as to whether they advance the technology before they are adopted.

Every manufacturing operation has a quality control department. Every accounting department has auditors. There are inspectors for construction sites at every stage of building. There are requirements for formal specification of construction and manufacturing before anything is built. Any serious software development organization has trained quality assurance professionals.

Information systems need the same formality in a group of people and processes to ensure higher levels of quality. Every serious organization with a large IT operation needs a data quality assurance program. They need to require formal documentation of all information assets and sufficient information about them to satisfy all development and user requirements. They need inspectors, auditors, and development consultants. They need an established methodology to continuously monitor and improve the accuracy of data flowing through their information systems.

Availability of Experts and Consultants

Before any technology can take off, it needs the attention of a lot of smart people. When relational technology got its rocket start in the late 1970s and early 1980s, there was research going on in several corporate research organizations (most notably IBM) and in many universities (most notably the University of California at Berkeley). The vast majority of Ph.D. theses in computer science in that era had something to do with relational database technology. An enormous number of start-up companies appeared to exploit the new technology. I did a survey in 1982 and found over 200 companies that had or were building a relational database engine. Today, less than five of them have survived. However, those that did survive have been enormously successful.

Data quality has the attention of a few smart people, not the large group that is desirable for a new technology to emerge. However, the number is increasing every year. Many university research efforts are now addressing this topic. The most notable is the M.I.T. TDQM (total data quality management) research program. There are many more university research efforts being aimed at this field every year. In addition, technical conferences devoted to data and information quality are experiencing significant growth in attendance every year.

A number of consultant experts have emerged who are dedicating their careers to the data quality topic. The number increases every year. The quality of these consultants is superb. Corporations should not hesitate to take advantage of their knowledge and experience.

Educational Materials

There is a clear shortage of educational materials in the field of data and information quality. Materials need to be developed and included in standard college courses on computer science. Corporations need to provide education not only to those responsible for data quality assurance but to everyone who is involved in defining, building, executing, or monitoring information systems. There should also be education for consumers of information so that they can more effectively determine how to use information at their disposal and to provide effective requirements and feedback to system developers.

Books and articles are useful tools for education, and plenty of them are available. However, more specific training modules need to be developed and deployed for quality to become an important component of information systems.

Methodologies

There have emerged a number of methodologies for creating and organizing data quality assurance programs, for performing data quality assessments, and for ongoing data stewardship. These can be found in the various books available on data or information quality. This book provides its own methodology, based on data profiling technology, for consideration. More detailed methodologies need to be employed for profiling existing data stores and monitoring data quality in operational settings.

If data quality assurance programs are going to be successful, they must rally around standard methods for doing things that have been proven to work. They then need to employ them professionally over and over again.

Software Tools

There has been a paucity of software tools available to professionals to incorporate into data quality assurance programs. It is ironic that on the topic of data quality the software industry has been the least helpful. Part of the reason for this is that corporations have not been motivated to identify and solve quality problems and thus have not generated sufficient demand to foster the growth in successful software companies focusing on data quality.

More tools are emerging as the industry is waking up to the need for improving quality. You cannot effectively carry out a good program without detailed analysis and monitoring of data. The area of data accuracy specifically requires software to deal with the tons of data that should be looked at.

METADATA REPOSITORIES

The primary software tool for managing data quality is the metadata repository. Repositories have been around for a long time but have been poorly employed. Most IT departments have one or more repositories in place and use them with very little effectiveness. Most people would agree that the movement to establish metadata repositories as a standard practice has been a resounding failure. This is unfortunate, as the metadata repository is the one tool that is essential for gaining control over your data.

The failure of repository technology can be traced to a number of factors. The first is that implementations have been poorly defined, with only a vague concept of what they are there for. Often, the real information that people need from them is not included. They tend to dwell on schema definitions and not the more interesting information that people need to do their jobs. There has been a large mismatch between requirements and products.

A second failure is that no one took them seriously. There was never a serious commitment to them. Information system professionals did not use them in their daily jobs. It was not part of their standard tool set. It appeared to be an unnecessary step that stood in the way of getting tasks done.

A third failure is that they were never kept current. They were passive repositories that had no method for verifying that their content actually matched the information systems they were supposed to represent. It is ironic that repositories generally have the most inaccurate data within the information systems organization.

A fourth failure is that the standard repositories were engineered for data architects and not the wider audience of people who can benefit from valuable information in an accurate metadata repository. The terminology is too technical, the information maintained is not what they all need, and the accessibility is restricted too much.

Since corporations have never accepted the concept of an industry standard repository, most software products on the market deliver a proprietary repository that incorporates only that information needed to install and operate their product. The result is that there are dozens of isolated repositories sitting around that all contain different information, record information in unique ways, and have little, if any, ability to move information to other repositories. Even when this capability is provided, it is rarely used. Repository technology needs to be reenergized based on the requirements for establishing and carrying out an effective data quality assurance program.

DATA PROFILING

The second important need is analytical tools for data profiling. Data profiling has emerged as a major new technology. It employs analytical methods for looking at data for the purpose of developing a thorough understanding of the content, structure, and quality of the data. A good data profiling product can process very large amounts of data and, with the skills of the analyst, uncover all sorts of issues in the data that need to be addressed.

Data profiling is an indispensable tool for assessing data quality. It is also very useful at periodic checking of data to determine if corrective measures are being effective or to monitor the health of the data over time.

Data profiling uses two different approaches to examining data. One is discovery, whereby processes examine the data and discover characteristics from the data without the prompting of the analyst. In this regard it is performing data mining for metadata. This is extremely important to do because the data will take on a persona of itself and the analyst may be completely unaware of some of the characteristics. It is also helpful in addressing the problem that the metadata that normally exists for data is usually incorrect, incomplete, or both.

The second approach to data profiling is assertive testing. The analyst poses conditions he believes to be true about the data and then executes data rules against the data that check for these conditions to see if it conforms or not. This is also a useful technique for determining how much the data differs from the expected. Assertive testing is normally done after discovery.

The output of data profiling will be accurate metadata plus information about data quality problems. One goal of data profiling is to establish the true metadata description of the data. In effect, it can correct the sins of the past.

Data profiling tools exist in the market and are getting better every year. They did not exist five years ago. Data profiling functions are being implemented as part of some older products, and some new products are also emerging that focus on this area. More companies are employing them every year and are consistently amazed at what they can learn from them.

DATA MONITORING

A third tool includes effective methods for monitoring data quality. A data monitoring tool can be either transaction oriented or database oriented. If transaction oriented, the tool looks at individual transactions before they cause database changes. A database orientation looks at an entire database periodically to find issues.

The goal of a transaction monitor is to screen for potential inaccuracies in the data in the transactions. The monitor must be built into the transaction system. XML transaction systems make this a much more plausible approach. For example, if IBM's MQ is the transaction system being employed, building an MQ node for screening data is very easy to do.

A potential problem with transaction monitors is that they have the potential to slow down processing if too much checking is done. If this is the result, they will tend not to be used very much. Another problem is that they are not effective in generating alerts where something is wrong but not sufficiently wrong to block the transaction from occurring. Transaction monitors need to be carefully designed and judiciously used so as to not impair the effectiveness of the transaction system.

Database monitors are useful for finding a broad range of problems and in performing overall quality assessment. Many issues are not visible in individual transactions but surface when looking at counts, distributions, and aggregations. In addition, many data rules that are not possible to use on individual transactions because of processing time become possible when processing is offline.

Database monitors are also useful in examining collections of data being received at a processing point. For example, data feeds being purchased from an outside group can be fed through a database monitor to assess the quality of the submission.

The most effective data monitoring program uses a combination of transaction and database monitoring. It takes an experienced designer to understand when and where to apply specific rules. The technology of data quality monitors is not very advanced at this point. However, this is an area that will hopefully improve significantly over the next few years.

DATA CLEANSING TOOLS

Data cleansing tools are designed to examine data that exists to find data errors and to fix them. To find an error, you need rules. Once an error is found, either it can cause rejection of the data (usually the entire data object) or it can be fixed. To fix an error, there are only two possibilities: substitution of a synonym or correlation through lookup tables.

Substitution correction involves having a list of value pairs that associate a correct value for each known wrong value. These are useful for fixing misspellings or inconsistent representations. The known misspellings are listed with correct spellings. The multiple ways of representing a value are listed with the single preferred representation. These lists can grow over time as new misspellings or new ways of representing a value are discovered in practice.

Correlation requires a group of fields that must be consistent across values. A set of rules or lookup tables establish the value sets that are acceptable.

If a set of values from a database record is not in the set, the program looks for a set that matches most of the elements and then fixes the missing or incorrect part. The most common example of this is name and address fields. The correlation set is the government database of values that can go together (e.g., city, state, Zip code, and so on). In fact, there is little applicability of this type of scrubbing for anything other than name and address examination.

DATABASE MANAGEMENT SYSTEMS

Database management systems (DBMSs) have always touted their abilities to promote correct data. Relational systems have implemented physical data typing, referential constraints, triggers, and procedures to help database designers put transaction screening, database screening, and cleansing into the database structure. The argument is that the DBMS is the right place to look for errors and fix data because it is the single point of entry of data to the database.

Database designers have found this argument useful for some things and not useful for others. The good designers are using the referential constraints. A good database design will employ primary key definitions, data type definitions, null rules, unique rules, and primary/foreign key pair designations to the fullest extent to make sure that data conforms to the expected structure.

The problem with putting quality screens into the DBMS through procedures and triggers are many. First of all, the rules are buried in obscure code instead of being in a business rule repository. This makes them difficult to review and manage. A second problem is that all processing becomes part of the transaction path, thus slowing down response times. A third problem is that the point of database entry is often "too late" to clean up data, especially in Internet-based transaction systems. The proper way to treat data quality issues is to use a combination of DBMS structural support, transaction monitors, database monitors, and external data cleansing.

1.10 Closing Remarks

As information systems become more of the fabric of organizations, they also get more and more complex. The quality of data within them has not improved over the years as has other technologies. The result is that most information systems produce data that is of such poor quality that organizations incur significant losses in operations and decision making. It also severely slows down and sometimes cripples attempts to introduce new business models into the organization.

There are many reasons data quality is low and getting lower. This will not change until corporations adopt stringent data quality assurance initiatives. With proper attention, great returns can be realized through improvements in the quality of data.

The primary value to the corporation for getting their information systems into a state of high data quality and maintaining them there is that it gives them the ability to quickly and efficiently respond to new business model changes. This alone will justify data quality assurance initiatives many times over.

Data quality assurance initiatives are becoming more popular as organizations are realizing the impact that improving quality can have on the bottom line. The body of qualified experts, educational information, methodologies, and software tools supporting these initiatives is increasing daily. Corporations are searching for the right mix of tools, organization, and methodologies that will give them the best advantage in such programs.

Data accuracy is the foundation of data quality. You must get the values right first. The remainder of this book focuses on data accuracy: what it means, what is possible, methods for improving the accuracy of data, and the return you can expect for instituting data accuracy assurance programs.

CHAPTER 2

Definition of Accurate Data

To begin the discussion of data accuracy, it is important to first establish where accuracy fits into the larger picture of data quality.

2.1 Data Quality Definitions

Data quality is defined as follows: data has quality if it satisfies the requirements of its intended use. It lacks quality to the extent that it does not satisfy the requirement. In other words, data quality depends as much on the intended use as it does on the data itself. To satisfy the intended use, the data must be accurate, timely, relevant, complete, understood, and trusted.

Some examples will help in understanding the notion of data quality in the context of intended use. The sections that follow explore examples of the previously mentioned aspects of data integrity.

Case 1: Accuracy

Consider a database that contains names, addresses, phone numbers, and e-mail addresses of physicians in the state of Texas. This database is known to have a number of errors: some records are wrong, some are missing, and some are obsolete. If you compare the database to the true population of physicians, it is expected to be 85% accurate.

If this database is to be used for the state of Texas to notify physicians of a new law regarding assisted suicide, it would certainly be considered poor quality. In fact, it would be dangerous to use it for that intended purpose.

If this database were to be used by a new surgical device manufacturer to find potential customers, it would be considered high quality. Any such firm would be delighted to have a potential customer database that is 85% accurate. From it, they could conduct a telemarketing campaign to identify real sales leads with a completely acceptable success rate. The same database: for one use it has poor data quality, and for another it has high data quality.

Case 2: Timeliness

Consider a database containing sales information for a division of a company. This database contains three years' worth of data. However, the database is slow to become complete at the end of each month. Some units submit their information immediately, whereas others take several days to send in information. There are also a number of corrections and adjustments that flow in. Thus, for a period of time at the end of the accounting period, the content is incomplete. However, all of the data is correct when complete.

If this database is to be used to compute sales bonuses that are due on the 15th of the following month, it is of poor data quality even though the data in it is always eventually accurate. The data is not timely enough for the intended use.

However, if this database is to be used for historical trend analysis and to make decisions on altering territories, it is of excellent data quality as long as the user knows when all additions and changes are incorporated. Waiting for all of the data to get in is not a problem because its intended use is to make long-term decisions.

Case 3: Relevance

Consider an inventory database that contains part numbers, warehouse locations, quantity on hand, and other information. However, it does not contain source information (where the parts came from). If a part is supplied by multiple suppliers, once the parts are received and put on the shelf there is no indication of which supplier the parts came from. The information in the database is always accurate and current. For normal inventory transactions and decision making, the database is certainly of high quality.

If a supplier reports that one of their shipments contained defective parts, this database is of no help in identifying whether they have any of those parts or not. The database is of poor quality because it does not contain a relevant element of information. Without that information, the database is poor data quality for the intended use.

Case 4: Completeness

A database contains information on repairs done to capital equipment. However, it is a known fact that sometimes the repairs are done and the information about the repair is just not entered into the database. This is the result of lack of concern on the part of the repair people and a lack of enforcement on the part of their supervisors. It is estimated that the amount of missing information is about 5%.

This database is probably a good-quality database for assessing the general health of capital equipment. Equipment that required a great deal of expense to maintain can be identified from the data. Unless the missing data is disproportionately skewed, the records are usable for all ordinary decisions.

However, trying to use it as a base for evaluating information makes it a low-quality database. The missing transactions could easily tag an important piece of equipment as satisfying a warranty when in fact it does not.

Case 5: Understood

Consider a database containing orders from customers. A practice for handling complaints and returns is to create an "adjustment" order for backing out the original order and then writing a new order for the corrected information if applicable. This procedure assigns new order numbers to the adjustment and replacement orders.

For the accounting department, this is a high-quality database. All of the numbers come out in the wash. For a business analyst trying to determine trends in growth of orders by region, this is a poor-quality database. If the business analyst assumes that each order number represents a distinct order, his analysis will be all wrong. Someone needs to explain the practice and the methods necessary to unravel the data to get to the real numbers (if that is even possible after the fact).

Case 6: Trusted

A new application is deployed that is used to determine the amount and timing of ordering parts for machinery based on past history and the time in service since last replacement for the machines they are used in. The original application had a programming error that incorrectly ordered 10 times the amount actually required. The error went undisclosed until a large order was sent. A great deal of publicity ensued over the incident. The programming error was fixed and the problem does not repeat.

The database was never wrong; the application was. The large order was actually placed and the database reflected the order as such.

Because of a fear of a repeat of the incident, the maintenance chief has chosen not to use the application nor the information within the database. He orders parts based on a small spreadsheet application he built to keep much of the same information, even though he often misses transactions and does not always know when new parts arrive in inventory.

Unless his confidence in the original application is restored, the database is of poor quality, even though it is entirely accurate. It is not serving its intended use due to a lack of believability.

2.2   Principle of Unintended Uses

The previously cited examples demonstrate that you cannot separate data from uses. To assess the quality of data, you must first collect a thorough specification of the intended uses and then judge the data as to its suitability for those uses. In a perfect world, database builders would gather all requirements and then craft a database design and applications to match them.

In the real world there is a serious problem when dealing with "unintended uses." These are uses that were not known or defined at the time the databases were designed and implemented.

Unintended uses arise for a large variety of reasons. Some examples follow:

- The company expands to new markets.

- The company purchases another company and consolidates applications.

- External requirements are received, such as a new tax law.

- The company grows its usage, particularly in decision making.

- The company migrates to a new, packaged application that has different needs.

This represents the single biggest problem with databases. Unintended uses proliferate at ever-expanding rates. You cannot anticipate all uses for a database when initially building it unless it is a database with unimportant content. In the real world you can expect (and in fact depend on) a large number of unintended uses appearing with surprising regularity. Each of these can cause a good database to become a bad database. Two things are needed: anticipation in database design and flexibility in implementations.

Need for Anticipation in Database Design

Database designers need to be schooled in the principles of data quality. By doing so, they will be able to avoid some data quality problems from occurring when unintended uses appear. In the least, they should be schooled to be diligent in the careful and thorough documentation of the content. This means that metadata repositories should be more prevalent, more used, and more valued by information systems groups.

Anticipation also includes questioning each database design decision in light of what might appear in the future. For example, name and address fields should anticipate the company's growth into markets in other countries where the structure and form of elements may vary. Another example is anticipating sales amounts in multiple national currencies.

Database and application designers should be discouraged from using confusing and complicated data encoding methods. Many bad techniques proliferated in the past that were the result of the limited capacity and slow speed of storage devices. These are no longer excuses for making data structures and encoding schemes overly complicated.

A good database design is one that is resilient in the face of unintended uses. This principle and the techniques to achieve it must be taught to the newer generations of information system designers.

Need for Flexibility in Implementations

We know that changes will be made to our systems. Corporations always change. They change so much that keeping up with the changes is a major headache for any CIO. Unintended uses is one of the reasons for change. When a new use appears, its requirements need to be collected and analyzed against the data they intend to use. This needs to be done up front and thoroughly. If the database is not up to the task of the new uses, either the new use needs to be changed or discarded, or the database and its data-generating applications must be upgraded to satisfy the requirements. This analysis concept needs to be incorporated into all new uses of data.

It is amazing how many companies do not think this way. Too often the data is force fit into the new use with poor results. How many times have you heard about a data warehouse project that completed but yielded nonsense results from queries? This generally is the result of force fitting data to a design it just does not match.

Database systems are better able to accept changes if they are designed with flexibility in the first place. Relational-based systems tend to be more flexible than older database technologies. Systems with thorough, complete, and current metadata will be much easier to change than those lacking metadata.

Most information system environments do a very poor job of creating and maintaining metadata repositories. Part of the blame goes to the repository vendors who have built insufficient systems. Part goes to practitioners who fail to take the time to use the metadata systems that are there. Part goes to lack of education and awareness of how important these things really are.

➤ *Organizations must improve their use of metadata repositories hugely if they have any hope of improving data quality and recouping some of the losses they are regularly incurring.*

2.3 Data Accuracy Defined

Data accuracy is one of the components of data quality. It refers to whether the data values stored for an object are the correct values. To be correct, a data value must be the right value and must be represented in a consistent and unambiguous form.

For example, my birth date is December 13, 1941. If a personnel database has a BIRTH_DATE data element that expects dates in USA format, a date of 12/13/1941 would be correct. A date of 12/14/1941 would be inaccurate because it is the wrong value. A date of 13/12/1941 would be wrong because it is a European representation instead of a USA representation.

There are two characteristics of accuracy: form and content. Form is important because it eliminates ambiguities about the content. The birth date example is ambiguous because the reviewer would not know whether the date was invalid or just erroneously represented. In the case of a date such as 5 February, 1944, the USA representation is 02/05/1944, whereas the European representation is 05/02/1944. You cannot tell the representation from the value and thus need discipline in creating the date values in order to be accurate. A value is not accurate if the user of the value cannot tell what it is.

Value Representation Consistency

Two values can be both correct and unambiguous and still cause problems. For example, the data values *ST Louis* and *Saint Louis* may both refer to the same city. However, the recordings are inconsistent, and thus at least one of them is inaccurate.

Why is consistency a part of accuracy? Although the values are different, anyone looking at them would have no trouble interpreting what the values mean. The answer is that inconsistent values cannot be accurately aggregated and compared. Since much of database usage involves comparisons and aggregations, inconsistencies create an opportunity for inaccurate usage of the data. Because all databases have a base level of unintended uses through the opportunity for ad hoc queries, data is inaccurate if it is inconsistent in representation.

Change-Induced Inconsistencies

Inconsistencies can also be caused by system changes that change the way information is recorded or that change the granularity of recording. Following is an example of how change in granularity might introduce inconsistencies: A company has a color field that only records red, blue, and yellow. A new requirement makes them decide to break each of these colors down to multiple shadings and thus institute a scheme of recording up to 30 different colors, all of which are variations of red, blue, and yellow. None of the old records are updated to the new scheme, as only new records use it. This database will have inconsistency of representation of color that crosses a point in time.

These types of changes are often not documented. The point in time of the changeover may also be fuzzy, wherein not everyone switches to the new scheme at the same time. If data mining and business intelligence software is used on this database for periods of time that cross the change, results will be inaccurate.

Valid Values

The definition of a value being valid means simply that the value is in the collection of possible accurate values and is represented in an unambiguous and consistent way. It means that the value has the potential to be accurate. It does not mean that it is accurate. To be accurate, it must also be the correct value. Defining all values that are valid for a data element is useful because it allows invalid values to be easily spotted and rejected from the database. However, we often mistakenly think values are accurate because they are valid.

For example, if a data element is used to store the color of a person's eyes, a value of TRUCK is invalid. A value of BROWN for my eye color would be valid but inaccurate, in that my real eye color is blue.

Missing Values

A data element that has no value in it may be either accurate or inaccurate. For example, a missing value in the data element COLLEGE_LAST_ATTENDED would be blank if the person it applied to had never attended college. On the other hand, a BIRTH_DATE value left blank would not be accurate because all of us have birth dates.

A blank for COLLEGE_LAST_ATTENDED may be accurate or inaccurate. If the person it applied to had attended college, it would be inaccurate. This is another case of valid but not accurate.

Missing values are very problematic in a database because of this characteristic. To be accurate in recording information, an optional data element should allow encoding a value for NULL. This is properly done by creating a separate field that indicates whether the value in the first field is missing or not. In this instance, the value in the primary field would be set to blank if no college had been attended. If the recorder just did not know the answer to the question, the NULL field would be set to indicate YES, meaning that the blank in the primary field did not apply.

Unfortunately, few systems are built to allow for this distinction. Even if they were, most data entry people would not get it right all of the time anyway.

Sometimes a system is created that supports a keyword that means empty. In the previous example, it might be "never attended college." This is a bad practice because it can make queries that do COUNT, GROUPBY, and other commands difficult or impossible to formulate correctly. Thus, it leads to inaccurate query results.

Poor design within a system for not making the distinction between "No value is OK" and "I don't know the correct value" is a common source of poor data quality.

Object-Level Accuracy

The concept of accuracy also applies above the data element level. Data elements are never recorded in isolation. They are value attributes of business objects such as personnel records, orders, invoices, payments, and inventory records. The business objects represent real-world objects or events, and each consists of one or more rows of one or more tables connected through keys. Object-level inaccuracies consist of objects that are missing, have missing parts, or that exist but should not.

For example, if a repair is done to a piece of capital equipment and the repair person just failed to complete and submit a record of the action, there would be a missing row or rows in the database. It is just not there. Any decisions made from the database can be flawed if the missing information would affect the outcome. Missing objects are very difficult to detect. This is an important component of accuracy because a database may have nothing but accurate data but be an inaccurate database because of missing information.

An example of missing elements might be found for an entity consisting of a master record and one or more subrecords. For example, a master record may consist of a record describing a rental object, and the subrecords are instances of renting. If one of the rentals is done without the record being added to the database, the database still looks accurate, but in fact is not.

Missing subrecords are very difficult to detect, whereas missing master records are generally easier to detect. For example, if the rental auto is sold and the master record deleted but not the subrecords, detecting the problem is easy.

An example of objects being present that should not be is a personnel database containing a record for an employee who left the company. The record was just not deleted when it should have been. These are also generally difficult to detect.

Object-Level Inconsistencies

The concept of consistency is also found at the object level. Databases are not static. Changes are being made all of the time. Large databases generally have data flowing into them from many different sources. If you have groups creating data with a different criterion for when to add an object (insert) or to remove an object (delete), you can end up with object inconsistency. This means that if you want to use the database to get information about object counts or data aggregations, you have the potential to get inaccurate results.

To guard against this, companies need to define birth and death rules for data objects and try their best to enforce them. They also need to define a method of determining when all of the data is consistent over some time period so that the data can be used intelligently. Figure 2.1 charts the scenarios discussed in this section in terms of what constitutes accurate versus inaccurate data.

2.4 Distribution of Inaccurate Data

The presence of wrong values will generally not be distributed evenly throughout the database. The reasons for this are as follows:

- Some data is more important than other data.

- Some inaccurate data tends to get recognized and fixed when used.

- How an element of data is used will affect the chances of inaccuracies being recognized.

- Flaws in data acquisition processes are not equal for all elements.

In every database there are data elements that are more important for an application than others. For example, in an orders database, the order number

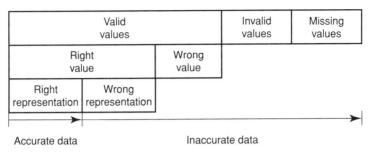

FIGURE 2.1   Breakdown of data within a set of data.

and customer number are more important than the order date. If the customer number is wrong, it will get recognized very early and get fixed. If the order date is wrong, it may never get recognized and fixed. In an HR (human resources) database, the employee's Social Security number is more important than the last education level achieved. A Social Security number error will get recognized and fixed very early, whereas the educational level achieved will probably never get recognized nor fixed. If a large number of errors occur on a frequent basis in important fields, a major issue erupts and the source of the errors is found and fixed.

Another factor is how a data element is used. A field that is used in computing an amount or for updating inventory levels is more important than one that is merely descriptive and is only printed on reports. Computations and aggregation fields will generally precipitate visual clues to errors, whereas fields not used for these purposes will generally not be recognized for their errors.

The tendency for data elements that are more important to be more accurate is why quality problems rarely surface through the initiating transaction applications. The major problems with fields important to the users of that application have already been recognized, and corrective action has been taken to ensure that they are of sufficient accuracy to satisfy their requirements.

The data inaccuracy problem surfaces when this data is moved and used for decision making. Many of the data elements used only to record secondary information about the transaction now become much more important. For example, trying to correlate promotions to educational levels requires that the "education level achieved" field be very accurate. This new use has a higher demand on this data element than the demands made from the HR application.

This is a major reason data suddenly appears to be awful even though the transaction applications have been running for years with no complaints. The new uses of the data place higher requirements for accuracy on some of the data elements than the transaction applications did.

Unfortunately, another dynamic comes into play regarding the chances of getting improvements made. The only way the data will come up to the level needed by the newer uses is for fundamental changes to occur all the way back to the transaction level. And yet, the farther away you get from the initiating application, the more difficult it is to get changes made. The people who own the data are satisfied with the quality and place low priority on complaints from decision support analysts. This situation screams out for data stewards and data quality controls.

2.5 Can Total Accuracy Be Achieved?

The short answer is no. There will always be some amount of data in any database that is inaccurate. There may be no data that is invalid. However, as we have seen, being valid is not the same thing as being accurate.

Data accuracy is much like air quality. You can never hope to get to 100% pure air quality within an area where people live and work. It is just not possible. However, most people can distinguish between good air quality and poor air quality, even though both have some level of imperfections. People value higher-quality air over lower-quality air; and they know the difference.

Data accuracy is the same thing. Improvements in the accuracy of data can change the perception of poor data quality to good data quality in most databases even though inaccuracies persist. It is a rare application that demands 100% accurate data to satisfy its requirements.

A database that has a 5% inaccurate data element rate will probably be very troublesome to most users. The same database at a 0.5% inaccurate rate would probably be very useful and considered high quality.

Another important concept to understand is that data inaccuracies arise for a variety of reasons. Some of these are

- wrong values entered

- data entry people who do not care to do the job right

- confusing and contradictory data entry screens or forms

- procedures that allow for data to not be entered or not be entered on time

- procedures or policies that promote entering wrong values

- poorly defined database systems

If you can identify and correct all of the sources except the first one, you can get to very high levels of data accuracy. You are left with only the case where I meant "blue" but entered "black." Data entry technology and best practices exist that can minimize the amount of these types of errors as well.

In almost all cases where poor data quality is reported, no effort has been made to identify root causes of wrong values. Without finding root causes, improvements in the quality are not going to occur. Whenever effort is spent to identify root causes and correct them, improvements follow. The improvements are almost always noticeable and impressive.

All other reasons tend to cause a clustering of data inaccuracies around the faulty process. These are easier to find and correct than the random errors that occur just because people enter data mistakenly. If all we had left were the random errors of people, the errors would be more evenly distributed throughout the database, would be small in number, and would have minimal impact on the uses of data.

So, the long answer is yes. You can get accurate data to a degree that makes it highly useful for all intended requirements.

2.6   Finding Inaccurate Values

Some of the inaccurate values can be found, but probably not all of them. In most cases a high percentage of inaccurate values can be found if enough effort is spent searching for them.

Figure 2.2 shows the general potential of any collection of data. In any collection there will be some data that is accurate and some that is not. This is shown by the first column. Of the data that is not accurate, some of it is valid and some of it is invalid.

There are two ways you can go about finding inaccurate data: reverification and analysis. If you want to be 100% sure that all values are accurate, you must use reverification. Even then, you cannot achieve this for many types of

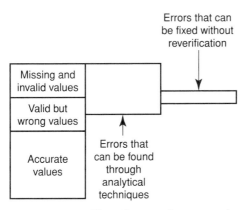

FIGURE 2.2   Chart of accurate/inaccurate values and those that are findable and fixable.

data. The reverification process may not be possible for some data. Reverification is done by people, and they may make mistakes in the reverification process.

The maximum potential of analytical techniques also falls short of perfect even if you employ all analytical techniques available.

Reverification

This means that you manually go back to the original source of the information and check every value. It is the only sure way to determine what values are right and what values are wrong. The reason for this is that analytical techniques cannot tell if a valid value is accurate unless there is a secondary source of information to correlate the value against.

Reverification is not always possible. For example, if the data records temperatures as of a point in time, it is impossible to go back in time and measure them again.

Reverification is also susceptible to errors. You would generally think that verifiers would be more careful than original entry people. However, this may not be true. In addition, the source of information that provided wrong information initially may continue to provide wrong information in the reverification. If someone lies about their age initially, they will probably lie about it in the reverification.

You would expect that a reverification would improve the quality of the data by some amount. It would catch more errors than it would create. However, you can never be sure that it catches them all.

Reverification takes a long time. If it were implemented as an operational technique to ensure the quality of the data before use, it would certainly violate the timeliness requirement for almost all uses.

The primary problem with reverification is that it is impractical for most databases. It is enormously time consuming and expensive. Reverification on databases that are continuously changing is extremely difficult if not downright impossible. For example, a web site that takes 10,000 orders per day is not likely to seek reverification of the information on every order. Companies are not willing or able to use this technique widely.

There are isolated cases for which reverification is practical. On small but important databases, it is not only possible but sometimes appropriate. For example, a database on capital equipment expenditures may use this technique. Another case is to use reverification on only part of the objects in a database. For example, an industrial supplier may verify order information on all orders over a certain amount of value or a certain amount of product.

Selective reverification may also be a technique used in monitoring a database. Random selection of transactions or records for reverification can be a good quality assessment tool either to spot developing problems or to instill confidence among users of the data. This improves the trust dimension of the quality of the data.

Analytical Techniques

Analytical techniques involve the use of software in conjunction with the skills of a data or business analyst to search through databases to find the presence of inaccurate data. Analytical techniques can be used against transactions as they are occurring, against databases as they are changing, or against databases on a periodic basis.

There are five categories of analysis that can be applied to data: data element analysis, structural analysis, value correlation, aggregation correlation, and value inspection. These are individually explored in Chapters 8 through 12. Each of these contributes to finding the presence of inaccurate data. However, not all of them can pinpoint the actual wrong values. The sections that follow briefly describe these types of analysis.

ELEMENT ANALYSIS

Element analysis involves looking at individual values in isolation to determine if they are valid. To do this you need a definition of what is valid and what is not. For example, a Social Security number must consist of nine numeric digits. If this is your only definition, you will find that all values that are blank, contain characters other than numeric or contain less than or more than nine digits. However, you can go further in your definition. The government employs a scheme of assigning numbers that allows you to examine the value in more detail to determine if it is valid or not. Using the larger rule has the potential for finding more inaccurate values.

Element analysis can include examination based on data type, length, range of values, list of discrete values allowed, patterns allowed, and any other information that is helpful. The more definition you provide, the more potential you have for finding invalid values.

A simplified but often overlooked technique for element analysis is visual inspection. This method involves looking at values to see if they belong to the data element or not. For example, you could not write a programmatic rule to find invalid names for names that contain valid characters. However, a human could look at the list and find wrong or questionable entries because of the superior human capability to deal with semantics and context. For example, names such as *Donald Duck*, *xwdcgex*, *Don't know*, and *Wouldn't tell me* would be spotted by the analyst and ruled to be invalid. You could not write a comprehensive enough rule to find these through a program.

STRUCTURAL ANALYSIS

Structural analysis techniques involve checking columns of values for unique-ness or consecutiveness, checking for orphans on collections of records with connecting parts, and checking for circular relationships. For example, no two employees can have the same employee number. Each employee record must have a corresponding emergency contact record, and each emergency contact record must belong to a valid employee record. An example of circular rela-tionships would be that a part cannot be used in the construction of itself.

Structural analysis techniques are used on collections of records. They can identify clear inaccuracies in the data. They generally isolate the error to a small number of records. They do not identify the offending values. Reverifi-cation generally is required to pinpoint the actual offender.

VALUE CORRELATION

Value correlation analysis involves checking collections of values against a rule that must hold true over the data. For example, if an EMPLOYEE_TYPE field indicates a part-time employee, the PAY_TYPE field must be hourly. This is a rule that applies to a subset of the records in the database. If it is vio-lated, an inaccuracy exists in the data. However, you cannot tell which value is wrong, EMPLOYEE_TYPE or PAY_TYPE. You just know that one of them is wrong.

Value correlation can be very simple or very complex. It may involve only values in a single row, values in multiple rows of the same relation, or values that cross over rows of multiple tables.

There is generally a large number of rules that can be written for cross-checking values to ensure that the set of values represents a valid combination. When a rule is violated, you cannot tell which value is the offender unless the rule involves only one data element. In addition, rules can be satisfied with completely inaccurate data. In the previous example, if the employee record showed EMPLOYEE_TYPE as part-time and PAY_TYPE as hourly, it would be satisfied even though it is possible the EMPLOYEE_TYPE field is inaccurate (i.e., it is really a full-time employee). In fact, both EMPLOYEE_TYPE and PAY_TYPE can satisfy the rule, even though both are inaccurate.

AGGREGATION CORRELATION

Aggregation correlation analysis is used to identify the presence of inaccura-cies through examining aggregated values over large amounts of data. For example, a rule may say that the count of orders by region for a week should be greater than 100 and less than 1,000. Violations would indicate that either data is missing or orders have the wrong date on them.

VALUE INSPECTION

Values can often be computed that allow the analyst to inspect them and determine if they are reasonable or not. Visual inspection differs from aggregation correlation in that it applies to cases where it is not possible to create a clear rule that defines the boundary between right and wrong. Small amounts of inaccurate data may not provide a clear indicator. However, clearly unreasonable data will jump out at the analyst.

For example, the distribution of values within a column may indicate that a problem exists. If 60% of the records indicate the same color of product even though you know that the colors should be approximately evenly divided over a set of 10 colors, the data is clearly inaccurate.

Aggregation tests can be applied to distribution of values, counts, sums, averages, and medians. They can also be used to compare aggregations between groups such as between sales regions.

In summary, element analysis is used to find only invalid values. Structural analysis, value correlation, aggregation correlation, and value inspection are used to find the presence of inaccuracies among valid values. They cannot identify the offending values but can determine with certainty that some of the values are wrong.

LOOKS LIKE A DUCK, WALKS LIKE A DUCK

Although it is clear that you cannot find all inaccurate data values in a database, there is clearly value in finding out what you can detect. If a database has inaccurate data within it, it is very likely that analytical techniques will surface enough of them to get a good picture of the health of the data. It is highly unlikely that all or most of the inaccurate values can hide out as valid values that successfully correlate through all rules. You will find enough inaccurate data, provided you do a thorough enough job of analysis.

You also do not need to worry about seeing only the tip of the iceberg. In most cases, the inaccuracies disclosed through analysis represent a significant portion of the bad values.

A quality improvement program will probably improve the accuracy of data that was not discoverable through analysis along with the inaccuracies that were discovered. This is a secondary effect. For example, if your analysis indicates that 8% of the records in a specific database have at least one wrong value, you implement changes targeting the areas you uncovered and then reassess to find that the new number is 1%. The actual improvement is probably greater than the 7% indicated because of the effect of improvements on values not discoverable through analysis. The result is that users may feel that

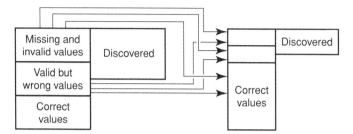

FIGURE 2.3   Effects of improvements.

a much bigger improvement has actually taken place. Figure 2.3 indicates cross-correlations in terms of the effects of improvements in the accuracy of data values.

2.7   How Important Is It to Get Close?

You can achieve very high levels of accuracy of data within a database if enough energy and resources are applied. Although data accuracy is only one component of data quality, it is clearly the single most important component. If the data values are just plain wrong, missing, or inconsistent, any attempt to use the data will be tainted. Every quality improvement program must begin by dealing with data accuracy.

Most decision support applications have a tolerance level for inaccurate data. Inaccuracies up to the tolerance level allow the application to provide high-quality decisions. The inaccuracies do not change the outcome from what it would be if the data were 100% accurate, provided the data inaccuracies are not unduly biased.

Above the tolerance level, the data will generate wrong decisions but will not be noticed because the decisions are not so bad. This is a dangerous situation because the company is acting in the wrong way to data that they believe to be good. It leads to inefficiencies that are not noticed. At some higher level of inaccuracies, the data becomes not believed and has no effect on decisions because it is not used. Figure 2.4 depicts the relationship of usefulness and accuracy as a step function influence on tolerance levels.

Most business analysts have no idea how to compute the tolerance levels for decisions they make. Because they have no idea how bad the data is, they must believe what they see.

This highlights two important aspects of working to improve the accuracy of data. First, you have a good chance of bringing the data accuracy back to the first area (the good place to be). You do not have to get to zero errors, you just need to get into the good zone. Second, you provide valuable information

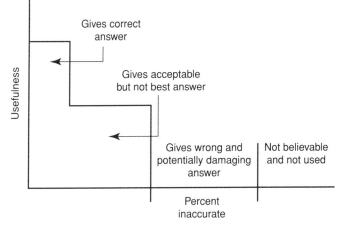

FIGURE 2.4 Step function influence on tolerance levels.

to the decision makers on the relative accuracy of the data. If you do not have an assessment program, you either blindly believe the data or mistrust it enough to either use it with caution or never use it.

Because decision-making efficiency is a step function of data accuracy, it follows that small improvements in the accuracy can lead to very large payoffs in value. If the quantity of inaccuracies is putting you in the wrong decision zone, and improvements move you into the zone of right decisions, the difference in value to the corporation can be enormous.

If you have no data quality program, there is probably a huge potential value in instituting one. You have no idea how much value is there because you are blindly using the data you have and have no idea how bad it is. The cost of lowering the percentage of inaccurate data will almost always pay off big for early improvements. As you get closer to zero errors, the cost will prove to be excessive in comparison to gain. However, you can get very close before the crossover occurs.

2.8 Closing Remarks

Data accuracy is the most visible and dramatic dimension of data quality. It is the easiest to expose, the easiest to make improvements in, often does not require system reengineering to achieve improvements, and often does not require reorganization of your corporation to accommodate it. Although you cannot get to perfect accuracy in your data, you can improve the accuracy to the point where it consistently provides information that drives correct decisions.

Data accuracy is a complex subject that needs to be fully understood. The concepts of valid versus invalid, inconsistencies in representation, object-level inconsistency, representation of values not known, and missing information are all part of defining accuracy.

There are two methods of determining the accuracy of data: reverification and data analysis. Neither one can guarantee finding all inaccurate values.

Reverification is generally too expensive and slow to be effective. Analytical techniques are easier to use. Analytical techniques require that you understand what the definition of "correct" is for each data element. Just as accurate data is the foundation component of data quality, analytical techniques are the foundation component of any effective data quality assurance program.

CHAPTER 3

Sources of Inaccurate Data

Before we can assess data correctness we need to understand the various ways inaccurate values get into databases. There are many sources of data inaccuracies, and each contributes its own part to the total data quality problem. Understanding these sources will demonstrate the need for a comprehensive program of assessment, monitoring, and improvement. Having highly accurate data requires attention to all sources of inaccuracies and appropriate responses and tools for each.

Figure 3.1 shows the four general areas where inaccuracies occur. The first three cause inaccuracies in data within the databases, whereas the fourth area causes inaccuracies in the information products produced from the data. If you roll up all potential sources of errors, the interesting conclusion is that the most important use of the data (corporate decision making) is made on the rendition of data that has the most inaccuracies.

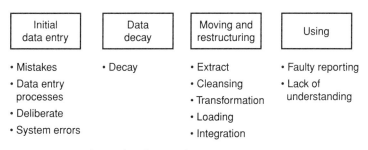

FIGURE 3.1 Areas where inaccuracies occur.

3.1 Initial Data Entry

Most people assume that data inaccuracies are always the result of entering the wrong data at the beginning. This is certainly a major source of data inaccuracies but not the only source. Inaccurate data creation can be the result of mistakes, can result from flawed data entry processes, can be deliberate, or can be the result of system errors. By looking at our systems through these topics, you can gain insight into whether systems are designed to invite inaccurate data or are designed to promote accurate data.

Data Entry Mistakes

The most common source of a data inaccuracy is that the person entering the data just plain makes a mistake. You intend to enter *blue* but enter *bleu* instead; you hit the wrong entry on a select list; you put a correct value in the wrong field. Much of operational data originates from a person. People make mistakes; we make them all the time. It is doubtful that anyone could fill out a hundred-field form without making at least one mistake.

A real-world example involves an automobile damage claims database in which the COLOR field was entered as text. Examination of the content of this field yielded 13 different spellings for the word *beige*. Some of these mistakes were the result of typos. Others were just that the entry person did not know how to spell the word. In some of the latter cases, they thought they knew how to spell the word, whereas in others they were just not able or willing to look it up.

Flawed Data Entry Processes

A lot of data entry begins with a form. A person completes a form either on a piece of paper or on a computer screen. Form design has a lot to do with the amount of inaccurate data that ends up in the database. Form design should begin with a basic understanding of quality issues in order to avoid many of the mistakes commonly seen. For example, having someone select from a list of valid values instead of typing in a value can eliminate the misspellings previously cited.

Another common problem is having fields on the form that are confusing to the user. This often leads them to enter wrong information. The field itself may be confusing to the user. If it is a field that is not commonly understood, or if the database definition is unconventional, the form needs to provide assistance in guiding the user through entry of values into the field. Sometimes the confusion is in the way the field is described in its identifying text or in its positioning on the form. Form design should always be subjected to rigorous quality testing to find the fields a normal user would have difficulty in knowing what to enter.

Data entry windows should have instructions available as HELP functions and should be user friendly in handling errors. Frustration in using a form can lead to deliberate mistakes that corrupt the database.

Forms are better completed by a trained entry person than by a one-time user. This is because the entry person can be taught how things should be entered, can become proficient in using the form mechanisms, and can be given feedback to improve the efficiency and accuracy of the data. A one-time user is always uncertain about what they are supposed to do on the form. Unfortunately, our society is moving by way of the Internet toward eliminating the middle person in the process and having end users complete forms directly. This places a much higher demand on quality form design.

The data entry process includes more than the forms that are filled out. It also includes the process that surrounds it. Forms are completed at a specific point or points in a process. Sometimes we have forms that are required to be completed when not all information is known or easily obtained at that point in the process. This will inevitably lead to quality problems.

An example of a data entry process I helped design a number of years ago for military repair personnel is very instructive of the types of problems that can occur in data collection. The U.S. Navy has a database that collects detailed information on the repair and routine maintenance performed on all aircraft and on all major components of every ship. This database is intended to be used for a variety of reasons, from negotiating contracts with suppliers, to validating warrantees, to designing new aircraft and ships.

When an aircraft carrier is in a combat situation, such as in Kuwait and Afghanistan, repairs are being made frequently. The repair crews are working around the clock and under a great deal of pressure to deal with a lot of situations that come up unexpectedly. Completing forms is the least of their concerns. They have a tendency to fix things and do the paperwork later. The amount of undocumented work piles up during the day, to be completed when a spare moment is available. By then the repair person has forgotten some of the work done or the details of some of the work and certainly is in a hurry to get it done and out of the way.

Another part of this problem comes in when the data is actually entered from the forms. The forms are coming out of a hectic, very messy environment. Some of the forms are torn; some have oil or other substances on them. The writing is often difficult to decipher. The person who created it is probably not available and probably would not remember much about it if available.

A database built from this system will have many inaccuracies in it. Many of the inaccuracies will be missing information or valid but wrong information. An innovative solution that involves wireless, handheld devices and employs voice recognition technology would vastly improve the completeness and accuracy of this database. I hope the U.S. Navy has made considerable improvements in the data collection processes for this application since I left. I trust they have.

The Null Problem

A special problem occurs in data entry when the information called for is not available. A data element has a value, an indicator that the value is not known, or an indicator that no value exists (or is applicable) for this element in this record. Have you ever seen an entry screen that had room for a value and two indicator boxes you could use for the case where there is no value? I haven't. Most form designs either mandate that a value be provided or allow it to be left blank. If left blank, you do not know the difference between value-not-known and no-value-applies.

When the form requires that an entry be available and the entry person does not have the value, there is a strong tendency to "fake it" by putting a wrong, but acceptable, value into the field. This is even unintentionally encouraged for selection lists that have a default value in the field to start with.

It would be better form design to introduce the notion of NOT KNOWN or NOT APPLICABLE for data elements that are not crucial to the transaction being processed. This would at least allow the entry people to enter accurately what they know and the users of the data to understand what is going on in the data.

It would make sense in some cases to allow the initial entry of data to record NOT KNOWN values and have the system trigger subsequent activities that would collect and update these fields after the fact. This is far better than having people enter false information or leaving something blank and not knowing if a value exists for the field or not.

An example of a data element that may be NOT KNOWN or NOT APPLICABLE is a driver's license number. If the field is left blank, you cannot tell if it was not known at the point of entry or whether the person it applies to does not have a driver's license. Failure to handle the possibility of information not being available at the time of entry and failure to allow for options to express what you do know about a value leads to many inaccuracies in data.

Deliberate Errors

Deliberate errors are those that occur when the person enters a wrong value on purpose. There are three reasons they do this:

- They do not know the correct information.

- They do not want you to know the correct information.

- They get a benefit from entering the wrong information.

DO NOT KNOW CORRECT INFORMATION

Not knowing the correct information occurs when the form requires a value for a field and the person wants or needs to complete the form but does not know the value to use. The form will not be complete without a value. The person does not believe the value is important to the transaction, at least not relative to what they are trying to do. The result is that they make up a value, enter the information, and go on.

Usually the information is not important to completing the transaction but may be important to other database users later on. For example, asking and requiring a value for the license plate number of your car when registering for a hotel has no effect on getting registered. However, it may be important when you leave your lights on and they need to find out whose car it is.

DO NOT WISH TO GIVE THE CORRECT INFORMATION

The second source of deliberate errors is caused by the person providing the data not wanting to give the correct information. This is becoming a more and more common occurrence with data coming off the Internet and the emergence of CRM applications. Every company wants a database on all of their customers in order to tailor marketing programs. However, they end up with a lot of incorrect data in their databases because the information they ask people for is more than people are willing to provide or is perceived to be an invasion of privacy.

Examples of fields that people will lie about are age, height, weight, driver's license number, home phone number, marital status, annual income, and education level. People even lie about their name if it can get the result they want from the form without putting in their correct name. A common name appearing in many marketing databases is Mickey Mouse.

The problem with collecting data that is not directly required to complete the transaction is that the quality of these data elements tends to be low but is not immediately detected. It is only later, when you try to employ this data, that the inaccuracies show up and create problems.

FALSIFYING TO OBTAIN A BENEFIT

The third case in which deliberate mistakes are made is where the entry person obtains an advantage in entering wrong data. Some examples from the real world illustrate this.

An automobile manufacturer receives claim forms for warranty repairs performed by dealers. Claims for some procedures are paid immediately, whereas claims for other procedures are paid in 60 days. The dealers figure out this scheme and deliberately lie about the procedures performed in order to get their money faster. The database incorrectly identifies the repairs made. Any attempt to use this database to determine failure rates would be a total failure. In fact, it was in attempts to use this data for this purpose that led to the discovery of the practice. It had been going on for years.

A bank gives branch bank employees a bonus for all new corporate accounts. A new division of a larger company opens an account with a local branch. If the bank employee determines that this is a sub-account of a larger, existing customer (the correct procedure), no bonus is paid upon opening the account. If, however, the account is opened as a new corporate customer (the wrong procedure), a bonus is paid.

An insurance company sells automobile insurance policies through independent insurance writers. In a metropolitan area, the insurance rate is determined by the Zip code of the applicant. The agents figure out that if they falsify the ZIP CODE field on the initial application for high-cost Zip codes, they can get the client on board at a lower rate. The transaction completes, the agent gets his commission, and the customer corrects the error when the renewal forms arrive a year later. The customer's rates subsequently go up as a result.

Data entry people are rated based on the number of documents entered per hour. They are not penalized for entering wrong information. This leads to a practice of entering data too fast, not attempting to resolve issues with input documents, and making up missing information. The operators who enter the poorest-quality data get the highest performance ratings.

All of these examples demonstrate that company policy can encourage people to deliberately falsify information in order to obtain a personal benefit.

System Problems

Systems are too often blamed for mistakes when, after investigation, the mistakes turn out to be the result of a human error. Our computing systems have become enormously reliable over the years. However, database errors do occur because of system problems when the transaction systems are not properly designed.

Database systems have the notion of COMMIT. This means that changes to a database system resulting from an external transaction either get completely committed or completely rejected. Specific programming logic ensures that a partial transaction never occurs. In application designs, the user is generally made aware that a transaction has committed to the database.

In older systems, the transaction path from the person entering data to the database was very short. It usually consisted of a terminal passing information through a communications controller to a mainframe, where an application program made the database calls, performed a COMMIT, and sent a response back to the terminal. Terminals were either locally attached or accessed through an internal network.

Today, the transaction path can be very long and very complex. It is not unusual for an application to occur outside your corporation on a PC, over the Internet. The transaction flows through ISPs to an application server in your company. This server then passes messages to a database server, where the database calls are made. It is not unusual for multiple application servers to be in the path of the transaction. It is also not unusual for multiple companies to house application servers in the path. For example, Amazon passes transactions to other companies for "used book" orders.

The person entering the data is a nonprofessional, totally unfamiliar with the system paths. The paths themselves involve many parts, across many communication paths. If something goes wrong, such as a server going down, the person entering the information may not have any idea of whether the transaction occurred or not. If there is no procedure for them to find out, they often reenter the transaction, thinking it is not there, when in fact it is; or they do not reenter the transaction, thinking it happened, when in fact it did not. In one case, you have duplicate data; in the other, you have missing data.

More attention must be paid to transaction system design in this new, complex world we have created. We came pretty close to cleaning up transaction failures in older "short path" systems but are now returning to this problem with the newer "long path" systems.

In summary, there are plenty of ways data inaccuracies can occur when data is initially created. Errors that occur innocently tend to be random and are difficult to correct. Errors that are deliberate or are the result of poorly constructed processes tend to leave clues around that can be detected by analytical techniques.

3.2   Data Accuracy Decay

Data that is accurate when initially created can become inaccurate within a database through time. The data value does not change; its accuracy does. Some data elements are subject to value accuracy decay and some are not. Some examples will illustrate the concept of decay.

Personal information in an employee database easily becomes wrong. People move, they change their marital status, they complete new education programs, they change telephone numbers. Most employees do not run into HR and fill out a form every time something changes in their life. The information in HR reflects the accuracy at the time they initially joined the company or the last time an update was done. Inventory-on-hand information can become wrong due to spoilage, parts taken and used, and new transactions not processed.

The value carried on the books for capital assets can change due to market demand changes, changes in the environment in which the asset is used, unusual wear and tear, or damage done and not reported. A state driver's license database indicates that a person has acceptable eyesight to drive without glasses. However, during the time since the license was issued, the person's eyesight may deteriorate to the point where she cannot safely drive without glasses. The inaccuracy will not be corrected until a renewal requires a new eye test.

All of these examples show that a change occurred in the object being represented in the database and the database was not updated to reflect it. Another way of saying this is that a transaction was needed to be processed and was not. However, these "missing transactions" are commonplace in the real world.

Not all data elements are subject to decay. Information defining an object generally does not decay, whereas information providing other information about the object generally can be subject to decay. Good database designers will note the decay characteristic of a data element as part of the metadata and will design processes to verify or update the information as needed by the consumers of the data. For example, in an inventory application, the data elements for PART_NUMBER, PART_DESCRIPTION, and UNIT_OF_MEASURE would not be considered subject to decay, whereas QUANTITY_ON_HAND, SUPPLIER_ID, and STORAGE_BIN_NUMBER would be subject to decay.

Another characteristic of decay-prone data elements is that the overall accuracy of the element tends to follow a sawtooth graph over time. Data is entered. Over time, the older data gets progressively more inaccurate (it decays). The accuracy of the element is determined by the mix of older data versus newer data, which tends to be more accurate. A corrective action occurs that pulls the data back into a higher state of accuracy.

In the previously cited examples, the corrective event for HR information may be an annual data review conducted with all employees; for inventory, an annual inventory exercise; for capital equipment, an annual reappraisal. Note that for the driver's license example there is no event that brings all or a set of records into accuracy at a single point in time. It is a continuous database with new records and renewals occurring on an individual timeline. This does not follow a sawtooth pattern because the decaying and correcting occurs continuously over the database. However, it does have an inaccuracy component due to decay that remains fairly constant over time. This relationship of accuracy and time is depicted in Figure 3.2.

An example of a good HR system is to have new employees verify all HR information immediately after initial entry into the database, request that employees review all personal information each time they make any change, and then request a specific review by the employee any time no review has been done in a year (or less if you can get away with it). Another mechanism is to make the review a part of the annual employee evaluation process. It would not hurt to monitor marriage and birth announcements as well.

Unfortunately, most companies are not willing to be that concerned about data decay accuracy issues. It is not because they have considered the cost of a continuous updating process to be higher than the cost of not being more accurate. It is more a case of not thinking about the problem at all. The cost of a corrective program is not very high once it has been put in place. It will generally return more value than it costs.

A proper way of handling decay-prone data elements is to identify them in the database design and indicate this in the metadata repository. Periodic events should be planned to update information to get the database to recover

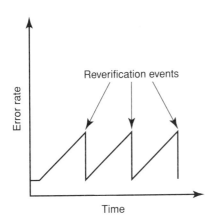

FIGURE 3.2 Accuracy of decayable elements over time.

from decay. The times that these events occur should be included in the database and/or the metadata repository so that database business users can know what to expect. The metadata repository should also include information on the rate of change that occurred in the periodic auditing event. A good data analyst knows the rate of decay and the probable accuracy index for any element at any given point in time.

3.3 Moving and Restructuring Data

Inaccurate data is often created from perfectly good data through the processes used to move and restructure data. These processes are commonly used to extract data from operational databases and put it into data warehouses, data marts, or operational data stores. It may also restage the data for access through corporate portals. This is an area often overlooked as a source of data inaccuracies and yet it contributes significantly to the inaccuracy problem. When you hear complaints that the data in a data warehouse or data mart is wrong and unusable, a major contributing factor might be flawed data movement processes as opposed to the data being inaccurate in the source databases.

Moving and restructuring data is commonly done through ETL (extract, transform, and load) processes. There may also be data scrubbing processes involved. Sometimes this is performed through packaged tools and sometimes through in-house-developed scripts or programs. When packaged tools are used, the errors are not coming from them but rather from faulty specifications used for them.

Entire classes of tools and software companies emerged to support this activity. The two primary tool categories are ETL and data cleansing. What was missing was tools to help understand the data in enough detail to effectively use the tools and to design decision support systems correctly. The recent emergence of data profiling tools is intended to fill this gap and is showing dramatically positive effects when used.

The irony of it is that most projects claim to be extracting the data and cleaning it up before it is moved into the data warehouses, when in fact they are making it dirtier, not cleaner. Data is generated and stored in a database based on the initiating application. This is generally a transaction system that collects the data and performs updates. The database is generally designed to meet the requirements of the initiating application and nothing more. The design of the data and the database is generally poorly documented and almost always not kept up to date.

There are also a host of other reasons for moving data to a database of a different structure. These include migration of applications to newer technology or to packaged applications. For many applications, this may be the first time they have been subject to a major reengineering effort. Another reason is the need to consolidate databases. Consolidations occur for two reasons: corporation mergers and acquisitions, and the need to centralize databases from local or divisional databases.

An important fact of migrations and consolidations is that you cannot leave the old data behind. Most databases require a continuity of information over long periods of time. You cannot move to a new personnel system and not move the existing personnel information behind. You cannot move to a new supply chain system and not move the inventory or the inventory history data. Figure 3.3 lists projects for which database restructure and/or data movement should be a serious consideration.

There are two major problems frequently found in moving and restructuring data. The first is that to effectively accomplish the movement of the data to another database you have to fully understand everything about the source database (and the target, if it is not a new database). The reality is nothing close to this. The other problem is thatthe source systems were never designed with the thought of having to give up their data to another database.

THE *software industry supported moving and restructuring data by creating two disjointed types of products: ETL products and data cleansing products.*

ETL products provide support for extracting data from source systems, transforming values in the data, aggregating data, and producing suitable load files for target systems.

Data cleansing companies provide support for processing selective data fields to standardize values, find errors, and make corrections through external correlation. Their target has been primarily name and address field data, which easily lends itself to this process. It has also been found to be usable on some other types of data.

In spite of very good software from these companies, a lot of data inaccuracies filter through the process and a

lot of new inaccuracies are generated. None of this is the fault of the products from these companies. They all execute as advertised. The problem is that they will not work correctly unless accurate specifications of the source data and the work to be done are entered. The problem is that the tools cannot help if they are fed inaccurate or incomplete specifications.

This has led to the emergence of a third product type: data profiling products. Data profiling is intended to complete or correct the metadata about source systems. It is also used to map systems together correctly. The information developed in profiling becomes the specification information that is needed by ETL and data cleansing products. This relationship is shown in Figure 3.4 at the end of this chapter.

- Migrate data to newly designed application
- Migrate data to packaged application
- Merge databases as a result of acquisition
- Merge divisional databases
- Build a data warehouse
- Build an operational data store
- Build a data mart
- Implement a CRM system

FIGURE 3.3 List of projects that require restructuring and movement of data.

This is particularly the case for a database of a different type, designed very differently and combining it with data from other sources.

Understanding Source Databases

Rarely do you have current, complete information available on transaction systems. Metadata dictionaries and repositories generally have very low accuracy. Even COBOL copybooks sport a high degree of mismatch between what they say and how the data is actually stored.

The poor attention paid to creating and maintaining accurate data in data dictionaries and metadata repositories is now hurting corporations to the tune of millions of dollars in unnecessarily complex data movement projects and/or in having to accept low-quality data (data that is even of lower quality than the source databases it is extracted from) for use in decision making.

The reasons for poor data quality in metadata repositories are many. Repository technology has lagged behind database design evolution. Repository solutions are generally insufficient in content to collect all the needed information. They are passive, which means that they can get out of step with the data without noticeable impacts on normal operations. There has been little motivation on the part of data administration staff to keep them current.

COBOL copybooks also become inaccurate over time. Changes to fields are often done without updating the copybook. A character field may be reassigned to be used for an entirely different purpose. If the physical definition of the field satisfies the new use, the copybook change is not needed to make the program work. This results in the field name and comment text referring to the old meaning and not the new meaning. This can, and will, mislead anyone using it to make changes or to extract data.

In many instances, valuable application information was found stored in the space defined to COBOL as FILLER. This is a common and quick-fix way of implementing a change and of completely bypassing an update of the copybook or any other documentation that may exist.

Overloaded Fields

Older, legacy applications are filled with "overloaded" fields. An overloaded field is one that has information about multiple, different facts stored in the same field.

An example of an overloaded field is where a mainframe application developer needs a new field that has a binary representation such as YES or NO. They do not want to waste the space for a new field (a common concern for developers in the 1960 to 1980 time frame). Instead of creating a new field, they decide to use an unused bit of another, existing field. This could be one of the spare bits within packed decimal fields for IBM mainframes or the sign bit of a numeric field that can never be negative. The result is an overloaded field. Other examples of overloaded fields are to use each bit of a single byte to represent the value for a different binary-valued field or to use free-form text fields to encode keywords that mean different things.

An extreme case discovered in one system was that a person's NAME field had the characters *DECEASED appended to it within the same NAME field if the person was dead. So, for example, the value *Jack Olson* meant who I am and that I am alive, whereas the value *Jack Olson *DECEASED* meant who I am and that I am not alive.

The problem with overloaded fields is that they are generally never documented. The copybook definitions and dictionary definitions usually document only the underlying field or, in the case of multivalued keyword fields, document it only as a text field.

Analysts designing data movement and restructuring processes often do not become aware of the overloading and either incorrectly transform and move the data or reject some or all of the values in the field as being inaccurate. In the process of rejection, they are losing correct information on each of the separate facts recorded in the field.

Another real example of overloading fields is where a legacy system developer used the sign bit on the PAY_RATE field to represent a different fact because this field should never be negative. Neither this convention nor the meaning of the bit was ever documented. When they upgraded to a new packaged application for payroll, they moved the field as it existed, innocently thinking that they did not need to investigate such an obvious field. When they ran their first payroll, 30% of the checks had negative amounts. This is an example of a situation in which you absolutely must verify the content of every field against your expectations when you lift it out of one system and place it into another.

Sometimes the information needed about existing databases is not recorded anywhere. You often need detailed information on missing or exception conditions. This is often not available. You also need information on accuracy. This is never recorded anywhere.

Matching Source Databases to Target Databases

This is tricky business. You first need to have a total understanding of both systems. You then need to match data elements to determine whether the result makes sense.

In matching data elements you are saying that a particular field in the source system contains the content you need to put into a particular field in the target system. Many times this is an obvious match, such as a PAYTYPE field in one system and a PAY_TYPE field in the other system. However, when you get below the surface, differences can emerge that are highly significant and can create enormous problems if not addressed. The types of problems that can occur are

- The actual representation of the values within the field may differ. One system, for example, may encode PAY_TYPE as H and S for hourly and salaried. The other may encode the same information as 1 and 2. You must look at the values to determine what is there.

- The scope of values may differ. One system may have two types of PAY_TYPE, and the other may have three types. Are the differences reconcilable?

- One system may record information to a lower level of granularity than the other system. For example, one may encode color as RED, BLUE, and GREEN, whereas the other system may have five values for shades of RED, four values for shades of BLUE, and so on. The issue then becomes whether the target system can deal with the differences.

- The systems may handle NULL or NOT KNOWN differently. One system may not allow them, whereas the other does. One system may record a NULL as a blank and the other system as the ? character.

- Special meanings may be attached to specific values in one system. For example, a policy number of 99999999 may mean that the policy number has not been assigned yet.

It is not sufficient that the target system have a field of the correct data type and length as the source system field. It is necessary that every value in the source system can be translated to an acceptable value in the target system that has exactly the same semantic meaning. Failure to do this will turn acceptable (accurate) values in the source system into unacceptable (inaccurate) values in the target system.

Another problem comes into play in matching data elements when there are a different number of data elements between the source and target systems. When the target system has a data element that does not exist in the source system, a determination needs to be made on what to do about it. The target data element may be eliminated from the design, NULLS inserted, or values manufactured for the field. In any case, the result is less than optimal. This problem is compounded when merging data from multiple sources wherein some sources have values for this field and other sources do not. The result is a target data element populated with highly questionable data. Any attempt to use the field to generate aggregations for groups will yield inaccurate results.

When the source system contains excess data elements, a decision needs to be made on whether the information is, in fact, needed in the target system. Generally it is okay to leave it out, provided it does not have structural importance to other data elements.

Source and target systems need to be matched at the structural level as well as at the data element level. This is a step often either not done or done very poorly. The result can be failures in attempting to move the data or, worse yet, inaccurate results in the target systems.

Structural matching involves checking to see if data element functional dependencies and referential constraints in the source systems match those in the target systems. This is discussed in detail in Chapter 9.

For example, if the data elements of one system are not part of a primary key and they correspond to data elements in the other system that are part of a primary key, an error can easily occur in trying to move the data. Another example is where in one system the DISCOUNT is applied to the order, and in the other system it is applied to individual line items within the order. If the target system has the discount on the order, a problem exists in trying to move the data.

A large number of errors are routinely made when trying to force data into a target structure in circumstances where the two systems are structurally different and not reconcilable. The reason so much force fitting is done is that the information about these differences usually does not surface until the actual implementation phase of projects. By then, the project team is trying to make things work at any cost.

Once data is understood and matched, the project must construct processes to extract the data from the source databases, run them through any data cleansing needed, apply transforms, and load the data into the target systems. Shortcomings in analyzing the source data and in matching elements and structures often lead to serious problems in executing these procedures or result in corrupt data in the target systems.

Extraction

Extracting data normally involves reading the source databases and building output files suitable for use in the subsequent processes. These output files are almost always expected to be in a normalized form. This means that they are tables of values, hopefully in "third-normal" form. (Normal forms of data are explained in Section 9.1.)

Source systems are not always easy to unwind into a set of normalized flat files. Depending on the complexity of how data is stored in the source systems, this can be a monumental task that is susceptible to all sorts of errors.

For example, a mainframe VSAM application covered by COBOL copybooks may store information in the same data file for many different records and have variations embedded within. Liberal use of the REDEFINE and OCCURS clauses can provide a challenging structural situation that must be studied thoroughly before developing the extraction routines.

A program cannot automatically figure this out for you. Many extraction programs have been constructed that automatically read the copybook and develop extraction logic from it. There are a number of problems with this approach. A REDEFINE may be used to recast the same facts or to indicate a different set of facts depending on some other value in the record. Only a human can determine which is meant. In one case you need to select the representation to include in the output; in the other you need to normalize the facts within the REDEFINE into separate data elements. A similar situation exists for OCCURS clauses. Do they represent n occurrences of the same fact or n different facts? One case calls for normalization into a separate file, and the other does not.

A company was trying to move a VSAM application for which over 200 different record types were encoded within the same VSAM file using a record type field to distinguish them and an equal number of record-level REDEFINEs. There were also liberal uses of REDEFINE and OCCURS within many of these record types. In essence, the user had cleverly defined an entire relational database structure within the VSAM file structure for a single file. Unfortunately, his cleverness caused great pains for subsequent analysts who needed to extract data from this file. As you might expect, he was no longer with the company when this was needed. Unraveling it into the proper relational definition was not easy.

Converting nonrelational structures to normalized files may also require key generation in cases for which the connection between records is done through positioning or internal pointers. Failure to recognize this and provide the keys will result in files that lack the ability to JOIN objects later or to enforce referential integrity constraints.

Extraction routines also need to handle overloaded fields. Often, they merely look at the source data as being in error and just reject the values or substitute a NULL or blank/zero value in its place. This is generating wrong information from correct information.

Source systems are often denormalized. Denormalization was a common trick used in earlier systems (especially early relational systems) to obtain adequate performance. Failure to recognize that the source data is denormalized results in denormalized flat files, which can lead to denormalized targets, which can lead to statistical errors when using the data. This is another area rarely documented in source systems.

The inverse is also true. Extraction routines that "flatten" data from hierarchical structures often generate denormalized flat files from structures that were correctly normalized. Most general-purpose extraction programs have the potential for doing this. For example, in an IMS database containing multiple segment types, if only one output file is generated for the entire database, it is denormalized if multiple occurrences of child segments are allowed for each parent instance. This output file will generate errors in the target system if the denormalization is not corrected somewhere else in the process.

Data Cleansing

Data cleansing involves identifying incorrect data values and then either correcting them or rejecting them. They deal with INVALID values in single data elements or correlation across multiple data elements. Many products are available to help you construct data cleansing routines. They can be helpful in improving the accuracy of data or they can result in less accurate data, depending on how carefully they are used.

Data cleansing becomes a problem when you lack an understanding of the source data and reject values that have special meaning. For example, if the source system had a convention of putting a value of * in a STATE field to indicate local state, the scrubbing routine may infer that * is invalid and either reject the row or put a null in its place. Even though the convention is unusual, it was correct in the source system, whose applications understood the convention.

Another problem is when data cleansing routines reject a value that is clearly correctable. For example, multiple representations of a name in a text field may include misspellings or alternative representations that are clearly recognizable for what they should be in the source systems. For example, the entry *blakc* is clearly a misspelling for *black*, and *Tex* is clearly an alternative representation of the text *Texas* (or *TX* if two characters are the convention).

A poorly designed data cleansing routine will reject these values and substitute a NULL or blank. The result is that there is no way of correcting it in the target system because the original wrong value is lost.

Data cleansing routines can identify wrong values but generally cannot correct them. They can correct values only through synonym lists or correlation against tables showing valid combinations of values. Most of the time they identify a wrong value but cannot correct it. The only alternative is to change the value to unknown (NULL in most systems) or to reject the row in which the bad value is contained. If it is rejected, they can either leave it out of the target (creating a bigger problem) or manually investigate the value and reenter it into the target after correction.

Leaving rows out has multiple problems. First, you are losing some data. The correct data in other data elements of these rows may be more important to the target than the result you get by leaving the entire row out. Another problem is that you may create a structural problem relative to other rows in the same or other tables. For example, if you reject an order header, the order detail records in a different file will become orphans. Rejecting one row may have the effect of causing many other rows to be rejected later, when referential constraints are enforced upon load.

Transforms

Transforms are routines that change the representation of a value while not changing the content. For example, in one system, GENDER may be represented by 1 and 2, whereas in the target it is represented by M and F. The transformation routine simply translates 1s to M and 2s to F. Transformation routines can be simple or complex. Failure to properly specify transformations can result in correct data in the source becoming wrong data in the target.

Two areas that commonly introduce problems are code page crossovers and currency translation. For example, if you are building a central data warehouse from data coming from divisions around the world, you need to pay special attention to the effects either of these may have on the outcome. Code page conversions can lose special country codes that translate the special characters of another country into the USA code page. This may generate a name value that looks invalid to the target system.

Another problem sometimes overlooked is where a source system stores a dollar value as an integer. The application programs "know" that they are supposed to insert the decimal point after position 2 (effectively dividing the stored value by 100). A transform needs to occur when this data is moved. If the analyst fails to recognize the convention, the values are moved over as if they were full dollar amounts.

Loading

The last step of the data movement process is loading data. You would think that this step would be a safe bet and that all of the damage that can be done has already been done to the data. Assuming you have properly defined the target database, you only need to deal with a few issues.

You need to ensure that all of the data gets loaded in order for the target to be in a consistent state. This sounds simple. However, if data is coming from dozens of sources, you need to ensure that all of the data from all sources gets there and gets loaded together to create a complete target system. One of the important issues of data warehouse and data mart design is ensuring that this is done and that the data is not released to the user community until a complete load is accomplished.

Another issue is what you do with the data that is rejected upon load due to data type, key definition, referential constraint, or procedure violations. As in the case of data cleansing, you must decide if you substitute a value to make the structure work, leave rows out of the target, or investigate the cause and enter the correct values.

The quantity of rejections will determine the best way to handle this issue. A good data movement process will have found all of these values before they get to the load process.

This section has shown that there are many opportunities to make mistakes in the process of extracting data from one system and moving it to another. The majority of these mistakes are mistakes of omission. The developer of the processes does not have a correct or complete set of information about the source systems in order to know everything that needs to be done. The scary part of this is that we continually plow through projects with very low-quality metadata for the source systems and try to fix or reconcile the problems after the fact.

The other problem is that when we look at the data in the target system and determine that it is of low quality we instinctively blame the source systems instead of considering the movement processes as the culprit. Since source systems are difficult to change, little is generally done about the situation. Often the target system is just not used because of a lack of confidence in the data. Much of the time, the target system quality can be improved immensely through fixing the data movement processes.

Figure 3.4 diagrams the steps involved in the data movement process. Clearly, the more effort you make in completing the first two steps properly the fewer mistakes you make in the other steps. Mistakes result in inaccurate data in the target systems. Eliminating the mistakes makes the target systems more accurate and more usable.

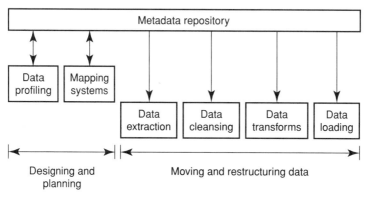

FIGURE 3.4 Steps in the data movement process.

Data Integration

The previous section covered what can go wrong when data is taken from one system to another. Data integration projects that fetch data from source systems and use them in new applications have all the same problems. They may be only fetching tiny amounts of data for each use. However, the data in the source systems, no matter how small, must be properly extracted, cleansed, transformed, and put into a form (usually a message) the target application understands. Virtually all of the topics covered for batch, bulk data movement apply to integration.

Failure to recognize this and do everything that needs to be done leads to inaccurate data being presented to new applications from correct databases. This can lead to incorrect processing of transactions because of wrong data values being presented to the integration transactions. This has a large potential for negative impacts on the business conducted through them.

3.4 Using Data

The final area where data goes wrong is the process of putting it into business objects such as reports, query result screens, portal-accessible windows, and the subsequent use of this by business professionals.

Data may be accurate, but if users do not understand the meaning of the data or the context within which it is presented, their interpretation and use of the data may be inaccurate. This again points to the problem of not having a good metadata repository that is maintained 100% accurately all of the time. This repository should contain information on what each data element represents, how the data within it is encoded, how to interpret special values, the source of data, the time periods last updated, and the quality levels last known for this data.

Quality levels are important because they can let users judge whether the data satisfies their needs or not. They should be able to determine from the repository the probable inaccurate rate within the data. This can be derived from periodic assessment, data monitoring tools, or both.

The user should have easy access to this information. What is needed is either a comprehensive help system on the business objects or an easy-to-use corporate portal on corporate data stores. If users have to call someone or jump through hoops to find out information about their data, they will just not do it. They will make their own assumptions about what the data represents and use it accordingly. Unfortunately, most companies do not have a good metadata repository and certainly do not have a good mechanism for non-IT professionals to access the information they do have.

3.5 Scope of Problems

By the time a report has been generated from a data warehouse, there have been a lot of opportunities for the data to go wrong. The errors just accumulate from initial data creation through decay, data movement, and use. No wonder so many data decision support systems are judged failures.

Some practitioners take comfort in believing that data accuracy problems are greater in legacy systems than they are in systems built more recently, systems on a relational base, or systems implemented through a packaged application. The truth is that there are many opportunities to create problems in all of these.

Relational systems are not immune to errors. This is particularly true of relational systems built in the 1980s. Much of the current protection capability of relational systems was introduced gradually throughout the 1980s. This included date/time data types, triggers, procedures, and referential constraints. Many of the older systems do not use these capabilities and thus leave themselves open to inaccurate data.

Packaged applications do not protect against bad data. They provide a framework for collecting and storing data, but only the using company generates and is responsible for the data. The packaged application cannot ensure that all data is collected, that all values are accurate, or that the fields are being used as intended. Using companies often make local customization decisions in order to force the packaged application to fit their way of doing business. This can lead to problems in extracting, moving, and interpreting data.

3.6 Closing Remarks

Inaccurate data gets into databases at a number of points and for a variety of reasons. Any program to improve data accuracy must address the issues across the entire spectrum of opportunities for error.

Data can be entered mistakenly, can be deliberately entered inaccurately, can be the result of system errors, can decay in accuracy, can be turned into inaccurate data through moving and restructuring, and can be turned into wrong information when inappropriately reported or used. Understanding all of these areas will make data quality assurance professionals more expert in analyzing data and processes for inaccuracies.

The common theme throughout this chapter is that knowledge about your data is the key to successful assessment, movement of data, and use of data. There is no substitute for a sound knowledge base of information about the data. Most metadata repositories fall short of the need. If a process similar to that shown in Figure 3.4 is used vigorously, updating the metadata repository at all stages, higher data accuracy will result for those making decisions from the data.

The area of metadata repositories is ripe for new development, meaningful standardization, and widespread deployment. It should emerge as the next most important technology corporations demand after they have made significant progress on data quality. The business case for repository projects will emerge as the cost of not having them (via inhibiting data quality improvement efforts) becomes more clear. The business value of data quality initiatives will generally depend on the ability of the corporation to maintain an accurate metadata repository. To the extent that it does not, it will not reap the maximum value from data quality efforts.

Implementing a Data Quality Assurance Program

For companies to create high-quality databases and maintain them at a high level, they must build the concept of data quality assurance into all of their data management practices. Many corporations are doing this today and many more will be doing so in the next few years. Some corporations approach this cautiously through a series of pilot projects, whereas some plunge in and institute a widespread program from the beginning.

The next three chapters cover the structure of a data quality program built around the concept of identifying inaccurate data and taking actions to improve accuracy. The assertion is that any effective data quality assurance program includes a strong component to deal with data inaccuracies. This means that those in the program will be looking at a lot of data.

The data-centric approach encompasses a methodology in which data is examined to produce facts about data inaccuracies. These facts are converted into issues. The issues are managed through a process of assessing business impacts that have already occurred or those that can potentially occur. Remedies are proposed, implemented, and monitored. You look at the data to find the issues, and you look at the data again after remedies have been implemented to see if those remedies worked.

Various ways of integrating the process with the rest of the data management team are explored. Each corporation must have a game plan on how they will initiate or get involved in projects and how they will interact with other departments. This can strongly determine the effectiveness of the effort.

Different ways of evaluating the business value of data quality assurance efforts are discussed. This is one of the most difficult topics to deal with in getting a program established.

CHAPTER 4

Data Quality Assurance

The previous chapters define accurate data. They talk about the importance of data and in particular the importance of accurate data. They describe how complex the topic really is. You cannot get to accurate data easily. They show that data can go wrong in a lot of different places. They show that you can identify much but not all inaccurate data and that you can fix only a small part of what you find.

Showing improvements in the accuracy of data can be done in the short term with a respectable payoff. However, getting your databases to very low levels of inaccuracies and keeping them there is a long-term process.

Data accuracy problems can occur anywhere in the sea of data residing in corporate information systems. If not controlled, in all probability that data will become inaccurate enough to cause high costs to the corporation. Data accuracy problems can occur at many points in the life cycle and journeys of the data. To control accuracy, you must control it at many different points. Data can become inaccurate due to processes performed by many people in the corporation. Controlling accuracy is not a task for a small, isolated group but a wide-reaching activity for many people.

Data accuracy cannot be "fixed" one time and then left alone. It will revert back to poor quality quickly if not controlled continuously. Data quality assurance needs to be ongoing. It will intensify over time as the practitioners become more educated and experienced in performing the tasks necessary to get to and maintain high levels of data accuracy.

This chapter outlines the basic elements of a data quality assurance program. It focuses on data accuracy, a single dimension of data and information quality. This is not to mean that the other dimensions should not also be addressed. However, data accuracy is the most important dimension, and controlling that must come first.

4.1 Goals of a Data Quality Assurance Program

A data quality assurance program is an explicit combination of organization, methodologies, and activities that exist for the purpose of reaching and maintaining high levels of data quality. The term *assurance* puts it in the same category as other functions corporations are used to funding and maintaining. Quality assurance, quality control, inspection, and audit are terms applied to other activities that exist for the purpose of maintaining some aspect of the corporation's activities or products at a high level of excellence. Data quality assurance should take place alongside these others, with the same expectations.

Just as we demand high quality in our manufactured products, in our financial reports, in our information systems infrastructure, and in other aspects of our business, we should demand it from our data.

The goal of a data quality assurance program is to reach high levels of data accuracy within the critical data stores of the corporation and then keep them there. It must encompass all existing, important databases and, more importantly, be a part of every project that creates new data stores or that migrates, replicates, or integrates existing data stores. It must address not only the accuracy of data when initially collected but accuracy decay, accurate access and transformation of that data, and accurate interpretation of the data for users. Its mission is threefold: improve, prevent, monitor.

Improvement assumes that the current state of data quality is not where you want it to be. Much of the work is to investigate current databases and information processes to find and fix existing problems. This effort alone can take several years for a corporation that has not been investing in data quality assurance.

Prevention means that the group should help development and user departments in building data checkers, better data capture processes, better screen designs, and better policies to prevent data quality problems from being introduced into information systems. The data quality assurance team should engage with projects that build new systems, merge systems, extract data from new applications, and build integration transaction systems over older systems to ensure that good data is not turned into bad data and that the best practices available are used in designing human interfaces.

Monitoring means that changes brought about through data quality assurance activities need to be monitored to determine if they are effective. Monitoring also includes periodic auditing of databases to ensure that new problems are not appearing.

4.2   Structure of a Data Quality Assurance Program

Creating a data quality assurance program and determining how resources are to be applied needs to be done with careful thought. The first decision is how to organize the group. The activities of the group need to be spelled out. Properly skilled staff members must be assigned. They then need to be equipped with adequate tools and training.

Data Quality Assurance Department

There should be a data quality assurance department. This should be organized so that the members are fully dedicated to the task of improving and maintaining higher levels of data quality. It should not have members who are part-time. Staff members assigned to this function need to become experts in the concepts and tools used to identify and correct quality problems. This will make them a unique discipline within the corporation. Figure 4.1 is a relational chart of the components of a data quality assurance group.

   The group needs to have members who are expert data analysts. Analyzing data is an important function of the group. Schooling in database architecture and analytical techniques is a must to get the maximum value from these activities. It should also have staff members who are experienced business analysts. So much of what we call quality deals with user requirements and business interpretation of data that this side of the data cannot be ignored.

   The data quality assurance group needs to work with many other people in the corporation. It needs to interact with all of the data management professionals, such as database administrators, data architects, repository owners, application developers, and system designers. They also need to spend a great deal of time with key members of the user community, such as business

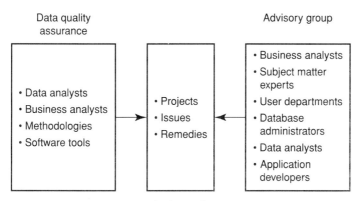

F I G U R E   4 . 1   Components of a data quality assurance group.

analysts, managers of departments, and web designers. This means that they need to have excellent working relationships with their customers.

THERE *is a strong parallel between the emergence of data quality assurance to the improvements made in software development in the 1970s and 1980s. Software development teams back then consisted mostly of programmers. They wrote the code, tested the product, and wrote the user manuals. This was the common practice found in the best of software development groups.*

In my first job at IBM I designed, developed the code, tested, wrote user documents, and provided customer support of a software product (Apparel Business Control System). It was a one-person project. Although the product had high quality and good customer acceptance, I believe it would have gone better and been a better product if I had access to professional writers and software quality assurance people.

In response to the continual problems of poorly tested products and very poor user manuals, companies started dedicating some of the programmers to ensuring the quality of code (testing) and began to hire professional technical writers. There was an immediate improvement in both the code and user manuals. As time went on, these two areas became established disciplines. Software development companies specialized in building tools for these disciplines; colleges offered classes and tracks for these disciplines.

The programmers that tested were no different from those that wrote the

code in the beginning. They made huge improvements only because they were dedicated to testing, worked with the programmers throughout the entire project, and brought another view to the use of the code. In time, they became even better as they developed very effective methodologies and tools for testing. Testing became a unique technology in its own right.

The cost of these programs is clearly zero. Every serious development group today separates code quality assurance from code development. Projects finish earlier, with higher-quality results. The projects spend less money (much less money) and use up less time (much less time) than they would if programmers were still doing the testing.

Data quality is emerging as a major topic 20 years later. The same evolution is happening. Making data quality the responsibility of the data management staff who design, build, and maintain our systems means that they do not become experts in the methodologies and tools available, do not have the independence to prioritize their work, and do not focus on the single task of ensuring high-quality data. Data quality assurance must be the full-time task of dedicated professionals to be effective.

One way to achieve a high level of cooperation is to have an advisory group that meets periodically to help establish priorities, schedules, and interactions with the various groups. This group should have membership from all of the relevant organizations. It should build and maintain an inventory of quality assurance projects that are worth doing, keep this list prioritized, and assign work from it. The advisory group can be very helpful in assessing the impact of quality problems as well as the impact of corrective measures that are subsequently implemented.

Data Quality Assurance Methods

Figure 4.2 shows three components a data quality assurance program can build around. The first component is the quality dimensions that need to be addressed. The second is the methodology for executing activities, and the last is the three ways the group can get involved in activities.

The figure highlights the top line of each component to show where a concentration on data accuracy lies. Data accuracy is clearly the most important dimension of quality. The best way to address accuracy is through an inside-out methodology, discussed later in the book. This methodology depends heavily on analysis of data through a process called data profiling. The last part of this book is devoted to explaining data profiling. Improving accuracy can be done through any of the activities shown. However, the one that will return the most benefit is generally the one shown: project services.

Any data quality assurance function needs to address all of the dimensions of quality. The first two, data accuracy and completeness, focus on data stored in corporate databases. The other dimensions focus on the user community and how they interpret and use data.

The methods for addressing data quality vary as shown in Figure 4.3. Both of these methodologies have a goal of identifying data quality issues. An

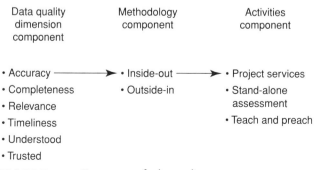

FIGURE 4.2   Components of a data quality assurance program.

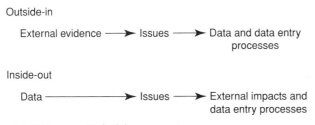

Outside-in

External evidence ⟶ Issues ⟶ Data and data entry
processes

Inside-out

Data ⟶ Issues ⟶ External impacts and
data entry processes

FIGURE 4.3 Methodology comparisons.

issue is a problem that has surfaced, that is clearly defined, and that either is costing the corporation something valuable (such as money, time, or customers) or has the potential of costing the corporation something valuable. Issues are actionable items: they result in activities that change the data quality of one or more databases. Once identified, issues are managed through an issues management process to determine value, remedies, resolution, and monitoring of results. The process of issue management is discussed more fully in the next chapter.

INSIDE-OUT METHOD

The inside-out method starts with analyzing the data. A rigorous examination using data profiling technology is performed over an existing database. Data inaccuracies are produced from the process that are then analyzed together to generate a set of data issues for subsequent resolution.

The analysis should be done by a highly qualified data analyst who understands the structure of the data. The methodology starts with a complete and correct set of rules that define data accuracy for the data. This is metadata. It consists of descriptions of the data elements, values permitted in them, how they relate to one another in data structures, and specific data rules that describe value correlation conditions that should always be true within the data. All of these categories are discussed at length in later chapters.

Of course, such a rigorous rule set for any operational database does not exist. The metadata that is available is generally incomplete and most likely inaccurate. The data profiling process described in later chapters is a process that completes and corrects the metadata, along with using it to find evidence of inaccurate data. This intertwined process has a very valuable by-product: accurate and complete metadata.

The process of determining the correct metadata inevitably involves conferring with business analysts and end users. The data analyst will detect a behavior in the data and require consultation to determine why it is so. This often leads to modifications to the metadata. These consultations are always productive because the question is always backed up by information from the data.

The data analyst should identify who in the user community will be the most valuable in consulting on issue identification and form a small, dynamic working group with them. In the end, they should always agree on what the final metadata is, and agree on the inaccurate data facts derived from the comparison with the actual data.

The inaccurate data evidence produced is a collection of facts. It may be explicit cases of wrong or missing values, or it may identify rules that fail without being able to say what values are wrong. For example, one fact may be that 30% of purchase order records do not have a supplier ID. Another may be that the employee birth date field has values that are invalid: too long ago or too recent. Another might be that the percent of the color BLUE in a database is too large. In this case, the analyst does not know which instances are correct and which are wrong; only that some of them must be wrong.

The facts are aggregated into issues. Some facts are issues by themselves. For example, the supplier ID problem may be the basis for a single issue. Others are aggregated into a larger issue. An example is that customer demographic fields in a marketing database contain numerous errors in all fields, possibly indicating a general problem with form design.

OUTSIDE-IN METHOD

This method looks for issues in the business, not the data. It identifies facts that suggest that data quality problems are having an impact on the business. It looks for rework, returned merchandise, customer complaints, lost customers, delays in getting information products completed, high amounts of work required to get information products produced, and so on. Interviews are done with users to determine their level of trust in the accuracy of data coming from the information systems and their level of satisfaction with getting everything they need. It may also include looking for decisions made by the corporation that turned out to be wrong decisions.

These facts are then examined to determine the degree of culpability attributable to defects in the data. The data is then examined to determine if it has inaccuracies that contribute to problems, and to determine the scope of the contribution. This examination is generally pointed at the specific problem. It is generally not a thorough data profiling exercise, although it could be expanded to that if the evidence indicates a widespread quality problem with the data.

This approach is generally the work of the data quality assurance team member with skills as a business analyst. It involves heavy participation on the part of outside people. It also requires conference sessions with user community experts. The result is a collection of data issues that are then tracked on the same path as those from the inside-out methodology.

COMPARISON OF METHODS

Neither approach is superior to the other: they both bring value to the process. However, they do not get to the same end point. Data quality assurance groups should use both methodologies as applicable.

Inside-out is generally easier to accomplish and uses less people time. A single analyst can analyze a great deal of data in a short time. The data quality assurance group can accomplish a great deal with this approach with the staff within their own department. The outside-in approach requires spending a lot of time interviewing people in other departments.

The inside-out approach is nondisruptive. You just get a copy of the data you want to analyze and do it offline. The outside-in approach requires scheduling time for others, thus interrupting their regular activities.

The inside-out approach will catch many problems the outside-in approach does not catch. For an outside-in approach to catch a problem, it must manifest itself in some external behavior, and that behavior must be recognizable as being not good.

An example of a hidden problem is a case in which missing supplier ID numbers on purchase orders causes a company not to get maximum discounts they were entitled to from suppliers. The purchase order volumes were summarized by supplier ID and, because the field was missing on 30% of the records, the amounts were low. The company was losing millions of dollars every year because of this and was completely unaware that it was happening. The inside-out approach catches this; the outside-in approach does not.

Another type of problem are those inaccuracies that have the potential for a problem but for which the problem has not yet occurred. An example of this is where an HR database failed to capture government classification group information on employees accurately. Many minority employees were not classified as minorities, nor were handicapped employees all being identified as handicapped. No problem may have surfaced yet. However, the potential for being denied contracts in the future because of these inaccuracies is waiting to happen. Inside-out analysis will catch this; outside-in will not.

The opposite is also true. The inside-out approach will not catch problems where the data is inaccurate but valid. The data can pass all metadata tests and still be wrong. This can happen either because the rule set is incomplete or because the data hides underneath all of the rules. An example is getting the part number wrong on orders. The wrong merchandise is shipped. An analysis of the data will not reveal inaccurate data because all of the part numbers are valid numbers. The outside-in approach catches these problems better. (The inside-out approach may catch this if the analysis finds the percentage of orders returned to be higher than an acceptable threshold. This is possible if a data rule or value test has been formulated. These topics are covered in Chapters 11 and 12).

There is another class of problems not detectable by either approach. The data is valid but wrong and also produces insufficient external evidence to raise a flag. Although these generally are of little concern to a corporation, they have the potential to be costly in the future if not detected. A data quality assurance program built exclusively using only one approach is generally going to miss some important issues.

Data Quality Assurance Activities

The data quality assurance team must decide how it will engage the corporation to bring about improvements and return value for their efforts. The group should set an explicit set of guidelines for what activities they engage in and the criteria for deciding one over another. This is best done with the advisory group.

There are three primary roles the group can adopt. This is shown as the last column in Figure 4.2. One of them, project services, involves working directly with other departments on projects. Another, stand-alone assessments, involves performing assessments entirely within the data quality assurance group. Both of these involve performing extensive analysis of data and creating and resolving issues. The other activity, teach and preach, involves educating and encouraging employees in other groups to perform data auditing functions and to employ best practices in designing and implementing new systems.

PROJECT SERVICES

The vast majority of projects being pursued by the IT organization involve repurposing an existing database. It is rare these days to see a truly new application being developed that does not draw from data that has already been collected in an existing application. Examples of projects that involve working with existing data stores are

- data migration to new applications (generally packaged applications)

- consolidation of databases as a result of mergers and acquisitions

- consolidation of databases to eliminate departmental versions of applications

- replication of data into data warehouses, data marts, or operational data stores

- building a CRM system

- application integration that connects two or more applications

- application integration that connects an older database to the Internet

There is a real danger in all of these applications of introducing errors through mistakes made due to a misunderstanding of the data. There is also a real danger in the data from the original systems not being of sufficient quality to meet the demands of the new use of the data. Both of these are classical concerns that if not addressed will certainly cause great difficulty in completing the projects, as well as unhappiness with the outcome.

The data quality assurance team can provide an invaluable service to these projects by profiling the data. By doing this they provide two valuable outputs: an accurate and complete metadata description of the data and an inventory of data quality problems uncovered in the process.

The metadata repository produced should be used to match target system requirements against the content and structure of the source systems. It is also the perfect input to developing processes for extraction, transformation, cleansing, and loading processes.

The data quality assurance team can use the inaccuracy facts to determine either whether the data is strong enough to satisfy the intended use or whether there is a need to establish new projects from the issues to drive improvements in the source systems. Of course, this applies to cases in which the source databases continue to live past the project, as is the case for replication and integration projects.

The data quality assurance team can also provide advice and oversight in the design of target database structures, as well as processes for collecting or updating data. They also have a good opportunity to get data checking and monitoring functions embedded in the new systems to help prevent future quality problems.

Why should the data quality assurance team perform these tasks, as opposed to the project teams? The answer is that the data quality assurance team are experts in data quality technologies. They are experienced in data profiling, investigation of issues, and fabrication of data quality problem remedies.

One of the most valuable outputs of data profiling at the beginning of a project is to learn that the project cannot achieve its goals because of the condition of the source data. When this happens, the project team can then make decisions about changing target design, changing target expectations, making improvements to data sources, or scrapping the project outright. This is the perfect place to make these decisions: before most of the project money has been spent and before most of the development work has been done.

Projects that do not perform a thorough review of the source data generally do not discover the match between the data and the project requirements until after much time and money has been spent. It is generally very expensive to repair the damage that has already been done and impossible to recoup the money spent and the valuable time lost.

STAND-ALONE ASSESSMENTS

A stand-alone assessment is a project organized for the purpose of determining the health of an existing database. The database is chosen because of suspicions or evidence about problems coming from the use of the data, or simply because it is an important data source for the corporation.

The data quality assurance team will generally execute the entire project. Using the inside-out method, they will profile the data, collect quality facts, produce issues, and then follow the issues through to remedies.

The advantage of assessment projects is that they do not require as much interaction with other project teams and can be scheduled without concern for other plans in IT. Of course, it makes no sense to schedule an assessment of a database that is about to get a facelift as a result of another project.

An assessment can be quite disruptive to other departments, even if no change activity is under way for the data source. Time from them will be needed to develop perfect understanding of the metadata and to interpret facts that come out of profiling. If remedies are needed, negotiations with IT and users will be needed to get them designed and implemented. It may also be quite disturbing to people to find out that they have been using flawed data for a long time without knowing it. The data quality assurance team needs to involve the other departments in the planning phase and keep them involved throughout the process.

It is important not to appear as an outside hit team trying to do damage to the reputation of the operational organizations. Involving them makes them part of the solution.

TEACH AND PREACH

This function involves training information system staff members on the technology available for data quality assessment, the techniques and best practices available for building and maintaining systems, and how to develop quality requirements and use them to qualify data.

Few information systems professionals come out of college with training explicitly targeted to data quality. The principles are not difficult to understand, nor are the disciplines difficult to use in daily practice. Educating them will improve all of the work they do.

The data quality assurance group should function as the experts in data quality. They should not keep this knowledge exclusively to themselves. The more they educate others in the corporation, the more likely the information systems will reach and stay at a high level of quality.

Preaching means that the data quality assurance department should encourage and insist that quality checkpoints be put into all projects. They should encourage upper management to be cognizant of the need for data quality activities. They should collect and advertise the value to the corporation realized from these activities.

The data quality assurance group should not depend exclusively on teaching and preaching. If that is all they do, the company will never develop the focused expertise needed to analyze the mountains of data and drive improvements.

4.3 Closing Remarks

If you want high data quality you must have highly accurate data. To get that you need to be proactive. You need a dedicated, focused group.

You need to focus on data accuracy. This means you need an organization that is dedicated to improving data accuracy. You also need trained staff members who consider the skills required to achieve and maintain data accuracy as career-building skills.

You need to use technology heavily. Achieving high levels of data accuracy requires looking at data and acting on what you see. You need to do a lot of data profiling. You need to have experienced staff members who can sniff out data issues.

You need to treat information about your data as of equal or greater importance than the data itself. You must install and maintain a legitimate metadata repository and use it effectively.

You need to educate other corporate employees in the importance of data and in what they can do to improve the accuracy. This includes the following elements.

- Business users of data need to be sensitized to quality issues.

- Business analysts must become experts on data quality concepts and play an active role in data quality projects.

- Developers need to be taught best practices for database and application design to ensure improved data accuracy.

- Data administrators need to be taught the importance of accuracy and how they can help improve it.

- All employees who generate data need to be educated on the importance of data accuracy and be given regular feedback on the quality of data they generate.

- The executive team needs to understand the value of improved data accuracy and the impact it has on improved information quality.

You need to make quality assurance a part of all data projects. Data quality assurance activities need to be planned along with all of the other activities of the information systems department. Assisting a new project in achieving its data quality goals is of equal or higher value than conducting assessment projects in isolation. The more integrated data quality assurance is with the entire information system function, the more value is realized. And finally, everyone needs to work well together to accomplish the quality goals of the corporation.

CHAPTER 5

Data Quality Issues Management

Data quality investigations are all designed to surface problems with the data. This is true whether the problems come from stand-alone assessments or through data profiling services to projects. It also does not matter whether assessments reveal problems from an inside-out or an outside-in method. The output of all these efforts is a collection of facts that get consolidated into issues. An issue is a problem with the database that calls for action. In the context of data quality assurance, it is derived from a collection of information that defines a problem that has a single root cause or can be grouped to describe a single course of action.

That is clearly not the end of the data quality effort. Just identifying issues does nothing to improve things. The issues need to drive changes that will improve the quality of the data for the eventual users.

It is important to have a formal process for moving issues from information to action. It is also important to track the progress of issues as they go through this process. The disposition of issues and the results obtained from implementing changes as a result of those issues are the true documentation of the work done and value of the data quality assurance department.

Figure 5.1 shows the phases for managing issues after they are created. It does not matter who performs these phases. The data quality assurance department may own the entire process. However, much of the work lies outside this department. It may be a good idea to form a committee to meet regularly and discuss progress of issue activity. The leader of the committee should probably be from the data quality assurance department. At any rate, the department has a vested interest in getting issues turned into actions and in results being measured. They should not be passive in pursuing issue resolution. This is the fruit of their work.

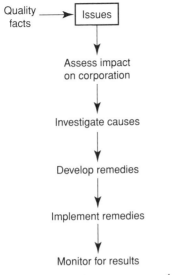

FIGURE 5.1 Issue management phases.

An issue management system should be used to formally document and track issue activity. There are a number of good project management systems available for tracking problems through a work flow process.

The collection of issues and the management process can differ if the issues surface from a "services to project" activity. The project may have an issues management system in place to handle all issues related to the project. They certainly should. In this case, the data quality issues may be mixed with other issues, such as extraction, transformation, target database design, and packaged application modification issues. It is helpful if data quality issues are kept in a separate tracking database or are separately identified within a central project management system, so that they can be tracked as such. If "project services" data profiling surfaces the need to upgrade the source applications to generate less bad data, this should be broken out into a separate project or subproject and managed independently.

5.1 Turning Facts into Issues

Data quality investigations turn up facts. The primary job of the investigations is to identify inaccurate data. The data profiling process will produce inaccuracy facts that in some cases identify specific instances of wrong values. Other cases identify where wrong values exist but identification of which value is wrong is not known, and in yet other cases identify facts that raise suspicions about the presence of wrong values.

Facts are individually granular. This means that each rule has a list of violations. You can build a report that lists rules, the number of violations, and the percentage of tests performed (rows, objects, groups tested) that violated the rule. The violations can be itemized and aggregated.

Metrics

There is a strong temptation for quality groups to generate metrics about the facts and to "grade" a data source accordingly. Sometimes this is useful; sometimes not. Examples of metrics that can be gathered are

- number of rows containing at least one wrong value

- graph of errors found by data element

- number of key violations (nonredundant primary keys, primary/foreign key orphans)

- graph of data rules executed and number of violations returned

- breakdown of errors based on data entry locations

- breakdown of errors based on data creation date

The data profiling process can yield an interesting database of errors derived from a large variety of rules. A creative analyst can turn this into volumes of graphs and reports. You can invent an aggregation value that grades the entire data source. This can be a computed value that weights each rule based on its importance and the number of violations. You could say, for example, that this database has a quality rating of 7 on a scale of 10.

THE GOOD

Metrics can be useful. One use is to demonstrate to management that the process is finding facts. The facts have little to no significance by themselves but can be circumstantial evidence that something is wrong with the data. When a data quality assurance department is trying to gain traction in a corporation, metrics can be a useful way to show progress.

Metrics can also be useful to show improvements. If data is profiled before and after corrective actions, the metrics can show whether the quality has improved or not.

Another use of metrics is to qualify data. Data purchased from outside the corporation, such as demographic data, can be subjected to a quick data profiling process when received. Metrics can then be applied to generate a qualifying grade for the data source. It can help determine if you want to use the data at all. This can be used to negotiate with the vendor providing the data. It can be the basis for penalties or rewards.

Qualification can also be done for internal data sources. For example, a data warehousing group can qualify data extracts from operational groups before they are applied to the central data warehouse.

THE BAD

The downside of metrics is that they are not exact and they do not solve problems. In fact, they do not identify what the problems are; they only provide an indicator that problems exist.

Earlier chapters demonstrated that it is not possible to identify all inaccurate data even if you are armed with every possible rule the data should conform to. Consequently you cannot accurately estimate the percentage of inaccuracies that exist. The only thing you know for sure is that you found a specific number of inaccuracies. The bad news is that there are probably more; the good news is that you found these. If the number you find is significant, you know you have a problem.

Corrective actions have these potential consequences: they can prevent recurrence of some errors that you can detect, they can prevent recurrence of errors you cannot detect, and they can continue to pass errors through. It is also theoretically possible that you would introduce new errors that may or may not be detectable.

The conclusion is that data profiling techniques can show the presence of errors but cannot show the absence of errors nor the number of errors. Therefore, any metrics derived from the output of profiling are inexact. This does not make them useless. On the contrary, the errors found are true errors, and if there are enough of them you have uncovered true problems.

You might conclude from the previous discussion that the number of errors reported is understated. This would be great if it were true. However, poorly defined metrics can actually overstate the error condition. This occurs when a single inaccurate value triggers multiple rule violations. This is difficult to detect and impossible to quantify. When you consider that the majority of rules will find the presence of inaccurate data but will not pinpoint the offending values, you can see why it is difficult, if not impossible, to find the true number of inaccurate values.

Comparing metrics can also be misleading if the yardstick changes between profiling exercises. As analysts gain more knowledge about a data source, they will add to the rule set used to dig out inaccuracies. Comparing two result sets that are derived from different rule sets results in an apples-to-oranges comparison. All presentations of quality metrics need to provide disclaimers so that the readers can understand these dynamics.

THE *following is an example of preventing recurrence of errors you never detected. A medical clinic's internal system records a code for the medical procedure performed, as well as the gender of the patient. It is discovered in data profiling that procedures are being recorded that are not possible for the gender code recorded. These are inaccuracy facts.*

However, the root cause is that the procedure codes are handwritten on paper forms and then sent to the data entry office. Many of them are illegible or missing. The data entry staff has no way of verifying the correct procedure and are motivated to get the data into the system rather than fix it. In addition to the procedure codes being invalid in the case of gender conflicts, there are probably many other procedure codes that are wrong. However, because they are valid procedure codes, they are not detected.

The remedy called for having the data entered directly online by the administrators of the doctors instead of transferring paper documents to a central data entry function. Because so many errors were noted, the new form displays a text description of the procedure when it is entered with a confirmation button. This helps the administrators confirm that they have entered the correct code.

Checks were put in for gender/procedure code conflicts, as well as other conflicts, such as invalid patient age/procedure code combinations. In addition, administrators were educated on the importance of correct procedure codes. Because of the better data entry procedures, the number of errors prevented not only included those that were detectable but many others that were not detectable through analysis.

An additional problem with metrics is that data quality assurance departments often believe that this is the end of their mission. They define their work product as the metrics. However, metrics do not define the source of problems nor the solutions. To improve data quality you need to follow through on getting improvements made. To hand the responsibility for this to other departments is a guarantee that the work items will sit low on priority lists of things to do and will not get done expeditiously. The data quality assurance department needs to track and drive the issues through to solution.

Metrics are not all bad. They are often a good shock factor for driving actions. When you give management a presentation that says the HR database records revealed 700 inaccurate values, this can raise eyebrows and produce a call for action. Knowing that you have 700 and that the real number is higher can be motivation enough.

Often a single fact is more shocking than statistical metrics. For example, telling management that a profiling exercise of the birth date of employees revealed that the youngest employee in the company has not been born yet and that the oldest was born before the Civil War is far more effective than a metric at getting across the point that improvements are needed *now*. (I did not make this up; it was an actual output of a data profiling exercise.)

Issues

The real output of the fact collection phase is a set of issues that define problems that need to be solved. A single statistic can result in an issue. For example, 30% of the purchase order fields have no supplier ID number. Alternatively, several facts can be grouped into one issue. For example, the customer name and address data is severely flawed: 5% of name fields have invalid names, 15% of address fields are inaccurate or blank, 12% of city fields are blank, 5% of city fields are misspelled, and 12% of Zip codes are invalid or blank. This single issue rolls up several inaccuracy facts into a single issue that needs to be addressed. Addressing each inaccuracy fact is an inefficient use of time.

Issues need to be recorded in a database within an issues tracking system. Each issue needs a narrative description of the findings and facts that are the basis for the issue. It is important to identify the facts and the data source so that comparisons can be correctly made during the monitoring phase. The information needed for the data source is the identification of the database used, whether samples or the entire database were used, the date of the extraction, and any other information that will help others understand what you extracted the facts from. In tracking the issues, all meetings, presentations, and decisions need to be recorded along with dates and persons present.

5.2 Assessing Impact

Each issue that has been created needs to be studied to determine the impact it has already had or potentially may have on the corporation. Somewhere along the line someone will ask the "so what" question about an issue. It is important to justify development and disruptive efforts to deploy corrective actions. It is important to document the value returned to the corporation for the time and cost spent pursuing issues.

This needs to be updated from time to time. It is usually impossible to compute the costs and benefits up front. One approach is to look at the facts and theorize on possible impacts. A brainstorming session with data analysts, business analysts, and others may be helpful. This will lead to activities to prove that the impacts have already occurred. Because impacts have not occurred does not mean they will not in the future. As the issues are worked through the entire process, additional information about impacts may become apparent. These need to be added to the impact section.

Impacts Already Happening

The impacts may not be obvious to anyone but may be very real. For example, an issue that states that suppliers exist in the supplier's database multiple times may lead to speculation that you are not getting large enough discounts for volumes purchased over a year. Investigation may uncover that this is true (one department orders under one supplier ID and another department uses a second supplier ID for the same supplier). You can easily compute the discount difference, the volume of purchases made, and the value lost to the corporation. The cost of this type of inaccuracy is totally hidden until the issue is identified and pursued.

Sometimes an issue is created from an outside-in investigation and the cost is already known. Tying the external cost to facts is part of issue definition. For example, the external manifestation might be that the accounts receivable department spends x amount of people time per month correcting wrong information on invoices. The facts are the number of blank or inaccurate values found during data profiling. The facts back up the assertion that invoices are not being prepared properly.

Further investigation may reveal that not only is time being wasted but that payments are being delayed by a certain amount for two reasons: one is the lag in time in getting invoices out, and the other is that invoices sent out without corrections get rejected by the purchasing company, causing yet further delays. In fact, there may be a group of invoices that are never collected due to data errors on the invoices. This is an example of a single visible cost leading to facts about inaccuracies, which lead to the discovery of more hidden costs.

One point to consider is that a significant accuracy problem on a data element may indicate a bigger quality problem. In the case of the missing supplier ID, it is clear that if 30% of the values are missing, there is a real possibility that the process is flawed and that the supplier ID is not available at the time the data is entered. It is unlikely that data entry staff are that bad at their jobs. It is also clear that this field is not involved in making the purchase or subsequent payments (it appears to cause no harm). The harm is all done in the secondary uses of the data. It is easy to speculate that if the data is not available at entry, data entry staff may also be entering wrong but valid values. The problem may be much larger than it first appears.

This is why you need to match inaccuracy facts to known manifestations. By seeing the actual data values in error and the data elements containing errors, you can often speculate about hidden costs that may be occurring.

Impacts Not Yet Happening

The most dangerous impacts are those that have not yet occurred. Seeing the presence of inaccurate data can sometimes lead to speculation about problems that could occur. These can have greater impact than those that occur on a regular basis but cost little to correct.

A simple example is the inaccurate birth dates of employees. There may have been no costs that have occurred yet for a new company that hires mostly young people. However, as this population ages, all sorts of government regulations about reporting, pension programs, and changing medical benefits when an employee reaches age 65 are at risk of occurring. These errors can also make decisions about hiring practices inaccurate and lead to wasteful efforts to adjust the company's mix of ages.

A business rule may require that a fast mode of shipment be used to ship certain materials that have the potential to spoil or decay. They may require refrigeration or avoidance of temperatures above a certain number. It may be that errors in the orders have caused a number of shipments to be made that violate the rule and no dire consequences have occurred. All values are valid individually, but the shipment mode rule for the product type is violated. By speculating on the potential for costs, the issues team may speculate about returned orders, merchandise that cannot be resold, and lost customers. However, that speculation may lead to the potential for real lawsuits, as the corporation may be liable for damage done to the purchaser trying to use spoiled merchandise.

This example may have been saving the company money (lower shipping costs) but creating a potential liability (lawsuits) that could severely damage or even destroy the company. This is why speculation on potential impacts is so important.

The process of assessing impacts will crystallize issues. It may result in issues being broken apart or issues being combined. As participants gain more experience, they will be better at sniffing out impacts both real and potential. As new participants join the process, they can benefit from the documentation of previous issues as a training device.

It should also be apparent that the documentation of the impacts of issues is highly sensitive information. The issues management process should provide for a high degree of privacy and safety of the information.

5.3 Investigating Causes

The next logical step in the process is to discover the causes of the inaccuracy facts. Remedies cannot be fabricated until more information is uncovered.

You need to perform a thorough study, in that the causes may not be what you think they are.

This chapter is not going to cover this topic comprehensively. This is a very large topic and beyond the scope of this book. However, a snapshot of some of the approaches is given to show the types of activities required.

Investigating causes requires talking to a lot of people in a lot of organizations. Assignments to investigators must to be done based on the substance of the issues. Participants from many organizations may be needed. The data quality assurance department should not try to undergo this step entirely with their own staff. Neither should they relegate this entirely to others. It is yet another place where the need for a larger team exists that gets guidance and leadership from the data quality assurance staff.

Investigation of the cause is not always possible. For example, databases purchased from vendors may be found to be defective. It is your responsibility to notify them of the problem and give them facts. It is their job to investigate the causes and correct them.

There are two basic approaches to investigating errors: error cluster analysis and data events analysis. The first is used to narrow down the sources of errors. The second is used to study the events that cause data to be created and maintained in order to help identify the root causes of problems. They can often be used together to efficiently complete the task.

Error Clustering Analysis

This type of analysis attempts to use information in the database to provide clues as to where the inaccuracies may be coming from. It starts with information about the specific database objects containing inaccuracies. For example, in an order database, it would start by identifying those orders that contain inaccurate data or that are suspected of having inaccurate data. Although many rules about data cannot identify specific data elements that are wrong, they can identify entire orders that contain the wrong data. The collection of all orders that have wrong values or rule violations constitutes the analysis set.

The analysis set may be defined narrowly (all orders violating a single rule) or broadly (all orders violating any rule). It depends on the amount of data in the analysis set and the importance of the individual rule. There is also the concept of rules having affinity. That is, for example, all rules that deal with the initial capture of the order information (a process clustering) or all orders dealing with customer name and address information (data semantic clustering).

Once the set of data is isolated that contains offending data, all of the data elements of the isolated set are used to determine if they vary in significant ways with the general population of data.

Common data elements that may reveal significant variances are data source location (branch office, geographic region, specific sales reps), customer information (first-time customers, Internet customers), dates (specific dates, days of week, range of dates), product type or characteristics (engine pats, volatile, expensive), or process steps completed (initial entry, order shipped, invoice created). You are looking for any factor that may indicate a starting point in examining the causes of the errors. Performing error clustering analysis can shorten the search for causes significantly through performing a relatively quick and simple test of data.

Data Events Analysis

This involves a review of all processes that capture data or change data. Data takes a journey from inception to one or more databases. It may have a single process event (data entry) or a number of events. The points of examination can be any or all of the following:

- data capture processes

- durations in which data decay can occur

- points at which data is extracted and added to a different data store

- points at which data is converted to business information

DATA CAPTURE PROCESSES

The process point at which data is captured represents the single most important place data can be made accurate or inaccurate. All data capture points need to be identified and examined. Some data is only captured once. Some is captured and then updated on an exception basis. Some data is captured and the business object updated or enhanced through a work flow process that may occur over a long period of time. Some of these points may take on multiple forms. For example, an order may be entered by the actual customer over the Internet, entered by a recording clerk from a form received in the mail, or entered by a company sales representative through a company client server application. This example shows three very different and distinct ways of entering the same business object.

Building a diagram of the data paths of a business object, identifying the distinct points of data capture, and specifying the characteristics of each is a time-consuming but extremely important task. Figure 5.2 shows some of the characteristics that need to be identified for each data capture or update point. Comments on these factors follow:

- Time between event and recording
- Distance between event and recording
- Number of handoffs of information before recording
- Availability of all facts at recording
- Ability to verify information at recording
- Motivation of person doing recording
- Skill, training and experience of person doing recording
- Feedback provided to recorder
- Data value support of getting it right
- Auto-assist in recording process
- Error checking in recording process

FIGURE 5.2 Factors in evaluating data capture processes in the data capture environment.

- *Time between event and recording:* In general, the longer the time differences, the greater the chance for errors. If the time lag is long enough, it also lends itself to missing or late information. Examples of long durations are cases in which forms are completed and mailed to a data entry location. The accuracy and timeliness would be enhanced if the time difference were eliminated through a more direct entry, such as through the Internet.

- *Distance between event and recording:* Physical distance can also be a factor. This reduces the opportunity for the person who is entering the data to verify or challenge information. For example, if the originator of data is in Chicago but the information is transmitted via telephone or paper to Kansas City for entry, you have a distance between the person who knows the right information and the one entering it. If there is confusion, the entry person has to either enter nulls or enter a best guess.

- *Number of handoffs of information before recording:* The first person to experience the event is most likely to be the one with the most accurate description of the facts. Each handoff to another person introduces the possibility of misreading written information, misinterpreting some else's comments, or not knowing information that was not passed on.

- *Availability of all facts at recording:* If the person entering the information has no access to the event, to the person who created or observed the event, or to databases containing important auxiliary information, they cannot fill in missing information or challenge information they see. For example, it is better for HR data to be entered with the employee sitting next to the entry person, as opposed to copying information from a form. Another example is to have a search function for customer identifiers available for order entry personnel.

- *Ability to verify information at recording:* This is similar to the previous issue, but slightly different. Can the data entry person get to correct information if they think the information provided is wrong? An HR data entry person could call or e-mail the employee if there is confusion. Sometimes the process makes it impossible to make this connection. Sometimes the process penalizes the data entry person for taking the time to verify questionable information. All entry points should allow for information to be either verified immediately or posted to a deferred process queue for later verification and correction if needed.

- *Motivation of person doing recording:* This is a complex topic with many sides. Are they motivated to enter correct information? Are they motivated and empowered to challenge questionable information? Are they motivated to enter the information at all? Someone entering their own order is motivated to do it and get it right. Someone entering piles of form information they do not understand could not care less if the information is entered correctly or completely. Is feedback provided? Is their performance measured relative to completeness and accuracy?

- *Skill, training, and experience of person doing recording:* People who enter the same information for a living get to learn the application, the typical content, and the data entry processes. They can be trained to do it right and to look for red flags. People who enter data on a form only one time in their life are much more likely to get it wrong. Sometimes there exists a data entry position that has not been trained in the application. This is an invitation for mistakes. Note that entry people who are making mistakes tend to make them repetitively, thus increasing the database inaccuracy level and thereby increasing the likelihood that it will be exposed through data profiling analysis.

- *Feedback provided to recorder:* Feedback is always a good thing. And yet, our information systems rarely provide feedback to the most important people in the data path: those entering the data. Relevant information, such as errors found in computer checks, should be collected and provided to help them improve the accuracy of data they enter.

- *Auto-assist in recording process:* Do the data entry programs and screens help in getting it right? A complex process can include pull-downs, file checking, suggestions on names, addresses, questioning of unusual options or entry information, and so on. Remembering information from the last transaction for that source can be very helpful in getting information right. Letting each data entry station set its own pull-down defaults can reduce errors. Providing the current date instead of asking that it be entered can improve accuracy. There are a lot of technology best practices that can improve the accuracy of information.

- *Error checking in recording process:* Evaluate the checking provided by the entry screen programs, the transaction path, and the database acceptance routines. Data checkers, filters, and database structural enforcement options can all be used to catch mistakes at the entry point. These are not always easy to identify because they require someone to dig around in code and database definitions. Many times these are not documented. Many times they are thought to be true but have been turned off by a database administrator to improve performance. Many times they exist but are not applied to all points of entry.

It is important to study all factors at each entry point, even though the investigation started by focusing on a single set of inaccuracy facts. This process may reveal other inaccuracies that were hidden from the profiling process or uncover the potential for problems that have not yet occurred. It may also uncover some locally devised practices that are good ideas and may warrant propagation as a formal methodology throughout the data entry community.

DATA DECAY

The analyst needs to identify data elements that are subject to decay and check for process steps that exist that will mitigate decay. Identifying data decay candidates is a business analyst topic best handled as work sessions with participants from multiple departments.

If the investigation reveals that no procedures are present to prevent decay, the analyst needs to determine the extent to which decay has contributed to currently visible problems or whether it presents the potential for future problems.

Decay problems are often not observable though data profiling because the values in the database are valid even though wrong. However, process analysis may suggest that the data is susceptible to decay problems. Sampling the data and testing it through object reverification may reveal hidden problems. These can become the subject of new issues split off from those that got you there.

DATA MOVEMENT AND RESTRUCTURING PROCESSES

Many errors can be introduced when data is extracted, reformatted, aggregated, and combined with other data. If the data source that was used for identifying the inaccurate data is not a primary data source, it requires examination of the processes that build that database from the primary sources.

The first question to ask is whether the problems also exist in the original data source, are part of the data movement processes, or are the result of an incompatibility with the target database structure or definition. Errors at this level often cause primary data sources to be blamed for problems not of their making.

One of the problems with this type of analysis is that the extraction, transformation, cleansing, and loading processes are often not well documented or are documented only in the proprietary repositories of individual products used for the separate steps. This requires expertise on each of these repositories and on the functions of the individual products used. This can lengthen the time required to perform the analysis.

Often data movement processes are locally developed without the aid of packaged tool software. The project team merely writes code for each step. In these cases, finding out what the team does may be difficult because much of it is probably not documented at all. This stresses the importance of being disciplined enough to create and maintain metadata repositories on all data structures: primary, intermediate, and summary. Information should also be kept on all processes that move data between them.

Review of upstream processes may be indicated by discovering information about quality problems in primary databases. This means that a situation discovered in a primary database that produces inaccurate data may lead to the discovery that upstream uses of this data are also flawed. You are basically asking the question "What is the data warehouse doing with this wrong stuff?" This process of examining known data flaws through to their final use can raise issues that were otherwise hidden.

CONVERSION TO INFORMATION PRODUCTS

Other places to look are the conversion of data from databases to reports, movement to OLAP cubes, staging data in corporate portals, and other business information products.

This type of review would normally only be done if the issue were created from concerns raised about these objects. Looking at wrong output does not always indicate that the data is wrong. The routines to extract the data and to compute from it, and the timeliness of this activity, can lead to inaccurate business information products from perfectly accurate data. Problems in the information products should be traced back through the system because they can often uncover previously hidden problems with other uses of the same data.

It should be clear that the process of identifying where errors creep into databases has many beneficial side effects. It can surface bad practices that are creating errors that were not detected in the initial analysis. It can detect bad practices that are not generating errors but have the potential for doing so. It can identify hidden problems in upstream copies of the data or uses of the data that were not known. This may lead to expanding the impacts section to include impacts already occurring and those that have not yet occurred. This process may lead to the consolidation of issues (discovery that the data entry process caused many of the issues) or creating new issues (the corporate portal is displaying flawed renditions of the data).

It may be helpful to document the bad practices independently for the benefit of future projects. Bad practices used in one application frequently find their way into other applications. The same team that implemented them in one case may have implemented them in other applications they also worked on. Having a list of bad practices can serve as a checklist of things to look for in subsequent investigations.

5.4   Developing Remedies

Remedies to quality problems can range anywhere from simply holding a training class for data entry personnel to replacing an entire application. Without remedies, the problems are likely to persist, if not get worse. Without remedies, the potential problems that have not yet occurred increase in likelihood of occurring.

Often the problems that exist in a database cannot be repaired. This is true when the number of errors make it impractical to seek out and repair the wrong ones. This is also true when it is no longer possible to obtain the correct information. The remedies are mostly designed to improve the quality of *new* data being entered into the databases as opposed to fixing the data that is already there.

There are a number of classical problems associated with this phase. The first is the trade-off of making quick improvements through patching an existing system versus taking a longer-term view of reengineering the data processes and application programs. The second is the trade-off between making changes to primary systems versus performing data cleansing to fix problems when moving data. Figure 5.3 lists some of the types of remedies that can be used for resolving issues.

Scope of Remedies

Remedies are changes to systems that are designed to *prevent* data inaccuracies from occurring in the future, as well as to *detect* as many of them as possible when they do occur. The scope of changes includes data capture processes,

- Improve data capture
  - Train entry staff
  - Replace entry processes
  - Provide meaningful feedback
  - Change motivations to encourage quality
- Add defensive checkers
  - Data entry screens
  - Transaction servers
  - DBMS implementations
- Add periodic monitoring
- Perform periodic data profiling
- Use data cleansing
- Reengineer and reimplement application
- Reengineer and reimplement data extraction and movement
- Educate user community

FIGURE 5.3 Data quality issue remedy types.

primary applications that create and update data, processes that move data between databases, and applications that generate information products. In short, everything is fair game to designing remedies.

DATA CAPTURE PROCESSES

Improving data capture processes can include actions such as redesigning data entry windows and associated logic, training data entry people, and instituting feedback reporting of quality problems to data entry people. Many small items like these can make large improvements in the accuracy of data.

At the other extreme is altering the business processes that include data capture and update. Changes in who enters data and when they do it can improve the efficiency of the processes and the likelihood that the data will be accurate. Getting the entry of data closer to the real-world event, having fewer people involved in the process, and having the entry people trained on the intent of the application can all contribute to better data.

Business processes can be altered to add data verification through additional means in cases where it is warranted. Business processes can be altered to eliminate incentives to provide inaccurate data.

More automation can be brought to the entry process wherever appropriate. Use of bar coding, lookup of previously entered information, voice capture of verbal information exchange between the person creating the data and the person entering the data for later replay, and verification are examples where automation can improve accuracy.

ADDING DEFENSIVE CHECKERS

Defensive data checkers are software that assists in enforcing rules at the point of data entry to prevent invalid values, invalid combinations of valid values, and structural problems from getting into the database in the first place.

Rule checking can be performed in multiple places and through multiple means. Data entry screens can be designed to check for valid values for encoded fields and to enforce values for required fields. Application server code can take the data for a transaction and perform further rule testing for more stringent value testing and multivalued correlation testing. The database implementation can employ the support of the DBMS software to enforce many structural rules, such as primary key uniqueness, primary/foreign key constraints, and null rule enforcement. The use of a separate rule-checking component can be added to the transaction flow to perform additional data rule checking.

A solution that might be chosen is to leave the application alone but change the database management system used in order to take advantage of a different DBMS's superior data-checking functions.

Data checkers can be moved more into the mainstream of the application. For example, several new Internet applications are checking the correlation of address information at the point of data capture and alerting the entry person when the various components are incompatible.

Defensive checkers cannot prevent all inaccuracies from getting into the database. Inaccuracies still flow through in cases for which values are valid individually and in combination but are just plain wrong. It is also generally impractical to test rules that involve large sets of data to determine correlation correctness.

ADDING DATA MONITORING

Data monitoring is the addition of programs that run periodically over the databases to check for the conformance to rules that are not practical to execute at the transaction level. They can be used to off-load work from transaction checks when the performance of transactions is adversely affected by too much checking. Because you can check for more rules, they can be helpful in spotting new problems in the data that did not occur before.

DATA CLEANSING

The use of data cleansing programs to identify and clean up data after it has been captured can also be a remedy. Cleansing data is often used between primary databases and derivative databases that have less tolerance for inaccuracies. They can also be used for cleaning up data in original source systems.

Data cleansing has been specifically useful for cleaning up name and address information. These types of fields tend to have the highest error rate at capture and the highest decay rates, but also are the easiest to detect inaccuracies within and the easiest to correct programmatically.

REENGINEERING APPLICATIONS

In extreme cases, the application that generates data can be overhauled or replaced. This is becoming more common as the solution to cases in which many data issues pile on the same data source.

Reengineering can apply to the primary databases where data is initially captured, as well as to the applications that extract, transform, and move the data to derivative data stores or to the derivative stores themselves.

This remedy rarely stands alone. All other remedies are specifically directed at solving a data quality problem. Reengineering generally will not be selected as a solution solely for data quality reasons. Data quality concerns become additional justification for making a change that has been justified by other business drivers.

Short-Term Versus Long-Term Solutions

Remedies need to be devised with consideration for the cost and time to implement. Time to implement must include the time lag before it is likely any project would start. Many of these remedies require negotiation with development teams and scheduling against many other competing tasks.

This often leads to a staged approach to implementation involving data cleansing and monitoring early and reengineering of applications later. It may also lead to implementation of throwaway efforts in order to effect some short-term improvements while waiting for long-term projects to complete.

Too often projects initiated from these remedies end up on a to-do list and then get dropped or continue to get prioritized behind other projects. A reason for this is that they tend to be too granular and are not competitive against bigger projects that promise greater returns.

Issues management should strive for as many easy or short-term remedies as possible to obtain quick improvements. For example, training data entry people, changing screen designs, adding checker logic, or setting expectations are easy to do.

Data cleansing can also be introduced as a short-term remedy to fill the void while more substantive changes are made. Data cleansing should always be considered a temporary fix.

These are tricky matters to manage. One of the dangers is that the temporary improvements become permanent. Managers think that because some improvements have been made that the problem is solved. They may think that data cleansing is a solution instead of a short-term coping mechanism.

This underlines the need to keep issues open as long as they are not fully addressed. If necessary, long-term remedies can be split off into separate issues for tracking.

This is also a reason to monitor the results of remedies implemented. After the short-term remedies are implemented, the profiling process should be repeated and the impacts reexamined. This allows quality problems and their associated impacts that remain after short-term remedies are implemented to be documented, sized, and used to justify the longer-term efforts.

Practical Versus Impractical Solutions

There is a real danger in this phase of overengineering remedies. A zealous data quality team can outline a number of measures that will have no chance of being implemented. It is important that the team performing the remedy recommendations include representatives from the IT and user organizations in order to avoid recommending something that will be rejected.

An example of overengineering is to require that all data rules discovered during the data profiling process be implemented as transaction checks or as periodic monitoring functions. Although this would catch many errors, in practice it has the potential of overloading the transaction path and causing performance problems. The rule set needs to be prioritized based on the probability of errors occurring and the importance of an inaccurate value. The high-risk rules should be added to the transaction path, moderate-risk rules should be added to periodic monitoring sweeps over the data, and low-risk rules should not be implemented. Periodic reprofiling of data may check the rules not implemented to make sure they are not becoming more of a problem; possibly once a year.

Note that a rule can be classified as high risk even though profiling indicates few if any violations have occurred. If the potential cost to the corporation of a violation is very high, it needs to be included in checkers even though there is no evidence it has already produced inaccurate data.

Another example is to call for a major company reorganization to obtain more reliable data capture processes. This should not be considered a remedy unless an awful lot of evidence exists to justify it.

Organizations resist change, and change does not always produce the expected results. If there is a perception that little is to be gained, this type of recommendation will never be approved.

Similarly, recommendations that require major changes to high-availability applications are less likely to get approved. The disruption factor on a major application can cost a company tons of money if it is not managed properly. These types of changes are not accepted easily.

Turning Remedies into Best Practices

As more and more issues pass through the process, the team will learn more about what types of remedies are most effective and what types of remedies can more easily be adopted. What you learn can be converted into best practices that can be employed in all new system developments. This is a good way to improve the quality of data coming from new systems before a data quality problem even exists.

This is a part of the role of the data quality assurance department. It feeds into their role of *preventing* problems.

5.5 Implementing Remedies

Implementing remedies almost always involves other departments, their budgets, and their staff. The quality team needs to present very solid cases for improvements.

Quality problems are identified and impacts assessed at a granular level. Trying to get implementation commitments on individual issues generates a great deal of resistance. Issues need to be combined into change initiatives that have a bigger impact on the value returned to the corporation. This also leads to efficiencies in implementation.

The data quality assurance team needs to monitor implementation because items often get accepted for implementation but never get done or get done improperly. This is another reason for periodic reviews of all open issues. You need to keep the problems highly visible until they are no longer problems.

5.6 Post-implementation Monitoring

It is important to continue monitoring databases after remedies have been implemented. This provides two distinct values: validating the improvement effort and checking for the occurrence of new problems.

Validating Changes

The need to measure the quality of data before and after changes accomplishes two things: it validates that the changes have had a positive impact, and it quantifies the value provided to the business. The next chapter covers the factors considered in justifying data quality assurance functions. It demonstrates that it is impossible to predict the effects in advance. The best indicator of the potential value of an investigation is the value returned from other, similar investigations. This demonstrates the need to measure again after changes.

Also remember that the real impact will never be known for sure. If an inaccuracy count of 5% was found before changes and only 0.5% after changes, a logical conclusion is that an impact has been made. However, the real but unknown rate before may have been 7%, and after, 1%. There is a sizeable impact, although the true statistical difference is not known. This underscores the need to keep metrics from being used as absolutes but rather as indicators of the direction and relative size of impacts.

If post-change monitoring does not show significant differences, the analysis of causes or the implementation of remedies was not successful. The issues team needs to circle back and rethink what they have done.

Sometimes changes have an unintentional negative impact. For example, performance may be severely degraded due to extra error checking, or the number of rejected transactions may become too high. The trade-off is between "Do I let incomplete and inaccurate information get through in order to get the transactions processed?" or "Do I insist on perfectly accurate information before any transaction can complete?". There is no need to compromise quality to obtain accurate information, although it may take a lot of work and innovative process design to achieve it. The first attempts may not prove to be the optimal solution, and additional attempts need to be made.

Impacts on the business process should also be observed and documented in the issue management system. These may be positive or negative. Often streamlining the business processes to obtain higher-quality data leads to other savings as well.

Continuous Checking

All information systems should be instrumented to provide ongoing monitoring of data quality parameters. Most older systems have little or no monitoring functions built into them. They should be retrofitted into systems when addressing important quality issues. They should be included when developing new applications or making major renovations to existing applications.

Monitoring can include a number of things: feedback on rejected transactions, periodic execution of rule sets over databases, and periodic thorough data profiling.

Feedback on rejected transactions is important because excessive rejection indicates poor business process design. It is easy to accomplish this, but it is rarely done. Indications of the quantity of rejects, the point of rejection, and the data elements causing the rejection provide valuable information to data quality assurance staff, application developers, and business process designers.

An example of this is to design an Internet order form such that every time the user has a SUBMIT function denied because of checking errors a quality packet is built and sent to the application server indicating the errors found. The alternative is to wait for a correct form completion and only send that. The last approach provides no feedback that could lead to better form design and less frustrated customers.

Continuous monitoring tends to become decoupled with issues tracking. This is because the monitoring mechanisms become more global in nature and take in monitoring of information relevant to many issues. At the least, the issue tracking system should identify the specific additions to monitoring functions performed as a result of that issue.

5.7 Closing Remarks

This has been a light trip through the process of developing, solving, and measuring the effectiveness of issues that come from data quality processes. The emphasis has been on how issues are created and managed that originate from data inaccuracy discoveries.

This treatment should cement the thought that data quality improvements are long-term and very public tasks. The data quality assurance group cannot function in isolation. The other departments engaged in the data acquisition, management, and use activities are very integral parts of the process and need to be included in the process at all steps. They also need to accept the goal of better-quality data and to welcome efforts rather than resist them.

Issues can have a very long life. I suspect that some of them can live forever. This leads to the need for formal treatment of them as business objects. It also calls for issues to be very accessible in their own database.

Issue resolutions are often considered interruptive to the normal flow of work through departments that develop and deploy information technology. They will tend to get sidetracked easily if not monitored and placed in front of management on a regular basis.

These activities need to become the normal flow of work. Monitoring data quality and making corrections to improve it should not be considered a nuisance, but should be considered a regular part of information systems operations. This chapter again highlights the need to coordinate the activities of data quality assurance with the complete information systems agenda.

I AM *not aware of any issues management software that has been developed specifically for data quality issues. The best available software is standard project management software, of which there are many flavors available. Most organizations are already using one or more of these packages. It would be helpful if some vendor addressed this topic specifically as it relates to data quality assurance.*

Issues management would make an excellent XML database application. The different phases and types of information are easy to generate standard tags for. Access to information over the Internet would be facilitated through this approach. This is important, considering the wide range of people who need to get involved in issues at one point or another.

CHAPTER 6

The Business Case for Accurate Data

It has historically been difficult for data quality advocates to get corporations to make significant commitments and spend adequate money to create and maintain an effective data quality assurance function. The business case has always been evident, but quantifying it, determining the opportunity for improvements, and comparing it to other corporate opportunities has always been difficult to do and frequently has been unsuccessful.

Data quality has too often been one of those topics that everyone knows is important but just does not generate enough enthusiasm to get something done about it. Most CIOs will tell you they should be doing more. However, they then prioritize it down the list and give it little support.

There are a number of reasons for the difficulties that have plagued data quality efforts. It is a tough topic to build a business case for. Many of the factors are purely speculative unless the work to correct them has already been done. This means you have to spend the money to find out if it was worthwhile or not.

This chapter outlines some of the factors and thought processes that come into play when trying to get commitments and funding for data quality activities. Each corporation addresses funding in its own unique way. It is not possible to lay out a justification path that works for all of them. It is helpful to understand the nature of the beast in order to build a workable business case strategy appropriate to your own corporation.

6.1 The Value of Accurate Data

You cannot place a direct value on accurate data. It is the cost of inaccurate data that builds the business case. It is much like advertising. You do not know what impact it will have on sales and you do not know what impact it has had on sales, but you do know that if you don't do it you lose a lot of sales. Inaccurate data can cost corporations millions of dollars per year; it can cause corporations to go out of business. If you have perfectly accurate data, you do not know what you saved. You only know that if you do not have it the costs will be significant.

Corporations have clearly been willing to accept poor data quality. Its prevalence across almost all corporations attests to the fact that corporations can survive and flourish with poor data quality. It is not considered a life-and-death issue, even though for some companies it can be. It is an issue of improving the efficiency and effectiveness of the corporation to make them better able to compete and better able to survive tough times. However, most executives would not believe that data quality issues would be a serious threat to their corporation compared to other issues that are more obviously real and serious threats.

A COMPARISON *to the auto industry's product quality story provides useful insights. The auto industry in the USA had a poor product quality record. Their manufacturing processes were inefficient and error prone. The products they sold were of very poor quality. However, they were all doing the same things with the same outcomes. The poor product quality did cost each of them money in operational costs, although it had no effect on their individual market share because of the uniform nature of the quality problem.*

The Japanese auto industry came along with higher-quality manufacturing processes and higher-quality autos. They reaped two rewards: operational
efficiencies and market share. The market share came out of the hide of the American auto companies.

The response was an immediate drive to improve quality throughout the American auto industry. A failure to do so would have spelled the end of any company who chose that route.

The same is true of data quality. As long as every corporation has the same degree of poor quality, they only incur lost operational costs. Any one of them has an opportunity to get ahead of competitors if they are the first one to improve data quality. They not only will decrease operational costs but will gain other competitive advantages over their competition.

Data quality is a maintenance function. Like HR, accounting, payroll, facilities management, and other maintenance functions, information systems provide a basic function that is a must for an effective organization to do its business. The efficiency with which you perform maintenance functions determines how effective you can be at your primary business functions.

Information systems are moving up the ladder in importance and are a critical business component today. Data quality is the issue within information systems that can make them effective or make them a hindrance to getting things done. It is a sound management practice to want the best and most efficient information management systems.

The money spent on data quality activities is aimed at eliminating costs currently being incurred by the corporation and removing the risk of costs that can potentially occur due to inaccurate data. Following is the rationale for an aggressive data quality assurance program:

- Without attention to data quality assurance, data is certain to have inaccuracies.

- These inaccuracies are normally very costly to a corporation.

- To improve data accuracy requires an active data quality assurance program.

- To maintain high levels of accuracy requires an active data quality assurance program.

A business case is the difference between what is gained and what it costs. Business cases are adopted only if this is believed to be positive. Business cases are also adopted only if they survive a test of comparison to other business cases competing for resources. Corporations cannot pursue all positive business cases. The trade-offs involve whether a proposal is required (such as implementing HIPPA), the degree to which the proposals are aligned to corporate visions, core competencies, and the risks involved in achieving the objectives laid out in the proposals. In other words, you are always competing for resources and attention.

It would be nice if the world were as objective as this. In reality we know that projects often get funded for more political and emotional reasons as well. The popularity of a certain topic within the outer community often influences decisions. This explains why data warehousing projects got so much attention in the early 1990s and CRM projects are getting so much attention now. Most of these very expensive projects had very thin business cases built for them before they were approved. The primary approval driver was intuition.

To determine value, you look for costs to the corporation that result from inaccurate data. The assumption is that if you eliminate the inaccuracies, the costs go away and that becomes the value to the corporation. It is generally not a one-time value because most of the observed problems repeat on a regular basis.

Typical Costs

Typical costs developed for the business case are the cost of rework, cost of lost customers, cost of late reporting, and cost of wrong decisions. All of these costs were incurred in the past and cannot be recouped. The business case assumes that these costs will be repeated in the future, and therefore you can estimate the future savings by just using the past costs.

It is difficult to identify all of the costs of inaccurate data up front. Those listed previously are visible and obvious. But even these have to be examined to ensure they are the result of inaccurate data and not other causes.

Other costs probably exist but have not yet surfaced. Many times bad data is driving a process that would not be necessary with good data, but no one associates it with bad data. Other times wrong decisions are made because of bad data, but the fact that it is bad is never discovered or, if discovered, the cause is not traced back to bad data. Another problem with most data quality business cases is that they do not identify the really big costs to the corporation.

Wasted Project Costs

One of the big costs is the enormously wasteful practice of implementing large projects that depend on existing databases without first understanding the extent to which the data and the metadata in them is bad. Every corporation has stories of cancelled projects and significantly delayed projects due to excessive thrashing over data issues. These issues arise during the moving of data due to inaccurate data or metadata. For some reason we never want to count these costs as part of the business case for data quality assurance activities. They are huge and visible.

It is not unusual to see wasted costs in the tens of millions of dollars for projects that seem never to get done or are cancelled before they get to their objective. The contribution of inaccurate data and inaccurate metadata to these failures is very high, often being the factors that torpedo these projects.

Costs of Slow Response to New Needs

The really big cost is the penalty the corporation suffers because these projects take too long to complete or complete with unsatisfactory outcomes. For example, the corporation trying to reach a new business model through the project is forced to continue on the less desirable business model because of their inability to move forward. This may be a temporary penalty, such as waiting for the project to complete, or a permanent penalty, such as the project getting cancelled.

For example, getting the information systems of two businesses merged after an acquisition done in one year versus three years is a huge advantage. Getting a CRM system completed and serving the sales and marketing organizations in one year is much better than working on it for three years and then cancelling it.

There would be an enormous savings if a corporation were able to respond to the need for new business models faster than any competitor, at lower cost than any competitor, and more accurately than any competitor. Clearly, corporations that have perfectly accurate data and perfectly accurate metadata can implement a new business idea faster and cheaper than a company that does not.

A corporation with significantly inaccurate data and metadata can either plow through the project, risking failure and long delays, or perform the data quality improvement work at the front end. In either case, the corporation with accuracy up front has gained a significant advantage on those that do not have it.

THE *CRM concept offers a good example. It promises to provide significant returns to corporations who can move to that model. Most major corporations have launched CRM initiatives or are planning to launch them.*

The record to date is miserable. Many analyst companies have reported the number of failed projects to be higher than 60%. Many of these projects have stalled or collapsed because of the difficulty in cleaning up data or integrating data.

However, over 30% of the projects get completed. *Those companies have zoomed ahead of the others. Those that had been paying attention to data accuracy issues are more likely to be among those that are done, in that CRM is basically an example of unintended uses being imposed over previously captured data.*

As you can see, all value lies in reduced costs. It is also apparent that many of these costs are not known, are hidden, and are very subjective. Some are being incurred on a daily basis, some are lurking in the background to potentially hit you in the future, and some are obstacles to your moving your business models forward in the future. The biggest component of costs are those that have not yet been incurred.

This characterization makes management inclined not to believe numbers brought to them. They know there are some costs. However, the business cases presented are either factual, meaning that they grossly understate the value, or are speculative, meaning that they cannot be certain they are that large or that they will ever happen. This leads to skepticism about any numbers in a proposal.

6.2   Costs Associated with Achieving Accurate Data

The costs of pursuing a data quality program start with the costs of creating and maintaining a central organization for data quality assurance. Developing temporary teams of people to attack specific problems and then letting them drift off to other assignments is not a useful approach to data quality. A central team is needed. There is plenty for them to do.

This team needs the usual resources to accomplish tasks. They need personal computers, software, availability of a database or two to store project information, training, and administration support. These costs can be considered general costs of performing data management, or they can be allocated to specific data quality projects.

The quality team will carve out activities such as a data quality assessment for a specific application. In pursuing this, additional costs are incurred by people outside the data quality team. They will be asked to spend time with the team, to provide access to data, and to participate in issues discussions and reviews. These costs are generally not counted toward data quality because these people are already being charged to their normal functions. If a department assigns someone full-time to be a liaison to the quality activities, it would probably be counted.

The real costs come when the quality team has conducted studies and has a list of issues with recommended remedies. The cost of implementing remedies can be very high. It can involve application renovation projects and the modification of existing applications to add checkers and monitors. Often they can be combined with other objectives to create a project that does more than just improve quality, thus mitigating some of the costs.

Another cost to consider is the cost of disruption of operational systems. Fixing data quality problems often requires changing application programs or business processes. The testing and deployment of these changes can be very disruptive to critical transaction systems. Downtime of even one hour to an important transaction system can cost in the tens of thousands of dollars.

6.3   Building the Business Case

It is helpful to separate the front-end project of assessing the quality of the data from the back end of implementing and monitoring remedies. The front end takes you through the remedy design phase of issues management.

Figure 6.1 shows the shape of the business case when this is done. An assessment project looks at data, develops facts, converts them to issues, assesses impacts, and designs remedies. One or more back-end projects are spawned to implement the remedies. They can be short-term patches to sys-

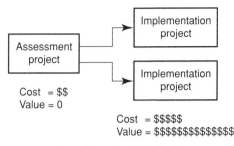

FIGURE 6.1 General model of business case.

A DATA *quality project can escalate into a cost of several millions of dollars. For example, an assessment project discovers many inaccurate data facts. This costs very little to find. In reviewing these with business analysts, they discover that many decision-making systems that feed off that data are corrupted, creating a serious potential problem. They also discover that the bad data is currently costing them a bundle.*

Moving to the remedy phase, they work with the IT department staff to find solutions. The problem is multi-faceted, with some of the blame going into improper data architecture. The application is old, using an obsolete data management technology.

A decision is made to scrap the existing application and database implementation and reengineer the entire application. Instead of building a new system, they decide to purchase a packaged application. This project escalates into a major migration of data and logic.

In parallel, the team determines that reengineering the entire data capture process is also in order. Bringing the application into the modern age entails defining Internet access to data as well an Internet data capture process. The jobs and responsibilities of many people change.

What started out as a small project mushroomed into a major initiative for the corporation. There were probably many other business drivers that pushed the decisions in this direction. However, data quality issues alone have the power to generate very large and costly projects.

---

tems followed by more substantial overhauls, or they can be parallel projects to improve multiple systems.

The assessment project is all cost and no value. This is because value is only returned if changes are made. The business case for doing the assessment project is the difficult evidence of value to be recouped from problems caused by that source of data and speculation about recoupable value not visible. Its business case is very speculative at both ends. Not only is value potential poorly known but the costs are also poorly known. The length of time to complete the assessment will not be understood until the project is fully engaged.

The implementation projects achieve the potential value. The business case for the implementation projects is determined by the assessment project. If done properly, it will have a thorough analysis of potential value to be recouped. It will also be much easier to estimate the costs of the project.

The front-end assessment project is not only the basis for the business case for the back-end implementation projects but an indicator of what can be accomplished through more assessment projects. As the company becomes more successful with projects, it becomes easier and easier to support new assessment projects. The goal of a data quality assurance group is to build on success not only by finding many useful facts but also in following through on the implementation projects to be able to measure the value achieved for the corporation.

The Case for a Data Quality Assessment Project

The model of front-end versus back-end projects described previously is instructive to use in comparing the two project activity types of stand-alone assessment versus services-to-projects. The stand-alone assessment project starts by selecting a data source that is suspected of having sufficient data problems to speculate that large gains are likely from quality investigations and follow-through.

Companies have hundreds if not thousands of data sources. Those that are usually considered ripe candidates for data quality assessment are those that are important to the primary mission of the corporation, those that are older, or those that have visible evidence of problems with data. It should be apparent from previous discussions that this is not a very scientific way of selecting what to work on first. The largest problems may not yet have occurred or may have occurred but are not visibly connected to data quality. In addition, the probability that a database has errors may be offset by the fact that the database is of low importance to the corporation.

The quality assurance group should inventory all information systems and then rank them according to their contribution to the business, the potential for them to be the target of new business models, and their potential to create costly problems if they are not accurate. The goal should be to get the corporation's information systems to high levels of quality and maintain them there. The process should select the databases first that have the most need to be at a level of high data quality.

Figure 6.2 shows some of the factors that should be considered in selecting what to work on first. Each of the categories should be graded on a scale of 1 to 10, for example, and weights assigned for each factor. This would give the

Factor	Rating	Weight
• Identified costs	—	—
• Potential for hidden costs	—	—
• Potential for future costs	—	—
• Importance to corporation	—	—
• Age of application	—	—
• Robustness of implementation	—	—
• Likelihood of major change	—	—

FIGURE 6.2 Project selection criteria.

team a basis for relative prioritizing. The resulting chart could be presented to management to help justify the work to be done. This becomes the basis for the business case.

IDENTIFIED COSTS

Identified costs include any problems, such as rework costs, that have already been identified. Quantification is very useful if possible.

POTENTIAL FOR HIDDEN COSTS

These are the potential for costs that are not visible. Identified costs may be an indicator that more costs are there. For example, if you know that 5% of customer orders are returned, you can speculate that the number of mixed-up orders is higher and that some customers are just accepting the mistake and not going to the trouble of returning the merchandise. A chart that shows the potential for additional wrong orders and the impact they have on customer loyalty can easily suggest that the cost is much higher than the visible component.

POTENTIAL FOR FUTURE COSTS

This is acquired by speculation on what could happen if certain data elements contained inaccurate information. Assessment of legal liabilities, potential for costly manufacturing mistakes, and the like can identify areas where the risk of not knowing if your data is accurate is not worth it.

IMPORTANCE TO THE CORPORATION

Data sources that serve the critical components of the corporation should be more important to study than others. Even if no visible problems exist, the risk of their being flawed and not knowing about it should carry some weight into the decision process. Conversely, the knowledge that the data is as clean as it can be carries some value.

AGE OF APPLICATION

The age of data source applications should be considered. Older applications generally have a large change history. This tends to promote problems with quality. They also tend to have the most inaccurate or incomplete metadata. Age should not be the only factor used to prioritize work, but it should certainly be one factor.

ROBUSTNESS OF IMPLEMENTATION

Applications that were built using modern DBMS technology, with data architecture tools, or with business rules accommodated in the design should be prioritized lower than applications built on obsolete technology and that gave little consideration to quality factors. The characterization should take into consideration whether quality promotion features such as referential constraints were used, not just that they were available.

LIKELIHOOD OF MAJOR CHANGE

The probability of a data source being the target of a business change is very important. Anticipating unintended uses can cause you to target a quality review and find and fix problems before they block your attempt to reengineer the business process they are a part of. Connecting data sources to projects that are in the planning phase is one way to do this.

The stand-alone project is all cost with no value. The justification is usually the expectation that value-generating issues will be found. This is why hard evidence of costs already being incurred has such large weight in these decisions. Because most of the costs are hidden at this stage, often one of less importance is selected.

The cost of conducting the assessment should also be estimated. Assessment projects involve a great deal of analytical activity regarding data. The factors that will influence the cost are the volume of data, the difficulty in extracting the data for analysis, the breadth of the data (number of attributes and relations), and the quality of the known metadata. Some sources can be profiled with very little effort, and others can take weeks or months to gather the data and metadata to even start the process.

Generally, the cost of conducting the assessment is not a critical factor. The value potential determined by the first part of the business case will drive the approval of the project, not the cost of doing the project. The primary difficulty in getting approval of assessment-only projects is that they are all cost without hard facts promising value.

The Case for Providing Services to Another Project

All active corporations execute several projects concurrently that are based on changing their business model or practices and that involve reengineering, reusing, or repurposing existing data. Examples of these types of projects are application migration from legacy to packaged applications, data warehousing construction, data mart construction, information portal construction, application consolidation due to mergers and acquisitions, application consolidation for eliminating disparate data sources, CRM projects, application integration projects joining Internet applications to legacy data sources, and on and on.

All of these projects have an existing data source or sources that are about to receive new life. These projects have the worst record of success of any class of corporate ventures ever attempted. They are plagued by budget overruns, missed schedules, and cancellations.

It is recognized that a major reason for the difficulties in executing these projects is the poor quality of the data and the metadata of the original data sources. It is also becoming increasingly recognized that discovering and correcting the metadata and discovering the data accuracy problems as the first step in these projects hugely reduces the risk of failure and shortens the time to completion while increasing the quality of the outcome.

It only makes sense that working from accurate and complete metadata will lead to better results than working with inaccurate and incomplete metadata. It also makes sense that knowing the quality of the data will lead to corrective actions that are necessary for the project to complete, as well as to meet its objectives.

The analytical approach to accomplishing this first step includes the same activities that are performed in a stand-alone data quality assessment project. It requires the same skills and produces the same outputs: accurate metadata, and facts about inaccurate data and issues. If the data quality assurance group performed this first step for these projects or with the project team, the business case becomes a no-brainer.

The justification of the project is not just that quality improvements will lead to value. It adds the justification that it will shorten the time to complete the project and reduce the cost of completion. The Standish Group has estimated that performing data profiling at the beginning of a project can reduce the total project cost by 35%. This is a very conservative estimate. However, it is more than sufficient to offset all costs of the assessment activity.

This means that performing a quality assessment on data sources that are the subject of a project is free: it returns more dollars and time to the project than it takes away. It is very different from the business case for stand-alone assessment projects in that it does not need to wait for remedy implementation to return its expense.

The story does not end there. The quality assessment also makes decisions within the project better. The project team may decide that improving the quality of the data source is a requirement for proceeding, thus spinning off a renovation project that will enable the larger project to succeed. It may identify changes to the design of the project that are necessary for success: changes to target system database design or packaged application customization parameters. The project team can decide to cancel a project early if the data assessment reveals that the data source cannot satisfy the project requirements in terms of either content or quality.

Additional benefits are the reduction in the potential for mistakes being made in the data flow processes for data between the original source and the target. It essentially prevents accurate data from being turned into inaccurate data.

It may also provide issues that can eliminate data inaccuracies in the source systems that are not directly needed by the project but that were discovered in the process. These inaccuracies may impact other projects using the same data, thus improving their quality. It significantly reduces the risk of failure of such projects while having the potential for several beneficial side effects.

Figure 6.3 shows this business case. The business case is just the opposite of that for stand-alone assessment. The cost is zero (actually negative), the value returned for the assessment project is high, and the value of implementation activities that result just add more value. The ability to estimate the cost and time of subsequent implementation activities improves.

Because of the unique business value for these activities, the data quality assurance department should include this as their primary function. Instead of avoiding data that is the subject of major projects, they should join with the projects and add value to them. The data sources involved in these projects are

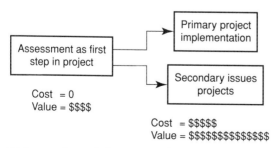

FIGURE 6.3 The business case for project services.

most likely the ones with the highest ratings for importance to the corporation and are most likely to have the highest rating for potential future problems.

The Case for Teach and Preach

Teach-and-preach activities involve educating information specialists in the principles of data quality and in the best practices for achieving better quality. The costs of such a program are relatively low. The potential return is obviously very high. The value is intuitive; it cannot be estimated or proven.

This is no different than wanting accountants to understand auditing or manufacturing staff to understand quality inspection techniques. Information specialists come to the corporation with poor data quality education and skills. It only makes sense that investing in their education is worth much more than the cost.

The outcome of continuous data quality education for information specialists will be better system designs and implementations, better awareness of quality issues (which leads to more exposure of problems), and better cooperation with data quality assurance staff and activities through higher appreciation of their value.

The Case for the Corporation

Spending money on improving data and information quality is always a trade-off decision for corporations. Data quality initiatives do not generally open up new markets, deliver new or improved products, or increase the number of customers. Competing with projects that promise these types of outcomes is always difficult.

There are three fundamental approaches to deciding whether to invest in data quality improvements and to what intensity the activities ought to be pursued. These approaches are described in the sections that follow.

DECISIONS BASED ON HARD FACTS

This type of decision requires defensible estimates of cost and value before funding is made. Demanding this for data quality initiatives will almost always result in no funding. Everyone knows that the value is there. It is just impossible to determine what it is before you spend the money.

Many corporate decisions are based on hard facts. For example, consider buying a software package that will reduce disk requirements for large databases by 40%. You can trial the software and see if it gets a reduction of 40%, plus or minus 5%, on samples of your data. If it does, you can take the worst case of 35%, compute the reduction in disk drives required, price the cost of the drives, and determine the total value. Compare this with the cost of the software package, and the business case is done.

Data quality initiatives do not work this way. Too often management wants a hard-fact case presented to them for data quality spending. Sometimes this is possible because of egregious examples of waste due to bad data. However, it is not a method that selects projects with the highest potential value. Even though this may grossly understate the potential for value, it may provide sufficient justification for getting started.

The negative about this is that one project gets funded and, when the specific case is corrected, the problem is considered solved. Providing hard-fact business cases can undermine attempts to justify other projects later. Management may expect all data quality funding to be based on hard facts because of the success of a single initiative. This leads down a very bad path.

DECISIONS BASED ON PROBABLE VALUE

Corporations often spend money on initiatives that promise returns that cannot or have not been estimated. Opening outlets in new cities, changing the design of a popular product, and spending money on expensive advertising campaigns are all examples of approving spending without hard facts about returns.

This is where data quality belongs. Those asking for funding need to exploit this approach as much as possible. Hard facts should be used to indicate the presence of value to be gotten, not the magnitude of the value. Management needs to be educated on the potential for finding value. Information about gains realized in early efforts or from other corporations are useful in establishing the case that unmanaged information systems generate inefficiencies by nature. The probability of coming up with a dry well is very low.

There is a lot of valuable information around about data quality. For example, most corporations could recoup 15% or more of operating profit if they could eliminate all data quality problems. Also, for example, the lack of understanding of metadata and quality of data can cost a project 35% or more of the total project budget. The argument is that if your corporation has not been paying attention to data quality, this type of return can be expected.

DECISIONS BASED ON INTUITION

Corporations also base decisions on intuition. Some of this is following fads. This is why some major vendors who push new ideas advertise on the Super

Bowl. The logic that says that managing the quality of data will make the corporation more efficient, more effective, and more profitable makes sense.

Executives should be made aware of the growing groundswell of interest in this area. It is not happening for no reason; corporations who adopt data quality initiatives become more successful than those who do not. Although this cannot be proven, it should be obvious.

MOST *large initiatives in IT are not created through hard facts or through credible estimates of probable value. They are created through intuition.*

An example is the movement to relational database systems in the early 1980s. The systems were unreliable, incompatible with prior systems, and showed very slow and unpredictable performance. They used much more disk space than other data storage subsystems. Whereas mature, previous-generation systems were benchmarking 400+ transactions per second, the relational systems could barely squeak out 20 transactions per second (at least on robust benchmarks, not the trumped-up benchmarks of some vendors).

There were virtually no hard facts to justify relational databases. There were no computations of probable value. There was only the vision that the software and the hardware they ran on would get better and that the productivity improvements for application development and the ease of satisfying new requirements from the data would be realized. Companies all over the planet rushed to relational technology only because of the vision.

Data quality is not a glamorous or exciting topic. It is not central to what a company does. It deals in negatives, not positives. It is difficult to get management's attention, and even more difficult to get its funding.

The best argument you can use is the one that says that placing your company in a position to rapidly respond to new business models can only be done by having and maintaining highly accurate data and highly accurate metadata for your corporate information systems. Failure to do that puts a serious impediment in the way of making any significant business model changes.

Data quality advocates should avoid being put into a position of conducting limited value-demonstration projects and in doing only projects that require hard facts. Far too much value is left on the table when this is done. They should try to get religion in the corporation and have a full-function mission established that performs stand-alone assessments, services to projects, and teach-and-preach functions across the entire corporate information system landscape. They need to be accepted as a normal cost of doing business, in that the penalty for not doing so is much higher.

6.4 Closing Remarks

This chapter establishes the case that data quality assurance should be a core competency. It describes how the team should prioritize the activities it pursues and how elements of business cases can be constructed.

Data quality projects have their best chance at getting support and being successful if they engage with the hot spots of the corporation. The more they integrate with other business activities, the more successful they will be.

Data quality assurance should not be a function that is outsourced. It is too central to the success of the corporation. Data quality expertise needs to be a core competency.

PART III

Data Profiling Technology

There are many technologies that apply to creating and maintaining an effective data quality assurance program. Professionals in this area need to be familiar with all of the primary ones: data profiling, data cleansing, metadata repositories, data filtering, and data monitoring. This book is focused on data accuracy. The most important technology for data accuracy is data profiling. The remainder of this book is devoted to that single technology.

Data profiling is defined as the use of analytical techniques to discover the true structure, content, and quality of a collection of data. It uses as input both any known metadata about the data and the data itself. The output of data profiling is accurate metadata plus additional information on content and quality of the data.

For purposes of data quality assurance, data profiling is a process used to discover the presence of inaccurate data within a database. The more data profiling you do, the more inaccuracies you dig out. The information discovered becomes facts used to form data quality issues that need resolution.

Data profiling is a new technology that has emerged in the last few years. Practitioners have been using ad hoc methods as a substitute for formal data profiling for many years. Because they lacked a formal methodology and analytical tools designed specifically for data profiling, the process was time consuming and relatively ineffective. Data profiling has matured into a formal and effective technology that enables the inside-out approach to data quality assurance.

The next chapter provides an overview of the data profiling process. It outlines the basic methodology and describes each of the data profiling categories. It also discusses the difference between discovery and verification techniques.

The chapters that follow drill down on specific steps of the data profiling process. They include techniques used to accomplish the analysis, as well as examples that demonstrate the process and value.

This part is not an exhaustive treatment of the topic of data profiling. That would take a large book by itself to accomplish. However, there is enough material here to develop a thorough awareness of the technology, understand how it works, and see how it can return value.

Data profiling applies directly to data quality assurance functions. It is also a valuable technology in developing new uses of data and in migrating data to other projects. When used in these projects, it can be viewed as either a development technology or a quality assurance technology. It provides an organized way of looking at data and delivering the metadata needed to make projects successful.

CHAPTER 7

Data Profiling Overview

This chapter begins the examination of the most important technology available to the data quality assurance team: data profiling.

Note to the reader: This text uses the terms *column* and *table* throughout the data profiling chapters in order to provide consistency. Data profiling is used for data from a wide variety of data sources that use different terminology for the same constructs. Consider *table* the equivalent of *file, entity, relation,* or *segment,* and *column* the equivalent of *data element, attribute,* or *field.*

The text uses the term *data profiling repository* to mean a place to record all of the information used in and derived from the data profiling process. Much of this information is metadata. However, I do not want to confuse the reader by referring to it as a metadata repository. A user could use an existing metadata repository for this information provided it was robust enough to hold all of the types of information. Otherwise, they could use the repository provided by a data profiling software vendor or fabricate their own repository. It is not unreasonable to expect that much of this information would subsequently be moved to an enterprise metadata repository after data profiling is complete.

7.1 Goals of Data Profiling

Data profiling is defined as the application of data analysis techniques to existing data stores for the purpose of determining the actual content, structure, and quality of the data. This distinguishes it from data analysis techniques used to derive business information from data. Data profiling is used to derive information about the data instead.

Data profiling technology starts with the assumption that any available metadata describing rules for correctness of the data is either wrong or incomplete. The data profiling process will generate accurate metadata as an output of the process by relying on the data for reverse-engineering the metadata and comparing it to the proposed metadata.

If data were perfectly accurate you would need to use only the information derived from the data. However, because most data stores contain data inaccuracies, the process requires the user to make decisions on whether the data is correct or the metadata is correct. When both are flawed, this can become a complex exercise.

Data profiling is a process that involves learning from the data. It employs discovery and analytical techniques to find characteristics of the data that can then be looked at by a business analyst to determine if the data matches the business intent.

Once the proper definition of data is arrived at, the data profiling methodology allows for computing the violations of the metadata that occurs in the data. This provides both hard instances of inaccurate data as well as evidence of the presence of inaccurate data for which determining the actual wrong values is not possible.

Data profiling cannot find all inaccurate data. It can only find rule violations. This includes invalid values, structural violations, and data rule violations. Some inaccurate data can pass all rule tests and yet still be wrong.

The data profiling process is directly applicable to the inside-out approach of assessing data quality. It is also useful beyond the data quality assessment function by providing valuable metadata and quality information to projects that are developing new uses of data or that are migrating data to different data structures.

Another goal of data profiling is to create a knowledge base of accurate information about your data. This information needs to be captured and retained in a formal data profiling repository. It needs to survive the data profiling process and serve many clients over time. It needs to be updated either as more is learned or as systems change. Data profiling may need to be repeated on critical data stores from time to time to ensure that the information continues to be accurate.

7.2 General Model

Figure 7.1 shows the general model of a data profiling process. The primary input is the data; the primary output is facts about the data.

Participants

Data profiling is usually done with a single analyst or small team of analysts performing most of the analytical work, and several other participants adding value to that analysis. The data profiling analyst is generally part of the data quality assurance team. This person should be well versed on data structures, data architecture concepts, data modeling, and analysis techniques. The analyst is not the one who needs to know the business purpose and meaning of the data, although it helps if she does.

Business analysts who understand the applications that work with the data being profiled must play an important role. The data analyst will bring intermediate results to the business analysts for semantic interpretation. The business analyst is the real authority on right or wrong rules. The data will suggest many rules and relationships that need to be verified.

IT staff members that built the application, maintain it, or manage the physical data can also be useful. When it comes to rule definition and verification, the application developers can provide a great deal of insight. The database administrators are helpful in providing the data to be used in data profiling and in explaining some of the structural issues that may surface in the data profiling process.

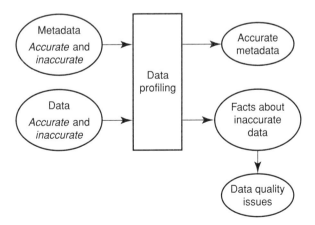

FIGURE 7.1 Data profiling model.

Other staff may be helpful in understanding situations discovered in the data. For example, people who create data, people who use reports, or people who perform ad hoc queries against the data can also be used to explain mysteries that arise.

It is helpful to periodically gather people from several of these disciplines into a room for a group review of the facts discovered by the data profiling analyst. This is often the most productive way to get through the mysteries to the truth: match the experts to the facts determined from the data.

SOME *business analysts are more than capable of driving the data profiling process. The key is whether they understand the basic principles of data architecture. If they do not, they will have difficulty getting through the structural analysis. They need to understand concepts such as null, primary keys, functional dependencies, referential constraints, and entity relationship rules.*

Some business analysts do understand these, and some do not. If they do, you have the best of all worlds: an analyst who can wade through the technology and who knows the business aspects of the data. If they do not, it is best that a partnership be created to get the work done.

Data Profiling Inputs

There are two inputs: metadata and data. The metadata defines what constitutes accurate data. If you had perfectly accurate and complete metadata, all you would need to do is compare the data to the metadata, and any violations are data inaccuracy facts. However, the metadata is almost always inaccurate and incomplete. This places a higher burden on attempts to use it with the data.

Data profiling depends heavily on the data. The data will tell you an enormous amount of information about your data if you analyze it enough.

METADATA

Metadata is essential for determining inaccuracies. You cannot tell if something is wrong unless you can define what being right is. That definition is metadata.

Appendix B shows a list of some of the information included in metadata. A data profiling repository should include all information the data management team and the business users require. This may include other information that is not included in that list.

Although you can be certain that what you know about the data before you start data profiling is going to be inaccurate and incomplete, you must start there. The existing information will provide a basic structure. This structure is essential to getting started.

The source of information starts with identification of the data source, the database or file technology it is stored in, and how to access the information. You need access to the data to perform data profiling. Access should be as unfettered and unfiltered as possible.

The next part is to collect metadata on the column-level layout of the data within the database or file system. How this is accomplished will generally be dependent on the data source. If the data is in a relational system, this information should be extracted from the relational database directory or catalog. If accessing an IMS or VSAM data source, you should look for a COBOL copybook or a PL/1 INCLUDE file that lays out the data. For other data sources, seek the appropriate source that gives you the layout that best represents the data according to the most likely extraction method.

Extract structural information that is available within the database management system. For example, in relational systems you can extract primary key, foreign key, and other referential constraint information. You can also examine any TRIGGER or STORED PROCEDURE logic embedded within the relational system to cull data filtering and validation rules being enforced. In IMS, the program specification block (PSB) gives insight into the hierarchical structure being enforced by IMS.

Seek out interface definitions to application programs that feed data to the data source. These can often add illuminating information about the expected content of the data. Collect any descriptions of the data that are available in existing data dictionaries, metadata repositories, or other documentation forms.

You may also want to collect application source code for programs that insert, delete, and update information in the database. These can be culled to extract data rules that are currently being enforced through the code. There are software packages available to assist you with extracting rules from source programs. Although this technique is possible, it is rarely done. Some reasons for not doing this are that the volume of source code may be extremely high, extracting rules is a difficult task because typical programming logic does not easily isolate rule logic, and the technical staff performing data profiling typically is not trained in the programming languages used (usually COBOL).

Looking for external process rules may also be helpful. Sometimes data rules are enforced through human procedures instead of through program or database logic. Procedure manuals used by data entry personnel may contain valuable rules.

All of this information should be recorded in a common place: the data profiling metadata repository. Recording in a common format will facilitate dealing with many disparate data sources.

It may be useful at this point to verify some of the information with other technical people to determine the completeness of your data-gathering exercise and to identify areas where others suspect wrong or missing information. In addition to talking to business analysts, it is probably just as important to discuss your findings with database administrators or application programmers. In fact, it would be useful for the data profiling analyst to work with them throughout the data-gathering phase.

DATA

The next step in the process is to extract some of the data from the data source. There are two reasons for doing this. Executing data profiling tasks can be CPU intensive, and most shops will resist doing this on operational systems. The interference with operational performance is normally prohibitive. The second reason is that you need to recast the data to a normalized form to effectively profile it. Data profiling can be done over data that is in less than third-normal form but may yield incorrect results. It is best to have it in third-normal form. However, you often do not know if it is in first-, second-, or third-normal form when you extract it. The data profiling process will reveal the form it is really in.

Extracting all of the data is clearly preferable to extracting only a sample. However, on very large data sources measuring in the hundreds of millions or billions of rows, using all of the data would be prohibitive for some of the analytical processes. Most data profiling is not done on supercomputers. In reality, the team may only have an NT box available. Some processes will be able to run in acceptable times over even very large amounts of data, whereas others will take a prohibitive amount of time to complete. On these large data sources, samples are generally more than sufficient to accomplish data profiling tasks.

Sampling is a very complex topic that can make data profiling accurate or inaccurate. Common mistakes in sampling are to draw too small of a sample, too large of a sample, having the sample biased through getting records that disproportionately represent only part of the population, or getting samples that violate structural rules. This book does not provide descriptions of sampling techniques. However, a practitioner should understand this topic well if mistakes are to be avoided. Sampling should be used only when necessary and only for data profiling steps that require it.

Extraction routines must be developed. These are normally easy to perform. However, they can become complicated when data structures include either of three common practices: field overloading, redefines, and repeating arrays (called OCCURS clauses in COBOL). These factors need to be identified and appropriate normalization performed in the extraction process to get a meaningful array of normalized files for data profiling.

Overloaded fields need to be broken into multiple columns. Redefines need to be analyzed to determine if they are the same facts being redefined by a different external view or whether they represent different facts based on the value in some other column. Repetitive arrays need to be analyzed to determine if they represent multiple occurrences of the same business fact or whether they represent truly distinct facts. These decisions all lead to a determination of the proper way to normalize. The last two of these decisions are semantic and cannot be determined from looking at the data definitions alone.

Some transformations are also helpful in the extraction process. Data that is bit encoded in the source can usually benefit from being converted to a character format in order to facilitate data profiling activities.

Sometimes extracting data generates errors or nonsense results. This generally occurs due to errors in the information provided that started the process. Often, COBOL copybooks inaccurately map the data as stored. Overloaded fields are often not documented. Sometimes the controlling values that determine redefinition mapping are not the ones actually used in the logic.

All errors need to be examined to determine why they did not extract correctly. Result data should be put into a displayable format and a reasonableness check performed to see if the data appears to map out according to the expected data layouts. Offset problems, columns in the wrong places, and so on will generally be visible in this cursory check.

The analyst may get into a repetitive process here by developing extraction routines, executing them, finding out that the results are nonsense, investigating the causes of the problems, adjusting the extraction routines, and trying again.

The data profiling analyst should verify all extraction logic and resolution of problems encountered with the keepers of the data source. This may be a database administrator or an application developer who knows the data source well. They can often shed light on the problems and catch mistaken choices made by the data profiling analyst.

The decisions to normalize REDEFINE or OCCURS structures are semantic decisions. They require interpretation of the intent of the data structure. To verify these decisions or even to make them in the first place, it may be necessary to consult with a business analyst.

MAPS *derived from programming materials often do not map correctly to the actual data. One study concluded that approximately 80% of COBOL copybooks incorrectly map to the data. Most IT shops I mentioned this to did not dispute this number.*

Typical mismatches include cases in which a column documented in the copybook is subdivided into two or more columns in practice, cases in which field overloading is done and not documented (COBOL specifications do not have constructs for overloading except in the case of REDEFINES that cover only one form of overloading), and cases in which programmers use a single column as a displacement anchor and do as they wish with the space behind it.

I have also observed on multiple occasions cases in which space in the FILLER specification is used for real data. I recommend that analysts always look at the content of FILLER for possible useful but undocumented data.

All of this comes about because a programmer needs to make a change in a hurry to an operational system and does not want to trigger a massive recompilation of hundreds of programs. They simply figure out how to accomplish the change in selected program logic and bypass the correct method of performing the copybook update. The change is made with minimum disruption of the system, and the copybook is forever corrupted.

Many issues may appear in the extraction process. Discovery of the need to separate overloaded fields should be documented because this will need to be done every time this data is accessed for new uses. The need to transform bit-level encodings to character representations must be documented for the same reasons.

All of the normalization logic needs to be documented, as this is important to get an accurate table representation of the source information. Key columns should also be included in the normalized representations.

Sometimes extraction fails due to problems in the data. For example, a column may be defined as packed decimal in the source system documentation, whereas attempts to convert this to a numeric variable in the extract representation may fail if the column is sometimes used for character data instead. The extraction routines may throw away the records containing errors or may substitute a zero for the invalid value. If this situation is found, the errors detected and the values changed need to be documented. One of the goals of data profiling is to find inaccurate data. If inaccuracies are detected in the extraction process and rejected from the output or changed to valid values, the data profiling steps will not catch them. This must be included in the set of inaccurate data facts disclosed.

If too many extraction issues arise, it may indicate that the data is unfit for the planned use. If this is the case, the data profiling analyst needs to specifically document the issues and try to quantify the magnitude of offending data. Some projects will not get past the extraction process, and rightly so. When this happens, they need to seek alternate data sources or launch a reengineering of the data source and its applications to improve the accuracy of the data before it is subsequently extracted.

EXTRACTING *data for data profiling can also be viewed as developing a common extraction process for all subsequent batch extractions of the data. Data profiling will be performed on the output of extraction, not the original data source. Therefore, any conclusions about quality or identified needs for transformations and cleansing will be based on the extracted representation of the data.*

If data profiling does its job well, the extraction routines should then be used for all subsequent draws of the data so that all logic built from the information developed through the data profiling process will be accurate. If you extract the data differently in subsequent project execution, the remedies developed through data profiling may be wrong or insufficient.

Data Profiling Outputs

The primary output of the data profiling process is best described as accurate, enriched metadata and facts surrounding discrepancies between the data and the accurate metadata. These facts are the evidence of inaccurate data and become the basis for issues formation and investigation.

METADATA

Metadata is both an input and an output. This is true because the data profiling process will both correct and expand the metadata gathered to start the process.

The data profiling process probably generates the most complete set of information ever assembled for this data. It is not only complete, it is accurate. It should be the basis for all subsequent development activities on projects that will use the data source that is profiled.

If purchased data profiling software is used, it will normally come with a data profiling repository to store this in. If you also maintain an enterprise metadata repository, you may want to copy the relevant information to that repository after profiling. This is also a good opportunity to determine how good the information is in your enterprise repository.

DATA QUALITY FACTS

The database of information gathered for data quality facts includes identification of rows and values that failed to pass the many rules used in the data profiling process. This information should include

- table and column name

- property rule

- invalid value list with frequency of each

- table and rowID containing the violation

- total number of rows tested

The rowID may be a list of rowIDs. There may be a number of rows that match the violation. If one rule violation encompasses multiple data rows, this should also be captured. Not all rules will identify a row set that can be recorded. As you will see later, some aggregation tests cover such a large amount of rows that detailing all rows accessed to generate the aggregate values would be impractical.

The collection of rule violations should be kept separate from the metadata. This set constitutes an instance of violations (those violations found in the specific extraction used to generate it). Over time, you may accumulate multiple result sets against the same metadata rule set. It may be helpful to put summary information about the result set in the data profiling repository.

LATENCY

Most people would claim that maintaining this information over time is impractical. If past history is any indication, they are correct. As much as we would all like to think we could create a true data profiling repository once and keep it current over time, the practical reality is that it never happens. It is therefore more practical to have a strategy of creating it the first time a data store becomes the subject of a quality assessment project or is used as a data source in any other type of project. It should then be upgraded through data profiling for any subsequent projects that require use of the information. Updating it should take considerably less work than starting over for each project that needs to use the data.

7.3 Data Profiling Methodology

Data profiling should follow a specific methodology to be most effective. The methodology provides for an orderly and logical progression of investigations that build information from one level to the next.

Data profiling methodology uses a bottom-up approach. It starts at the most atomic level of the data and moves to progressively higher levels of structure over the data. By doing this, problems at lower levels are found and can be factored into the analysis at the higher level. If a top-down approach is used, data inaccuracies at the lower levels may confuse the process and make it difficult to establish the true data rules. This is why a top-down approach will not work effectively in the face of data inaccuracies. Many analysts will correct data inaccuracies at each level before moving to a higher level. This is done to make the higher levels of data profiling more successful.

Process Steps

Figure 7.2 shows a diagram of the major steps in the data profiling methodology. Each step concentrates on a specific type of rule, builds or verifies the rule definitions, and then uses this to find discrepancies between the data and the rules.

Data profiling users often only go partway through the methodology. They find so much useful information in the first step or two they believe they do not need to go further. Eliminating steps in the process leaves open the opportunity for missing facts about inaccurate data. You will find fewer of the potential data inaccuracy facts that are there to be found. The ones you miss may be more useful than the ones you find.

The diagram is a general concept. In practice, a single inaccurate value can cause rule violations in all steps. That does not mean that only one instance of rule violation per inaccurate value is valuable to detect. Each rule violation has a unique business implication. Thus, a single inaccurate value can explode into

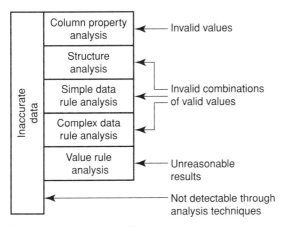

FIGURE 7.2 Data profiling steps.

multiple external problems. It is important to know all of the violations to understand the full potential of impacts possible from the inaccuracy.

Each of the steps, introduced in the sections that follow, is the topic of a separate chapter. The chapters go into greater detail with real examples of the rules and the type of investigative thought required to be effective.

Column Property Analysis

This type of analysis looks at the values stored in a single column independent of all other columns. It is the subject of Chapter 8. The metadata includes properties for each column that define what a valid value is within that column.

For example, a property might be that the DEPARTMENT_ID column is numeric and must be in the range of 100 to 999. A value of 010 would be output as an invalid value.

The property list for each column is really a rule set involving only a single column. The more properties included, the more bad values that can be found. The more complete the property definitions, the more opportunity exists for finding bad values.

Too often analysts use the database column specifications as the properties list. This is generally too limited to find most invalid values. The database specifications usually include physical storage properties and are not refined or specific enough to be used for invalid value testing.

Sometimes analysts confuse the column property list with domain definitions. These are different objects. A column may be required to conform to the definition of one or more domains but have additional restrictions that apply only to that particular use of the domain. This concept is described in the next chapter.

Violations of properties discovered are all inaccurate values. However, not all inaccurate values are found through this process. Values that are invalid but for which you do not have a test are not found. Neither are values that are valid but not correct.

Structure Analysis

Structure analysis uses rules that define how columns relate to each other to form tables and how tables relate to each other to form business objects. A business object is the data that describes a single business event or thing. For example, the data for a single customer order is a business object. The order object may consist of multiple parts, such as an order header, customer information, delivery information, and product line items. Each part would consist of one or more columns. The parts are normally stored in separate data tables. The collection of data for all orders is a database or a part of a database. This is shown in Figure 7.3. A full description of structure analysis is provided in Chapter 9.

The structure rules define the columns that uniquely identify a specific business object or table within the business object. It also defines rules for how tables relate to each other. For example, the order has an ORDER_ID column that defines each order uniquely. The order line items are identified by the ORDER_NUMBER column plus the PRODUCT_ID column. There can be one to many line item parts for each order.

Structure analysis deals with primary keys, primary/foreign key pairs, redundant data columns, column synonyms, and other referential constraints. It also deals with the sticky problem of denormalized data sources.

This is a very important component of data profiling. Every business object has a natural structure. This structure is often not known nor reflected accurately in source system definitions. For example, denormalization is rarely documented anywhere.

Knowing the columns that define the connections between object tables and knowing the rules on how tables of business objects relate to each other is essential in attempting to move data to other data structures that may have a very different set of structure rules.

In addition to the definition of how parts of a business object relate to one another, it is also important to discover how one business object relates to other business objects. For example, the order object above may relate to a customer master business object through the CUSTOMER_NUMBER column. These interobject relationships are important to know when databases

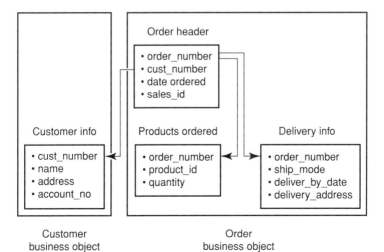

FIGURE 7.3   Example of a business object.

are being reengineered or migrated to packaged applications. These outward connections may need to be reengineered as well to maintain consistency.

Database management systems often provide support for structural rule enforcement. Relational systems are generally very good at this. However, there are many opportunities for rules not to be tested or defined to the DBMS system. Nondatabase systems data sources, such as flat files, can contain may cases of rule violations. Identifying these inaccuracies in the data is very important if the data is to be moved to a well-defined target database system. That system will most likely reject the load of the data whenever it encounters rule violations. Discovering these in advance can avoid costly backtracking in data movement processes.

Structure analysis is particularly useful for completing and correcting the metadata. In addition, violations identify specific cases where inaccurate data exists. However, because each structure rule involves more than one column or more than one row of a single table, violations only reduce the set of rows within which inaccurate data exists. They cannot identify which specific values within that set are wrong. The outputs describing the inaccurate data facts are the structure rule identifier, relation, and rowID sets within which the violation occurs.

Simple Data Rule Analysis

Once you have identified all of the invalid data values within columns and all of the structure rule violations, it is time to get more specific about rules that require that values across multiple columns within a business object be acceptable combinations of values. These are defined as data rules. A data rule is a rule that specifies a condition that must hold true across one or more columns at any point in time.

Data rules are a subset of business rules. Business rules include several types of rules that are not data rules. For example, a rule that says that IF LICENSE_TYPE = 'HEAVY_EQUIPMENT' THEN CURRENT_DATE – BIRTH_DATE > 21 YEARS is a data rule. A rule that says that IF CUSTOMER_TYPE = 'GOLD' THEN SET DISCOUNT = '10%' is a process rule and not a data rule. Both of them are business rules.

The data profiling analyst and the business analysts would normally collect or speculate about rules that should hold true over the data. These are converted to executable logic and then tested against the data. This is truly an iterative process that does double duty: solidifying the set of rules in the metadata and identifying specific sets of rows in the data that violate them. The output about inaccurate data facts is again relation and rowID sets connected to rule identifiers.

Because data rules involve more than one value, they cannot tell which value within the error set is wrong, only that the combination of values is wrong. A full description of simple data rule analysis is provided in Chapter 10.

Complex Data Rule Analysis

More complex data rules require values to conform to the rule over multiple business objects. An example might be a rule that says that a specific customer cannot be both a retail customer and a commercial customer. This requires finding all of the customer records for each customer and then checking for this condition within the set of records for each customer.

The only difference between this set of rules and the set described for single business objects is that the amount of data needed to test the rule is greater, involving the data of multiple business objects and identified violations, such as inaccurate data that is hidden within a much larger set of data rows. However, this may not always be true. Sometimes the rule can isolate the set of rows that contain the inaccurate values to as few as one row.

It is often not productive to capture all rows that constitute the set of rows within which the inaccurate data exists and store it in the inaccurate data fact table. It generates too many values that have no analytical value. However, it is valuable for these cases to record the ruleID and the number of specific violations of the rule. A full description of complex data rule analysis is provided in Chapter 11.

Value Rule Analysis

Sometimes the existence of inaccurate data can be spotted through aggregation numbers that are obvious to the analyst as being unreasonable. For example, seeing the frequency of occurrence of each value in a column may indicate that one or more values have far too low or far too high a frequency. This may lead the analyst to the conclusion that data is not being entered correctly.

Often it is not possible to convert these into hard rules that say that a particular value should be precisely x% of the data or that it should fall in a specified range. The analyst should collect these types of queries from the business analysts and run them against the data, presenting the results back to the business analysts for reasonable checks.

Examples are cardinality, counts, sums, averages, medians, frequencies, standard deviations, and so on. Any computed value that can be used to test the collection of data for completeness or reasonable values can be used. A full description of value rule analysis is provided in Chapter 12.

7.4 Analytical Methods Used in Data Profiling

Within each data profiling step there can be processes for discovery, assertion testing, or value inspection. The analyst uses outputs of these processes to make decisions. Each type of activity is explored in the sections that follow.

Discovery

Discovery includes processing that reveals facts about the data the analyst may not know or suspect. In this regard it is similar to data mining techniques.

An example of discovery is to execute a program that analyzes the patterns in text columns to determine if they may be date values, coded values following a specific character encoding pattern, single text strings, multiple text strings, or multiple text strings connected with special characters such as = or :. If a dominant characterization is found over a high percentage of the data, the analyst is a long way toward establishing the true properties of the column. The discovered property may be different from the one implied in the documented data type (usually just CHARnn) or in the name or description of the column.

Discovery can be applied to a number of variables that are common across columns. For example, it is easier to execute a range computation for all numeric columns and then to compare against the expected range.

Using this same example, discovery can be more powerful than assertion testing through exposing the true range rather than only exceptions to the expected range. If the discovery returned a true range of 100 to 200, all well within the expected range of 0 to 10,000, the huge discrepancy would indicate something wrong with the expected range or quite possibly that the column is used for a different business purpose than documented.

This same effect can be true of discrete value lists, text string lengths, and other factors where the actual list of values, although all valid, may indicate a problem in the definition of the data. A data quality problem may be hiding within the valid set that is exposed through discovery but not through verification. Simple examples are columns with all values being the same (essentially a NOT USED column) or columns with a very high incidence of one value that cannot be true in the real world, which indicates a problem in data capture. For these reasons, it is always better to discover facts about the data rather than to merely construct assertion tests.

Discovery is also possible for complex tests, such as finding functional dependencies. This is very important in order to determine the true structure of data if you intend to transform the structure and match it to another structure. If you only test the dependencies you think are true, you will miss others.

Assertion Testing

Assertion testing refers to processing that takes a known or suspected fact about the data and checks to see if the data conforms and, if not, reveals the instances where it does not. A good data profiler performs both types of investigation. Generally, discovery precedes assertion testing because discovery can uncover new rules.

An example of assertion testing is where you believe a column has a range of 0 to 10,000. You construct a query to test this assertion. The query returns all values that are not in this range.

Only rules involving single-column content or structural components that hold true over all of the data are reasonable candidates for discovery. Other data rules that are simple or complex have to be formulated and tested by crafting a query that exposes the violations. There is endless potential for such rules.

Data rules can come from existing documentation, application program logic, or from work sessions with business analysts. Some of these data rules will be conjecture until they are verified by data and business analysts.

All data rules need to be tested against the data to determine conformity. A lack of conformity needs to be investigated to determine if the rule should be discarded, if the rule should be modified, or whether the data is inaccurate. This decision is purely and simply a semantic decision that should be made through collaboration between the data profiling analyst and the business analyst.

Again, rules can be written too broadly and hide problems that could have been exposed if the rule were more restrictive (data hiding inside the rule). For example, if a series of dates need to be in order (BACKORDERED_ DATE <= SHIPPED_DATE <= RECEIVED_DATE), it may be that for a significant number of orders all three dates are the same. All orders would pass the rule. However, it may be that it is impossible or unreasonable for this condition to be true all of the time or even a high percentage of the time. It may be necessary to create a second rule as NOT(BACKORDERED_DATE = SHIPPED_DATE = RECEIVED_DATE). This says that the dates cannot be all the same and isolates the ones that are.

This second data rule may yield instances of accurate data (false positives) because sometimes having two of the dates the same is acceptable. However, the output can be reviewed to see if real inaccuracies are also reported from the data rule.

Visual Inspection

An additional form of analysis is through visual inspection. Many of the clues of data inaccuracies are not easily formulated as boundaries, limits, or rules. Visual inspection of the data can lead an analyst to the conclusion that something is wrong with the data (possibly very wrong). Typical value computations that may be used are

- frequency distribution of values over a column

- sums, totals of values over a column for a relation, or groups within a relation

- comparing counts or totals from one data source to another

- values with counts less than some interesting threshold

- text strings

Text strings present an interesting example. Consider a free-form text column used to capture the name of a company. The properties description of the column says that it is a column containing characters and can be from 1 to 30 characters in length. The description may also disallow leading blanks. However, embedded blanks would have to be allowed. It may also be refined to disallow other special characters, such as the following: #$%^&*(). This provides a reasonable filter against invalid entries.

However, this filter will allow many obviously invalid names that pass the previously described test. You cannot put in a test that requires more than two characters because it would disallow the company I2. Note that this name also includes a numeric character, so that cannot be disallowed either.

By visual inspection, you would be able to spot invalid names such as *Don't know, Not provided, A company, 1235 main street,* or *Chicago, IL.* These would all pass the properties verification test but not a visual inspection.

You cannot visually inspect all names in a five-million record customer database. However, you can programmatically look for names that suggest errors, thus significantly lowering the scope of names to inspect. For example, your screen could look for names beginning with lowercase characters, containing numbers, or containing other special characters that might, but rarely do, appear in names. You can also look for names that appear more than once in the database, in that entry operator conventions such as *Don't know* tend to appear multiple times.

Metadata Verification

The data profiling analyst needs to constantly review the metadata against testing results. Much of the metadata confirmation and development is a reflection of the business meaning of the data. Much of the interpretation of what constitutes inaccurate data is also semantic. The data profiling process will uncover a number of surprises from the data. Each surprise needs to be investigated to determine if the interpretation of the data given in the metadata is correct and the data wrong, or whether the data is right and the metadata is wrong. Input from others is generally needed to make these determinations.

Work groups consisting of the data profiling analyst, business analysts, and other subject matter experts should meet periodically to review the data as it evolves. These reviews can be done in a meeting or over the Internet. The important point is to use the computed data and compare it to metadata rules that are being proposed. Because the data is being used for the computations, there should be no disagreement about what is present, only discussion of what it means.

There is a specific value in ensuring completeness of each step before continuing to the next step. This will become more evident as the process steps are reviewed. It is therefore not a good idea to wait until the data profiling analyst has completed all of the steps before involving the other team members.

Iterations and Backtracking

Although the methodology calls for logically progressing through the steps and trying to complete and verify the results in each step before going to the next step, it is sometimes useful to backtrack. For example, performing structural analysis may reveal that the understanding of the content of a specific column is not what you think it is. This may require that you go back to value analysis and revisit that column before retrying the structural analysis part.

Software Support

Data profiling analytical techniques require special software to be effective. As you can see from this section, it depends on the ability to execute a wide variety of functions against a lot of data. The functions are too pervasive to support tuning through typical database administration methods. You would have an excessive number of indexes on the data if you tuned each process and rule.

Although you can perform some of the functions through standard query and reporting tools, you cannot perform all of them. Some of the more productive functions cannot be done through standard tools. You need to look for or develop specialized data profiling software to support strong data profiling activities.

7.5 When Should Data Profiling Be Done?

Clearly, data profiling should be done on all data quality assessment projects as well on all IT projects that either move data to another structure or migrate or consolidate data. If a data quality assurance department uncovers significant facts about a data source through the outside-in method, they should profile the data source after the fact to determine the extent of inaccuracies and to discover any additional inaccuracy problems that may exist in the same data.

It is important to do all steps of the data profiling process whenever used. Analysts that think they can bypass a step because they understand the structure or believe that rules are enforced by the application programs will often be surprised by discoveries that go beyond what they think. The biggest task in data profiling is generally getting started, gathering known metadata, and getting the data extracted. Once you have done all of this and gone through the first step of data profiling, the other steps do not add that much more time to the process. Ending early has risk or missing inaccuracies, but costs little to finish.

Important databases should be reprofiled periodically. The rationale is that changes to applications are occurring all of the time. Industry experts have consistently estimated that production applications incur a change of 7% every year. Many of these changes have the potential to introduce new opportunities for generating inaccurate data. Other changes, such as business process changes or personnel changes, can introduce the possibility that data accuracy will deteriorate.

Once data profiling has been done on a source one time, much of the initial work has already been done, making a reprofiling exercise go much faster. Data profiling should be done on data sources after remedies have been implemented and a period of time passes for them to have an impact. This is a good way to measure the effectiveness of the remedies as well as to ensure that new problems have not been introduced.

Data profiling of secondary, derivative data stores is also helpful. For example, data profiling the data warehouse can reveal problems that are unique only at the data warehouse level. Aggregating and integrating data from multiple data sources can generate conditions that are illogical and discoverable only in the aggregation. For example, two data sources that maintain the same information at different levels of granularity will populate a data warehouse column with unusable data. Each data source would pass data profiling just fine.

7.6   Closing Remarks

Data profiling is described in this book as a generic technology. Any specific implementation of software and process to support it will be more or less complete for each step. For example, in value analysis you could invent new analytical techniques endlessly to micro-define what is acceptable. Similarly you can invent rules for business objects seemingly endlessly.

DATA *profiling is emerging as a unique and independent technology. However, analysts have performed data profiling throughout the years on all projects. You always have a phase of collecting information about data sources, mapping to targets, identifying issues, and crafting remedies.*

The difference is that the analyst lacked a set of analytical tools designed specifically for the task of data profiling. They used ad hoc queries to test data. As a result, they generally did not have the time or resources to perform rigorous data profiling. They shortchanged the part about looking at the data. This meant that they tended to accept the gathered descriptions of data even though they cannot be trusted. The result has been a high rate of project failure or significant overruns.

One very experienced analyst once told me that he had been doing projects

for 20 years and at the beginning of each project he promised himself that he would do it right that time. Doing it right meant thoroughly looking at the data to verify all gathered facts about the data, to uncover undocumented issues, and to discover the true state of data quality. In every case, he ended up stopping his investigation early in the project because of the enormous time and resources required to complete a comprehensive examination. In all cases the project suffered later because of information about the data that was missed.

The emergence of a discrete methodology backed by software explicitly crafted for these tasks has greatly reduced the time and effort required to perform thorough data profiling. This is enabling data quality staff to use this approach effectively.

It is easy to get into "analysis paralysis" in performing data profiling by trying to micro-define correctness to the ultimate level and then burn up machines for days trying to validate them. At some point the process yields too little for the effort to be worthwhile. Practitioners need to find the right balance to get the most value from the work being performed.

Although overanalyzing data is a risk, you rarely see this as the case. The most common failing is not to perform enough analysis. Too often the desire to get results quickly ends up driving through the process with too few rules defined and too little thinking about the data.

Used effectively, data profiling can be a core competency technology that will significantly improve data quality assessment findings, shorten the implementation cycles of major projects by months, and improve the understanding of data for end users. It is not the only technology that can be used. However, it is probably the single most effective one for improving the accuracy of data in our corporate databases.

CHAPTER 8

Column Property Analysis

Analysis of column properties is the process of looking at individual, atomic values and determining whether they are valid or invalid. To do this, you need a definition of what is valid. This is in the metadata. It consists of a set of definitional rules to which the values need to conform.

In the industry, these types of rules are generally not referred to as rules. They are commonly referred to as domain definitions, column specifications, column descriptions, or column properties. However, they can all be considered rules because they provide a definition of what can be put into a column. For example, a column specification that the length of a column is 10 characters is basically a rule that says the maximum length is 10. All of the specifications for the content of an individual column are rules that restrict the values that can be considered valid. They are generally not expressed in a rule language or rule syntax.

8.1 Definitions

To understand this chapter you need to know how certain terms are defined and subsequently used. These terms are *column, domain, properties, null,* and *field overloading.* These terms are notorious for having different meanings, depending on the author or product using them. Defining how they are used in this text will reduce the risk of confusion. Figure 8.1 shows how these terms relate to one another.

Table

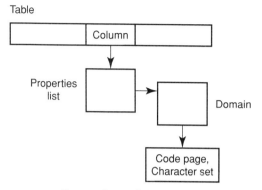

FIGURE 8.1 Definitional elements.

Columns

The most basic element of a database is an individual column. In some systems this is called a field or an attribute. It refers to a place to hold a single fact about a single business object that is stored in the database.

Columns are the elements of a database that generally have the most definition. This is because the database or file systems require a layout of the records, rows, or segments. This layout describes each data column as it appears in the database. This is essential for the database system to work properly. This definition usually consists of a NAME entry followed by a physical description of the requirements for storing the data. The following is an example.

```
EMPLOYEE_NAME    CHARACTER 35
BIRTH_DATE       DATE
UNIT_PRICE       DECIMAL (5,2)
```

This basic definition is required for the database or file system to find the data when processing a query statement. It also provides the minimal definition so that the database system can properly store the data. The database system will generally allow any value in a column that fits the shape and size provided for it.

These descriptions are also needed for application programmers to know how to treat each column. This is often the only definition that exists for a column. The COBOL copybook file, the PL/1 INCLUDE file, and the relational database CREATE TABLE specifications are very often all you will find for columns (or for anything else, for that matter).

There may exist other documentation for columns. This would typically be in a data dictionary or metadata repository. These descriptions would provide for a more restricted view of what can be stored in a column plus text descriptions of the business meaning and intended use of the data. It may provide a different, more expressive NAME entry for the column. This would be done in cases in which the database systems or the programming language used to access data has restrictions on the length of a column name, thus making it impossible to make names expressive at the physical level.

Relational database systems generally provide for a short text and/or a long text to allow documentation of the meaning of a column. The short text is frequently used to provide a longer descriptive name for a column. These can be extracted from the DBMS catalog.

Looking at how a column is described in leading text on data entry forms can also be helpful in establishing the meaning beyond what is implied by the column name. To fully understand a column you generally need more information and rules than what is available. The available metadata is generally incomplete. The metadata you have can be inaccurate, even if it comes from a database or programming source code file. In fact, it is often inaccurate. You need to be skeptical about its accuracy.

Domains

A domain is a named object that defines the acceptable values for encoding one specific business fact. Domains are not columns. They are standards. They are standards that should be applied to the definition of business data objects. A column is a specific instance of a business fact being defined within a business object. The domain is a generic definition not attached to a physical instance of its use. A column is the physical instance of its use.

The concept of domains is to define the basic rules for encoding common business elements independently of the applications that will use them. If application developers are responsible enough to use them, they will significantly enhance the usability, understanding, and maintainability of the applications across the corporation. They will eliminate the enormously wasteful practice of each individual programmer or data designer inventing multiple ways of expressing the same business fact across the corporation.

A well-disciplined corporation will have a metadata repository that has domains defined and easily available to all developers. It will also have an application development quality assurance function to ensure that they are used and used properly. The metadata repository will link the domains to the columns that use them to enhance the ability to interpret application data and to easily map the impacts of proposed changes.

This sounds so good. And yet, few corporations actually do this. Examples are explored in the sections that follow.

DATE DOMAIN

A date domain may be defined as a date between the day 01/01/1900 and the day 12/31/2099 inclusive, of the format *mm/dd/yyyy*, where *mm* is the month, *dd* is the day of the month, and *yyyy* is the year. This is a typical date domain definition for the United States.

A column that contains dates such as ORDER_DATE may use the date domain with additional restrictions on the range. An example is 01/01/1996 through CURRENT_DATE.

An enterprise may define several date domains: USA format dates, European format dates, year of the emperor dates, and so on. If the enterprise deals with very old dates, they may need a date domain that goes back thousands of years and has the BC/AD designation as well. This may be required for dating art, for example, or for encoding historical or geological events.

The corporation ought to have the discipline to define date domains as needed and then construct column definitions containing them from the standard domains, and to impose additional restrictions at the column level. RDBMS systems all internalize dates for columns specifying the DATE data type, making the external format immaterial. Using this capability greatly eliminates many potential errors in handling dates.

IN *1987, when IBM added date support to DB2, I decided to provide my customers with conversion routines to automatically convert dates contained in CHARACTER or INTEGER columns to the new DATE data type. To do this, I surveyed a limited customer base of about 10 DB2 users, asking them to provide me with the formats they were using in DB2 columns for expressing dates.*

They returned 94 different formats. One customer alone contributed over 40 formats. Some were CHARACTER formats, and some were INTEGER formats. I could not have imagined that people could think up that many different ways of expressing the same fact. I would have expected information system organizations to be more disciplined about data representation. I was wrong.

In addition, we all know about the debacle of Y2K, in which just finding all the columns that had dates in them and then building conversion routines for the dozens of formats used cost the IT departments around the world hundreds of billions of dollars. If database systems had better date support earlier and/or if customers had better discipline earlier, the costs would have been billions of dollars less. A little discipline, please!

ZIP CODE DOMAIN

This one is also instructive. The USA postal code calls for a Zip code on addresses in the format of *nnnnn-nnnn*, where *n* is a numeric character between 0 and 9, inclusive. However, the enterprise may decide that the shorter version is also acceptable, in that most people do not remember or provide the four-digit extension. Thus, the standard for the enterprise may be that Zip codes are in one of two formats: *nnnnn* or *nnnnn-nnnn*. They may choose to represent the short version as *nnnnn-0000* instead of *nnnnn*. They should not allow both short versions to be used.

However, if you want to include Canadian addresses, the previously described standard does not work. They use six characters, with the first three separated from the last three by a blank in the format *cnc ncn*, where *n* is a number between 0 and 9 and *c* is an alphabetic character from A to Z. They do not have an extension.

You can go beyond the United States and Canada because there are postal codes in most countries. However, they all have their own unique definitions.

You have two choices when defining domains for international addresses. You can define a domain strictly for each country, or you can generate a least common denominator domain definition that satisfies all of them. This might be that the Zip code is ALPHA/NUMERIC of variable length to a maximum of 10 characters. However, the least common denominator approach is not very useful in checking data for accuracy; just about anything will pass the test.

UNIT OF MEASURE DOMAIN

In this example, the unit of measure of various products produced or sold by the corporation is defined. In this case, the domain is an itemized list of values with their definitions. For example, you might use LB for pound, MT for metric ton, CT for carton, and EA for each.

The purpose of this domain is to create the proper definition for each of these so that individual data entry people do not make up their own versions and create a representation inconsistency problem. In fact, it is easy to build a pull-down list with acceptable values and their meanings.

The domain should encompass all units of measure that are needed for the corporation. This could also include units of measure that are not currently being used in anticipation of product line expansion in the future.

A few notes about domains. Domains should follow external standards wherever possible. There are countless standards groups in the world, many of which are restricted to one subject or one industry. These are very useful in finding standard domains that apply to your corporation.

An entire study of the topic of domain gets into micro-issues and macro-issues. A micro-issue is defining just what is meant by ALPHA, ALPHA-NUMERIC, and so on. It takes into consideration different alphabets and country code set issues. For example, the term *alphacharacter* means something different to someone in Russia than it does to someone in the United States.

Macro-issues include building hierarchies of named domains. In the Zip code example, the corporation may define a Zip code domain for each country. They could then combine country domains into superdomains for use by columns. For example, they might define a domain as USA-CANADA ZIP CODE, which inherits the domains of USA and CANADA. Another super-domain might be INTERNATIONAL ZIP CODE, which inherits the definitions from all Zip code domains. In this hierarchy, each subdomain may inherit the domains of individual character sets.

In this last example, the Zip codes are truly defined at a low enough level to identify invalid Zip codes from any country. However, it may require an excessive amount of computer processing cycles to do the validation.

Domains make all the sense in the world. It is so logical to take each business fact that you want to record information on and define precisely what constitutes correctness. But do not expect many to have done this. In practice, you will find many columns built from ad hoc domain definitions that have no similarity to other columns containing the same fact.

Property Lists

The term *properties* refers to rules for values that are permitted within a single column. Each column should have a base definition that includes one or more domain definitions.

The column property list is more than just the domain's restrictions. It also includes other factors. Figure 8.2 shows the basic list of some properties that are possible in a column. Some of these are domain properties; others are not. For example, the data type, length restrictions, range of acceptable values, and list of acceptable values would normally be found in the domain definition. Rules such as unique rule, consecutive rule, and null rule are not domain rules but additional rules imposed on a specific use of the domain.

A unique rule says that each value in the column must be different from all other values in the column. A consecutive rule says that the column values must be unique but also that no values between the highest and lowest can be missing (for example, check numbers in a check-issued table). The consecutive rule generally applies to an integer column but may also apply to a single-byte alphabetic column.

- Name; business name
- Business meaning
- Domain name
- Data type
- Character set, code page
- Length restrictions (shortest and longest, variability)
- Acceptable values
  - Discrete list of acceptable values
  - Range of acceptable values
  - Text field restrictions
  - Character patterns
- Null rule
- Unique rule
- Consecutive rule

FIGURE 8.2 Typical properties.

A column can be defined in terms of a domain plus additional factors that apply only as the domain is used in that column, or it can fully define itself without a domain definition. For example, an ORDER_NUMBER domain might say that it is a five-digit number between 10001 and 99999. In the ORDER_HEADER table, there is a column named ORDER_NUMBER. Its properties are that it contains the ORDER_NUMBER domain plus a requirement for UNIQUE, NOT NULL, and CONSECUTIVE. However, the ORDER_DETAIL table also has a column called ORDER_NUMBER. In this table it again uses the ORDER_NUMBER domain, but the unique rule is NOT UNIQUE because you can have many details per order, the null rule is again NOT NULL, and the consecutive rule is NOT CONSECU-TIVE because it permits multiple occurrences of the same number. There is another column called LAST_ORDER_NUMBER in the inventory table, which shows the last order received for that item of inventory. In this case, the business meaning is that it is only the most recent order received for this item. It again uses the ORDER_NUMBER domain. However, the properties are NOT UNIQUE, NULL permitted by using a blank because some items may have had no orders yet, and NOT CONSECUTIVE. This is shown in Figure 8.3.

Column Names

One of the most important properties of a column is the column *name*. Having a name that indicates the nature of the content is extremely valuable in performing data profiling as well as in constructing other processes for using the data. Most analysts and application developers tend to overdepend on the

DOMAIN   ORDER_NUMBER
A value that uniquely identifies each order received.
It is assigned by the order-processing application auto-
matically when a new order is inserted into the database.
Data type = NUMBER
Length = 5 digits
Range of acceptable values = 10001 through 99999

Columns:

ORDER_HEADER.ORDER_NUMBER
Domain = ORDER_NUMBER
Unique Rule = UNIQUE
Consecutive Rule = CONSECUTIVE
Null Rule = NOT NULL

ORDER_DETAIL.ORDER_NUMBER
Domain = ORDER_NUMBER
Unique Rule = NOT UNIQUE
Consecutive Rule = NOT CONSECUTIVE
Null Rule = NOT NULL

INVENTORY.ORDER_NUMBER
Domain = ORDER_NUMBER
Unique Rule = NOT UNIQUE
Consecutive Rule = NOT CONSECUTIVE

FIGURE 8.3   Example of domain versus property definitions.

name to indicate content. A name such as QUANTITY_AVAILABLE is more descriptive than a name such as AQ003BZ.

In some cases, column names are prefixed or postfixed with codes to indicate application or department. This reduces the number of characters available for meaningful semantics and makes the result less useful.

Columns sometimes have descriptive names and sometimes do not. As systems get larger and larger in the number of columns, the use of descriptive names becomes less likely. Many older application development tools, DBMSs, and file systems restrict the length of a name, making it very difficult to use descriptive names.

The analyst should always have a descriptive name associated with every column. This name may not be possible to use for application development but is very useful for metadata purposes. The analyst should generate a name if one is not available and should not worry about the length of the name.

The descriptive name should be as precise as possible. For example, a column named EMPLOYEE_NAME is much more descriptive than one named merely NAME. When you are working with hundreds or thousands of columns, having a more complete descriptive name is very helpful.

Null

The term *null* is one of the most controversial terms in database circles. There are many definitions and theories about how to handle the null condition, most of which the application development world completely ignores. When they ignore it in application design, the data entry people often invent their own conventions for dealing with the missing information, creating problems for data accuracy.

The null condition is the case where a value is not available for a column. A value may not be available for a number of reasons, such as

- The originator of the data refuses to provide the value.

- The entry person does not know the correct value.

- The column is not applicable for that particular instance.

- The value for the column is to be provided in a later step of the business process.

It is possible for applications to be designed such that each column could be entered as a value or a checklist for each of the reasons cited previously. The reason for no value could be recorded, and everyone would know how to interpret the value.

However, this never happens. What happens in practice is that the application stores a blank for character columns, stores zero for numeric columns, or uses the relational definition of NULL, which only allows one indicator for all conditions.

Other practices are found in legacy systems for which application designers decide to build a convention for NULL into a database or file system that does not support NULL indicators. In this case you see things such as *?*, *Not provided*, or *9999.99* put into the columns as values. The application programs "understand" that these mean no value provided.

Sometimes data entry people make up their own conventions. This occurs when the entry person does not know the value but the data entry procedure requires that something other than blank be provided.

Data profiling property lists need to record the conventions used for the NULL condition. If the conventions are bad design or can lead to quality problems, this should become a data quality issue. In the meantime, the data profiling process needs to be able to sort out nulls from real values.

Field Overloading

Field overloading is a term for a number of practices that are today considered bad data design but were commonly used in the past. It refers to the practice of using a single column for recording more than one business fact.

Field overloading is common in legacy systems. They were almost never a part of the original application design. However, as changes occurred in an application and the need for new columns arose, developers found it more convenient to piggyback columns than to create new columns. Creating new columns meant that record or segment lengths needed to be longer, which meant that databases needed to be unloaded and reloaded and that application programs not related to the change needed to be modified or at least recompiled. To avoid these expensive disruptions, they just overloaded fields that had unused bit capacity to handle the new information.

In addition to creating a difficult condition to detect and handle, the overloading was usually not documented. Because COBOL and PL/1 have no convenient way of specifying overloading, the programmers just did not document the fact at all. The splitting of the bits to separate columns was always done in the logic sections of the application programs (under the covers, so to speak). Following are some of the ways field overloading is done:

- Let text columns contain multiple facts as words or keywords.

- Steal unused bits of packed decimal column to use for binary information.

- Use the sign bit of a numeric column that cannot be negative for binary information.

- Use a column conditionally, meaning, for example, that if one column has a value of X, this column means *this* and otherwise *that*.

Column property analysis cannot be performed on overloaded columns without first splitting them into discrete, single-fact columns.

8.2 The Process for Profiling Columns

Figure 8.4 shows a schematic of what goes on when profiling columns. There are two goals to the process: (1) define the properties that determine what values are acceptable in the column and (2) find occurrences of violations of those properties (inaccurate values). This process looks at values in isolation. The examination concerns itself solely with the values stored in each column without any regard for how these values relate to other values in the business objects. That is covered in later steps of the data profiling process, as described in later chapters.

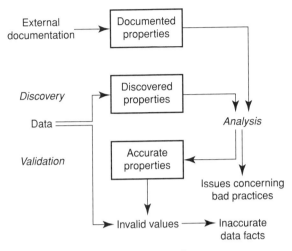

FIGURE 8.4 Column property analysis process.

Gathering Information

The available metadata needs to be captured in a data profiling repository used for the data profiling process. This includes as much information as is available about each column, regardless of whether it is complete or accurate. These are referred to as documented properties.

Sources of information can include programming specifications such as COBOL copybooks or PL/1 data definitions, database specifications such as DDL for relational systems, data entry screen specifications, data entry procedure manuals, data dictionary descriptions, and metadata repository information. The original metadata will provide a framework for identifying columns and their properties.

Discovery from Data

The data should be examined for each column to determine what is in it. This should be done independently from the metadata gathered. The reason for this is that gathering the information is generally not difficult to do, provided column boundaries can be found. Some properties of columns are difficult to discover without prior knowledge or discovery software. For example, automatically determining that the data type for a character column is really "date" is not easy to do without special software.

However, it is not rocket science to determine the cardinality, the range of values, whether the content is numeric or character, the range of the length of values, uniqueness, and the use of special-characters blanks, question marks, or strings that may indicate NULL. This should all be computed from the data.

You obviously cannot look at each data value in a column containing thousands or millions of instances to determine what you have. You need computational support. The ideal support is a program that computes the properties from the data and then allows the user to verify against the documented properties. If there is a mismatch, either the data is in error or the documented property is either inaccurate or incomplete.

If you lack a discovery-based program, you need to develop queries against the data for each column in order to determine the information you need to make a judgment whether the data is in conformance with the documented properties.

Trying to perform discovery of column properties against data that is not in tabular form is very difficult and is typically impractical. This is the essential argument for extraction of data to be profiled into tabular form as a part of the data profiling process.

Verification of Results

The next step is to match the content of the data to the documented properties. The matching process is both physical and logical. The goal is to determine if any differences are caused by inaccurate data or by inaccurate metadata. In looking at differences, there is a need to look at the results from two perspectives: inaccurate values and accurate values.

Values determined to be outside the scope of the documented properties would normally be considered inaccurate data. However, given the high suspicion about the accuracy of documented properties, the violations may suggest that the metadata is wrong. It is not at all unusual for data to be used for a fact that is different from the initial purpose of the column. It is also possible that the parameters are too restrictive, that the correct specification for valid values should be larger than specified in the properties. This examination may very well result in the metadata being revised as a result of investigating these differences.

Considering the accurate values is also useful in judging the metadata. For example, if a column is specified as having a length of 30 bytes and the discovery process determines that all entries are 1 byte in length, a strong suspicion is raised that the metadata is referring to some other column.

This process of matching the metadata to the discovered properties of the data should be done in a group setting. The data profiling analyst, business analysts, subject matter experts, and possibly data designers, database administrators, or application developers should be included. They need to approach the exercise from the point of view of rigorously determining what the correct property list is for each column and where it deviates from the discovered data and the extent of quality issues.

The output of this process is an accurate property list for each column. Another output may be a number of data quality issues surrounding situations that should be addressed to avoid future problems in using the data. The use of improperly defined encoding schemes, field overloading, inconsistent representations of NULL conditions, and the lack of domain standards across multiple columns are all good candidates for quality improvement issues.

Validation of Data

The last step is to process against the data one more time after the property lists are determined to be accurate. This allows identification and enumeration of all violations of the property lists. These are inaccurate data values.

These results need to be recorded in the data profiling repository as well. Ideally, these will be linked to each column specification in the repository.

This process is different from the discovery process previously described. In the discovery process you are computing characteristics. In the validation step you are computing the difference between the rules in the property list and the data. You may find that sample data is sufficient for discovery, especially on very large data sources, but that the entire data source needs to be used for validation.

It is a good practice to reconvene the data profiling review group used to determine the accurate metadata to review the outputs of the validation step. Additional confirmation can be achieved that the metadata is correct, as well as educating everyone on the amount of inaccurate values found in the data.

The results need to be recorded as inaccurate data facts. These facts are subsequently aggregated into data quality issues, as defined in Chapter 5.

8.3 Profiling Properties for Columns

This section discusses each of the types of properties that apply to columns and shows examples of using them to find invalid values. The property list may include within it a domain definition that provides some of the properties. Not all property lists will have the same rule property types, in that some only apply to specific cases.

Business Meaning

The business meaning of a column is a very important property. It says what should be stored in the column semantically. A simple statement of what the column is encoding is important in determining if the column is, in fact, being used for that purpose. A look at some of the data values returned from discovery, along with the discovered properties, is necessary to satisfy the reviewers that the column is not being used for something else.

This is an area that is often overlooked. It is so simple to just look at some of the values to verify that the content appears to be what you think it is. It is amazing how people decide what is stored in a column merely from a COBOL programming label.

Programmers have often decided to use an existing column that is no longer needed to store the values for a new requirement. This rarely results in a change to the programming specifications for that column. As a result you have program documentation that says a column is one thing, when in reality the information recorded is something different.

For example, a label of SOCIAL_SECURITY_NUMBER would be expected to contain Social Security numbers. In one real case, examination of actual data content revealed that the values stored could not be Social Security numbers. Further investigation revealed them to be fishing license numbers.

Other factors besides visual inspection of the data values can be used. For example, if the lengths of the data values are much shorter than the maximum length, the column has probably been repurposed.

ONE *of the easiest conditions to discover is that a column is not being used at all. This is indicated by the column having only one value in it (usually a blank for text columns or zero for numeric columns).*

It is amazing how often this is not known and the column is copied to decision support databases and used in decision support computations. All you have to do is look. In one case over 200 of these columns were found in a single database. The data management people were totally unaware of this situation and would have propagated these columns to their data warehouse had they not discovered it.

An unused column can contain more than one value. It may have been used for a period of time and then stopped being used. This is normally suggested by a very large number of empty values. Examination of the rows they are contained in will generally reveal whether the real values are recent or old. This will indicate whether it is a column that was used and then stopped being used or one that was recently added.*

Recently added columns have their own problems when being propagated. Moving data for a block of time that includes periods where the column was not used can seriously distort decision support aggregations, graphs, and reports.

One last thing to do in establishing the business meaning is to ensure that the column has a good descriptive name in the data profiling repository. If the name provided is not representative of the content nor long enough to precisely indicate the content, a better name should be constructed to use during the data profiling process.

Storage Properties

Storage properties are a subset of column properties defined to the database or file system that allow them to store the data in proper containers. This includes data type, length, and precision for numeric fields. The basic rules that govern the shape of the values in a column are rarely violated because they are usually enforced by the database system or file system. However, surprises can often be found even here.

PHYSICAL DATA TYPE

Most database or file systems have the notion of physical data typing that defines the form of data that can be stored in a column. Figure 8.5 shows a list of typical data types. It is assumed that the user will pick the data type that best represents the intended use of the column.

However, all data except BINARY and DOUBLEBYTE data can be represented as character values. For example, a number column can be stored in a CHARACTER data type by just typing numeric characters such as 12345.67.

EVEN *BINARY and DOUBLE-BYTE data can be put into a CHARACTER column if the database or file system uses either a fixed CHARACTER or a separate length column for VARIABLE CHARACTER fields.*

Only when the storage system locates the end of a column through the binary zero value can this not be done. For example, DB2 allows any coded values to be stored in CHARACTER fields.

The reasons for storing noncharacter data in character data types are many. One is that the system being used may not support the data type of the data. This is common for DATE, TIME, and TIMESTAMP data types. It may also be true of the FLOAT data type. Flat files commonly support nothing but character columns. The famous comma-delimited format of ASCII files is an example of a format for which everything must be in character format.

- CHARACTER
- VARIABLE CHARACTER
- INTEGER
- SMALL INTEGER
- DECIMAL
- FLOAT
- DOUBLE PRECISION
- DATE
- TIME
- TIMESTAMP
- BINARY
- DOUBLEBYTE

FIGURE 8.5 Typical data types.

A second reason is that the user may intend to store values that are not represented by the data type. For example, a DATE data type cannot be used if you intend to store blanks for *Date not known* or *99/99/9999* to mean something special. If the domain you plan to use is not pure, the database system may reject a value you want to store because it requires perfect conformance. This excuse is usually a lame one that covers up poor data design in the first place.

Another reason is that you are accepting data from an external source that has used some of these nonconforming values in fields. If the original data source has values that do not conform, you have two choices: transform them to NULL or put them into a character column to preserve the original nonconforming values. If you are trying to perform assessment on the data, keeping the original values, even if wrong, can provide good feedback to the originator of the data.

The major problem with storing noncharacter data in a character data type is that it invites corruption. Because the database system will accept anything in the column, you are getting no advantage of filtering out bad values using the DBMS support. Legacy systems are notorious for this, as are external data feeds. If it can be corrupted, you can bet it will be.

NOT *only does the liberal use of CHARACTER invite wrong values to be stored, it also brings out the creativeness of data entry people. They invent all sorts of conventions for storing values in them to mean different things. For example, if a discount percentage is not known, they might* enter NOT KNOWN *or* CALL SALESMAN. *After a while, the data can contain a variety of information that is all valid but rarely useful. However, this lack of discipline will frustrate, if not destroy, attempts to use the data for a new purpose.*

It is important not to accept the data type as used by the database or file system when profiling data. You need to discover the true data type of the data and then filter the data against that. This is a perfect example of improving on metadata you collect in the beginning. Discovering the true metadata can be done through discovery software or through visual inspection of values. Once you are confident of the content, you can then reprocess the data to find violations. If you have a database system that enforces data types, finding the violations can be done through a LOAD step after specifying the proper data types to the target.

LENGTH

The length field is not usually considered very important. It usually only decides the width of the column used by the database or file system to store the values for a column. It is always wide enough; otherwise, values would not fit, and either inserts and updates would fail or data would have been truncated. In any case, the problem would have been fixed a long time ago.

However, examination of length issues can sometimes be important. For character fields it is valuable to see the distribution of lengths over the column. This can indicate multiple things. The most important is to see if the column is being used for the purpose intended. A quick length check of actual data values can often lead to the conclusion that the column is not what it purports to be. For example, if all values in a 30-character column are only two characters wide, a high suspicion is raised.

It can point to individual inaccurate values. For example, if in a NAME column 5% of the values have a length of one character, they deserve visual examination because they are probably inaccurate names.

It can point to waste in storage, which is not an inaccuracy problem. If all values never exceed 5 bytes in a 30-byte-wide character field, you can save space. If all values are the same or near the same length in a VARIABLE CHARACTER column, it should probably be changed to CHARACTER. If the distribution of lengths is highly variable, converting from CHARACTER to VARIABLE CHARACTER can be helpful.

For numeric columns, the length should be commensurate with the range of values found. This can lead to shortening an INTEGER column to SMALL INTEGER to save space.

PRECISION

The actual precision required and number of positions to the right of the decimal point can be computed for each value and a distribution chart developed that shows the number of values for each precision. This can show the variability in precision and may help determine whether the data type selected is appropriate. For example, if all values show even integer values, but the data type is decimal or float, a change may be indicated. It may also raise the question of whether the column is being used for its intended purpose.

Valid Value Properties

Once the basic storage shape of the column is determined and the business meaning validated against some of the values, the process of digging out invalid values can begin. This is a process of specifying one or more value properties for each column that test the database values against specific values allowed. The properties will take different forms based on the type of data.

The more detailed the property definitions, the more inaccurate values can be found. Property definitions narrow the list of acceptable values. In some cases you can say simply that these are the only values allowed. In other cases it is impossible or impractical to itemize all valid values. The property definitions just set boundary conditions that valid values must meet. Actual values may meet the boundary conditions but still be invalid.

The types of property definitions that are possible in specifying valid values are shown in Figure 8.6. Each of these is explained in the sections that follow.

DISCRETE VALUE LIST

Many columns support only a small list of specific values. These may be real words or encoded values that represent real words. For example, the STATE column supports only a small list of valid state codes. These may be spelled out, or they may be the standard two-character state codes. Another example is a COLOR column, which would normally be a full word but in some cases

- Discrete value list
- Range of values
- Skip-over rules
- Text column rules
  - Token keywords
  - Embedded blanks, special characters, case
  - Line enders
  - Leading, trailing blanks
  - Code points
- Character patterns
- Special domains

FIGURE 8.6 List of valid value rule types.

(where the color is limited to a few values, such as Red, Green, and Blue) may be encoded (such as R, G, and B).

The first phase of value profiling is to validate the list of acceptable values. Instead of taking the list of values you believe to be the correct list and scanning for exceptions, it is a better practice in this phase to itemize the actual values stored, along with their frequency within the column. This approach will allow you to compare the actual values in the data to the valid value list in the rule.

In comparing the values you may discover the need to expand the valid value list. You may likewise discover that some of the values are not used at all. This may lead you to shorten the valid value list after investigation to determine the reason for the values being missing. You may also discover values that have disproportionately too many or too few values. This may lead to investigations that discover abuses in data entry. In other words, you may discover that the pull-down list default value occurs too many times, leading to the conclusion that it is being selected when the entry person either is too lazy to find the correct value or does not know the correct value.

RANGE OF VALUES

Ranges of values are typically used on numeric, date, time, or timestamp data. A typical range might be 0 >= value <= 1000 on QUANTITY_ORDERED, or HIRE_DATE BETWEEN 01/01/1985 AND CURRENT_DATE.

Ranges can be used on character data as well. For example, if product identifiers always begin with a letter in the range of A through F, a range check on the first character can be used to screen out invalid values.

As in the case of discrete values, it is better to initially let a program determine the range of values in the data instead of processing the data against the expected range. Producing a distribution list of values may be useful but also may be impractical if the number of discrete values is too large. In this case it is wise to include in the output the values close to the edge (the 100 smallest and 100 largest values, for example).

The purpose of doing it this way is to validate the range. If all of the values are hiding well within the range, possibly the range is too liberal and could be narrowed. Likewise, seeing the invalid values on the edges may lead to widening the range.

It is also helpful to see the most frequently found values within the range. This may be what you would expect or may surface a surprise.

THESE *examples show how an analyst needs to look within valid values to find inaccurate data that "hides under the rules." Bad practices in creating data tend to be repeated, which often lead to clues within the set of valid values. Any clues as to the existence of inaccurate data need to be surfaced and investigated.*

The perfect example of this is the HR department that used their supervisor's birth date for new employees that failed to provide a birth date on the hire form. This date showed up a surprisingly high number of times, thatß led to an investigation that revealed the bad practice. The date was perfectly valid and was hiding within the range of valid values.

A PRACTICE *used sometimes on older legacy systems is to store a dollar-and-cents value as an integer. This saves space. However, the value stored is 100 times the real value. The decimal point is implied and is provided by the pro-gram by dividing the integer by 100 when it is used. This convention will generally be noticeable by examining the range of values against the business meaning of the column.*

SKIP-OVER RULES

These rules exclude specific values within a range. They usually apply to date and time columns.

For example, a HIRE_DATE entry may have a further restriction against the date being a weekend or holiday. There are standard routines available that will return the day of week for any date. This combined with a list of holidays for each year could be used to screen for invalid dates within the acceptable range.

These types of tests are generally considered excessive and are not done. However, if it is very important that the date be exactly correct, they may be worth doing.

TEXT COLUMN RULES

Text data is the most difficult to put rules to. As a result, most data profiling efforts do no checking of the internal content of text fields. However, many text fields can have rules applied to them that get inside the column and dig out inaccurate entries.

Some text fields are actually used to store information that could be specified as another data type. For example, often numbers or dates are stored in text fields. These should be tested against their true data type and not by rules described here.

The simplest text column is one that contains only a single word. The words that are allowed typically require no leading blanks, no embedded blanks, and no special characters, and consist of just letters of the alphabet. Often the list of valid values is either too long to itemize or not known in advance. An example is a column for CHEMICAL_NAME. The rules just described can be included in a check of the data.

The next level up is a text column that allows multiple words separated by blanks and possibly allows embedded special characters. The special characters allowed are usually restricted to items such as the period and comma. Examples are CITY, NAME, and COLLEGE_NAME. You would not want to allow special characters such as &*%$#@? to be embedded in them. You can also build a scanner for this set of rules.

Some text fields hold one or more keywords. For example, a column may include a provision for text such as GRADE = MEDIUM, SIZE = LARGE, DESTINATION = CHICAGO. These types of columns substitute the keyword construct for having separate columns for each keyword. In this way they can pack a lot of information in a smaller space if the keywords possible are many and the occurrence of them is sparse. In most cases this is poor data design, but expect it to exist in older systems. Profiling data involves a lot of dealing with poor data design. Keyword text columns can have a special routine built that checks the syntax required and that finds violations.

Totally generic text columns allow just about anything. Some contain text fragments, which may include special characters such as line enders and carriage returns. An example is SHIPPING_INSTRUCTIONS. There is not much you can do about checking these types of columns.

The best way to profile text columns is to execute a discovery program that returns its best opinion of the type of column and identifies the existence of blanks and individual special characters. This aids in determining the true characterization of the content and in determining that it is truly a CHARACTER column.

It is important to record the expected content of these columns, because moving them through extraction/transformation and load processes can cause failures over unexpected special characters if not known in advance. Many a data movement process has been torpedoed by line enders and carriage returns embedded in text columns.

Another factor to take into account is the code page the data comes from. Data coming from Europe, the Far East, or other places can include text columns with code points that may fail tests devised solely for USA text.

PATTERNS

Sometimes text columns have single words that are a coded value for something that must follow a specific character pattern to be valid. A common example is a PRODUCT_IDENTIFIER. An example of a pattern follows.

- The first character indicates the type of product, which can be A, B, or C.

- The next three characters identify the division that produces it, which are numeric digits.

- The next character indicates storage requirements: R, S, H.

- The next five characters are numeric digits that identify the unique product.

In these cases, a specific rule check can be constructed for the column to find all occurrences that violate the rule. In this example, you may even want to check uniqueness of the last five digits independently from the rest of the value.

Patterns are never checked by the database systems and thus are subject to violation. Many times they are not documented in advance. Through special software you can discover the patterns of single-word columns. They will identify the patterns and the percentage of values that support the rule. This can be helpful in determining if a pattern exists and in confirming or denying a pattern rule that comes with the metadata.

MULTIPLE CONFLICTING RULES

In some cases it is possible to have a column that supports multiple rules that are distinct from one another. An example might be a ZIP_CODE column that supports USA and CANADIAN pattern rules. Another example is a TELEPHONE column that supports USA, CANADIAN, and MEXICAN TELEPHONE_NUMBER patterns.

It is okay to have this condition as long as the rules can be tested with an OR condition. As we shall see in the chapter on simple data rules, it is helpful to be able to correlate the pattern rule to a value (such as COUNTRY_CODE) in another column. However, this is not required to build rule sets. For example, a PRODUCT_IDENTIFIER column may contain product codes from two different companies that have recently merged.

SPECIAL DOMAINS

Some columns contain values from a well-known domain. Examples are SOCIAL_SECURITY_NUMBER, ZIP_CODE, TELEPHONE_NUMBER, and STATE. These domains can usually be universally defined with rules that apply to all occurrences in all databases. The value in having these domains around is that they will help you identify inconsistencies in representation within a column as well as across columns in the same or multiple databases. For example, does the SOCIAL_SECURITY_NUMBER follow a pattern of 999999999 or 999-99-9999? It is very helpful to be able to identify these differences, in that this is a common cause of problems in integrating or aggregating data.

Empty Condition Rules

Every column has one or more rules regarding the NULL condition. The rule may be that none are allowed. It may allow values indicating the NULL condition but not restrict itself as to what they may be, leaving the door open to inventions by people entering data. This is a common condition in legacy systems.

Software can be used to scan for values that may indicate missing values. They can search for things such as blanks, *?, none, **no value*, and any others that are found to exist in data. If such values are found and judged to be NULL condition indicators, they all need to be documented in the repository because they must be transformed to a common indication when data is moved.

Sometimes the NULL indicators are descriptive. For example, you might find the words *Don't know, Not applicable*, and *Did not provide*. This may be valuable information to retain. It may be wise to raise a data accuracy issue so that they could be standardized into a separate column to avoid inaccurate query results in the future.

A lot of the NULL indications are bad data design practices or bad data entry practices resulting from a lack of complete data design. Again, identification of the actual rules being used is helpful in dealing with the data when it is repurposed or in launching a source system improvement project. Knowing the rule is so much better than not knowing the rule.

Other Descriptive Information

It is useful to add other information for columns in the repository that can help in understanding the likelihood of data being inaccurate. This may lead to not having to run tests over a column. This information may be useful to others in the organization when they subsequently try to repurpose the data. Although this is useful information, it is rarely documented in metadata.

CONFIDENCE

One of the factors is a "confidence" factor that the data is accurate in some respect. For example, if the column is stored in a row of a relational database system and the column is declared as UNIQUE and NOT NULL, you can be assured that all values are indeed unique and that there are no nulls. This does not mean that the NULL condition has not been codified in some data value that the relational system cannot recognize as a NULL. However, along with the UNIQUE constraint, the likelihood of codified NULL conditions is very slim because they could occur at most one time.

Another example is DATE data typing in database systems that enforce valid dates. The DBMS will absolutely ensure that all dates stored are valid dates. You do not need to scan for this. You may still want to see date values on a value/frequency graph to help spot cases in which a single date is used too often or to apply a range check to make sure all dates are reasonable. However, you do not have to worry about any values being invalid dates.

The analyst may determine that the database system has a STORED PROCEDURE included that enforces ranges, discrete value lists, or patterns. Discovery of this procedure not only helps document the rules but increases the confidence that the values are in conformance with the rule. One danger here is to believe that the procedure has been applied to all values in the column. It may be that the procedure was added recently or changed. Older values may not have been processed by the procedure and therefore can be exceptions to the rule.

Extracted data screening logic from source code of the application programs is less reliable in building confidence. This is because it leaves open other means of data getting into the database or being changed afterward. For example, a database administrator could change any value through a simple SQL statement without going through the application program.

Another characteristic to record is the susceptibility of the column to have its values decay in accuracy over time. This is purely an external business analyst call because there is no way of programmatically identifying these columns.

Another factor to look for is the probability of an inaccurate value in a column being recognized and fixed. This again is a purely external semantic condition of the column. For example, in a payroll application, the PAYRATE column is more likely to get recognized if wrong (and fixed) than the DEPARTMENT column. The confidence factor for the one column being accurate is higher than the confidence factor for the other column. Scorekeeping on confidence factors will lead you to placing more emphasis on rule generation and testing of columns of lesser confidence than those of higher confidence if you lack the resources to exhaustively profile every column.

TIME-RELATED CONSISTENCY

Another factor to examine is whether the column has had a change in the way data is encoded at one or more points in time in the past. The result is that the data is inconsistent in representing the real world, depending on how old the information is. There will be multiple time periods of the data within each of which there is consistency but across time periods little or no consistency.

There are programmatic methods of finding potential inconsistency points. However, these are very complex. This area of data profiling technology is very new, with little maturity in implementations. However, you can employ heuristic techniques to find them. One simple method is to divide data into samples coming from different time periods (such as three-month intervals), profiling them to determine the value/frequency pairs, and then comparing the results across sample sets.

To find the actual point of inconsistency you can sort data by CREATE_DATE and then select each value to determine the earliest and latest date that value appears in the data. This may reveal the inconsistency points as well as the data values that were impacted by the change.

You can also develop a process of computing for each column the earliest date any value other than blank or zero are found. This can identify those columns that were added or new values introduced to the database, as well as the point in time they were added.

Using this approach is very time consuming and should not be used over all columns or even over very many of them. You can select columns that you are suspicious of having inconsistency points and test them this way.

It is important to understand that all data inconsistencies are not the result of changes to the way data is recorded. The inconsistencies may result from a business model change such as dropping a product line, the impact of external factors such as a recession, or other factors. Determining whether an inconsistency point is relevant to the data profiling exercise or not is a semantic call involving business analysts and subject matter experts.

Inconsistency points need to be recorded in the data profiling repository. This will benefit potential future users by allowing them to make decisions on how far they can safely go back in the data for their intended purposes. Using data across inconsistency points can distort decision support computations.

8.4   Mapping with Other Columns

One of the most important uses of value property analysis outputs is in mapping columns together between systems. You may be moving data from one system to another. You may be summarizing data from one system into summary columns of a target system. You may be combining data from two or more source systems into a single column of a target system.

If the target column is not populated, mapping is done at the properties level only. If you have a property list for the target and have developed a property list for the source through data profiling, mapping can proceed. If the target is already populated, its property list should have been generated or validated through data profiling. This provides more information to map to and increases the confidence in the accuracy of the mapping.

Business Meaning

The first check is at the business meaning level. Is the business meaning of the columns the same or are they different? The physical content may make them look the same but in fact they may not be. The business analysts must ensure that you are not mixing apples and oranges.

Storage Properties

The data types for the corresponding columns being mapped need not be the same if the content can be transformed. For example, dates stored in a CHARACTER column may be able to be mapped to a DATE column without a problem. If all values in the source system are valid dates, the column is transformable.

Length checks also must be performed. The target only needs to be large enough to hold the largest value found in the source. It does not need to be as large as defined in the source. This applies to CHARACTER length columns, integer/small integer columns, and decimal precision. For example, a 30-character column can be mapped to a 25-character column if all values found are 25 characters in length or less.

Value Properties

The valid values as determined by discrete lists, ranges, text rules, and null value rules need to be compared. This needs to be done even if the target is not populated, because you do not want to put data into a target that violates any of the target rules.

Value lists need to be mapped at the individual value level to determine if the encoding of one system is truly identical to that of the target. The semantic meaning of each value needs to match across the systems. You can map different encodings by mapping values together that mean the same thing even if their representation is different. This provides the input to data transformation processes that need to be executed when the data is moved.

Ending up with values that cannot be mapped because of differences in ranges or discrete value lists or other rule differences exposes invalid mapping data. These are values that are valid in the source system but not valid in the target system. The user must determine on a column-by-column or value-by-value basis what needs to be done with these values.

ONE *of the most common mistakes made in moving data is to automatically assume that a 1-byte CHARACTER column in one system can be mapped to a 1-byte CHARACTER column in the other system without looking at the data. A real example is the gender code that in one source system was encoded 1 and 2 and in the target system was encoded F and M. Additionally, a second source system was encoded M and F but had some other curious values stored. In this example the user moved the data without looking at values and created a mess in the target system.*

8.5 Value-Level Remedies

The column property analysis process discovers a variety of facts about the data. Some of it is identifying specific, inaccurate values. In addition, you end up with a rigorous rule set for defining what is stored in each column. You also identify bad data design, bad data entry processes, and data representation inconsistencies.

It is important to collect all of the facts before you fabricate remedies. The totality of issues should be used to determine what to do with all of the facts. The facts support decisions. Some of the remedies that can be supported at this level of data profiling are examined in the sections that follow.

Intended Use Decisions

If the data is being profiled as part of a project, a judgment can now be made as to whether the data contains the information needed for intended uses and has the quality to support the requirements of the intended uses. This is not the final decision point but is an important one.

It is far better to scrap a project at this point than to spend millions of dollars developing a new system that cannot succeed because the data cannot support it. If the data is inconsistent with the intended use, sometimes the target system can be modified to work with the data available. Most packaged applications have a number of customization options that can be examined to determine if they can be used to conform more to the source systems.

Improving Source Systems

Whether data profiling the data for stand-alone assessment or for use on a new project, the requirement to upgrade source systems can be examined at this point in regard to issues involving individual values. The data might suggest improvements to source data structure design, source data capture procedures and programs, or application program changes. Even when the purpose of data profiling is to match data to target systems, an important side effect can be the discovery of enough issues to warrant a secondary project to upgrade the source systems. This may not be just to help the new system but to add value for the source system applications.

Standardizing Data Representation Across Systems

Data profiling often reveals wide differences in data encoding across systems. This is an excellent time to review the various practices being used and to define standard methods of representing data. This can then be set as the standard and used for future application development, making changes to existing source systems, or building transformations to have the data land in target systems in the standard form.

Building Data Checkers

Data profiling discovers, develops, and executes a lot of rules for the purpose of digging out inaccurate data values. These rules can be used to build data checkers that can be installed in operational systems to catch bad values at the source. Checkers can be built into data entry screens, into transaction applications, or into DBMS functions, or they can be used to check databases through batch processing on a periodic basis.

You never want to put all rules into the checkers. They would run forever and hopelessly clog up the operational systems. However, selective use of rules can improve overall accuracy considerably.

Checkers can include more than just rules. They can include synonym lists of frequently found wrong values and the correct values to change them to. This is particularly valuable in resolving misspelled words and inconsistent representation problems. The wrong values discovered in data profiling can be turned into synonym lists to be used to clean data.

Checkers are particularly good for qualifying data coming into the corporation in the form of data feeds. It not only catches errors but provides the basis for negotiating improvements from the provider of the data.

Building Transformations for Moving Data

One of the most important outputs of profiling values is input to building data transformation routines for use in moving data. This applies to mapping valid values to corresponding valid values in the other system and to cleansing wrong values by substituting correct values.

It is very common for transformation routines not to include logic for handling the NULL condition. This is a source of many problems in trying to get data moved and aggregated. Data profiling should have identified all of the relevant information needed for proper handling and transformation of NULL values.

Cleansing Data Before Performing More Data Profiling

It is often valuable to clean up some of the data problems before moving to later steps of data profiling. This is because data inaccuracies and inconsistencies can distort the discovery processes of later steps. This is a choice the analyst must make carefully, because decisions made in later steps will be made on the transformed data, not on the original source data.

It is not recommended that you clean up data for later data profiling by eliminating rows with values that are inaccurate or by converting inaccurate values to NULL. This can distort follow-on steps in ways that are not helpful. Cleanup should be restricted to standardizing data representation, standardizing NULL condition representation, and changing misspelled words.

Meetings with management may also be indicated at this point in order to discuss data suitability for future use and to discuss general problems with data quality. This would normally be done after all data profiling is complete. However, the quality of the data may be so poor that aborting the data profiling process may make sense at this point. Poor-quality data will very likely frustrate attempts to perform subsequent data profiling steps.

8.6 Closing Remarks

Checking the content of individual columns is where you start data profiling. It is the easiest place to find inaccurate data. The values uncovered are clearly inaccurate because they violate the basic definition of the column.

You not only find inaccurate values, you find bad practices. This can lead the way to improving data encoding methods, use of standardized domains, use of standardized representations of the NULL condition, and even improving the storage requirements for some data. By looking at more data from more columns, your analysts will become experts at identifying best practices for column design.

Another large benefit is that you determine and document the correct metadata for each column. This alone is a huge benefit for subsequent projects and people who intend to use this data.

This step is the easiest to use for qualifying data feeds coming into your corporation from the outside. Column property analysis will tell you up front the general quality level of the data.

Data profiling can be very time consuming and expensive without software designed specifically for that purpose. Having to fabricate queries for each of the properties that apply to each column can be a laborious job. It may take three or more hours to examine each column in full detail using ad hoc methods. For a database with hundreds or thousand of columns, this is a lot of time. This can be reduced significantly with more efficient software.

CHAPTER 9

Structure Analysis

Having completed an analysis of individual column properties, the next step is to look at structure constraints that are, or should be, defined over the data. This may reveal additional problems in the data.

There are two issues to look for in structure analysis. One is to find violations to the rules that should apply. This points to inaccurate data. The other is to determine and document the structure rules of the metadata. This can be extremely valuable when moving data, mapping it to other structures, or merging it with other data.

Structure rules are often ignored when looking at data. This can have serious consequences when trying to extract the data for use in other data structures. The primary reason for ignoring them is that the analyst is not familiar with the basic concepts of database architecture. This makes structure analysis difficult. It is important that this step be performed by someone who has the right background. Any analyst can learn the basic concepts and should take the time to do so.

9.1 Definitions

It is not the intention of this book to provide a thorough education on database structure rules. The definitions provided here are brief and intended only to clarify how terms are being used in this chapter. Definitions of the terms used in this section are needed for the same reason as the previous chapter: these terms tend to be used in different ways by different authors and database systems. Defining how they are used here may head off some confusion.

The rule discussions in this book assume that data is being represented in a table, row/column format. Many source systems do not represent data this way. However, to profile data it is helpful to extract the data into table format. This can almost always be done, although the effort may be considerable. The topic of extracting data is not covered in this book.

It is assumed that an extraction has been done and that all data is represented in table format. This is not to say it is properly normalized. It need only be in first-normal form. Normal forms are defined later in this chapter. The data profiling process should determine the degree to which it is normalized and demonstrate the structure needed for other normal forms.

Functional Dependencies

A major structural element discussed in this chapter is the functional dependency. Functional dependencies are used to unlock the natural structure of business objects as defined by the data. A column in a table is considered a functional dependency of one or more other columns in the same table if it has only one value for any specific value set of the other columns.

Said another way, a functional dependency has a LEFT-HAND-SIDE (LHS) consisting of a set of columns that determines the value of a single column on the RIGHT-HAND-SIDE (RHS). A functional dependency is said to hold over a table if, for all rows where the values of the LHS columns match, the values in the RHS column are the same. This is shown in Figure 9.1.

The LHS of a functional dependency can consist of more than one column. In this case it takes the concatenated values of all columns to determine the LHS. When this is the case, it does not matter what the order is of the columns on the LHS.

Another property is that the columns on the LHS should be the minimum columns necessary to uniquely determine the value of the column on the RHS. Clearly, if A and B determine C, then A and B and D also determine C. However, the presence of D adds no additional meaning to the dependency.

Clearly, if EMPLOYEE_ID determined BIRTHDATE, then EMPLOYEE_ID and any other column would also determine BIRTHDATE. For example, EMPLOYEE_ID and HIREDATE also determine BIRTHDATE. HIREDATE should not be included in the dependency LHS definition because it is not necessary to uniquely define BIRTHDATE.

A number of functional dependencies can exist that share the same LHS but determine the value of different columns on the RHS. For ease of handling, these can be combined into a single functional dependency representation wherein the RHS includes all columns that have a functional dependency on the same LHS.

Relation = PERSONNEL

PERSON_ID	NAME	ADDRESS
1345	Mary Smith	123 Broadway
2879	Joe Smith	123 Broadway
3011	Mary Smith	34 E. Elm St.

Functional dependencies:

LHS → RHS

PERSON_ID → NAME

PERSON_ID → ADDRESS

Consolidated dependency:

PERSON_ID → NAME, ADDRESS

Relation = PROJECTS

PROJECT_ID	TASK_ID	START_DATE	STATUS
A345	F001	06/15/02	C
A345	F002	06/22/02	S
A789	F001	08/15/02	N
A789	F002	08/15/02	N
A789	F003	08/15/02	N

Functional dependencies:

LHS → RHS

PROJECT_ID, TASK_ID → START_DATE

PROJECT_ID, TASK_ID → STATUS

Consolidated dependency:

PROJECT_ID, TASK_ID → START_DATE, STATUS

FIGURE 9.1 Functional dependencies.

Functional dependencies are a metadata definition of structure in a table. Discovered functional dependencies are those that are true for the data in the table at the time discovery is performed. The metadata and discovered functional dependency sets may be different.

If the table has inaccurate data in it, a functional dependency set that is supposed to be true may be untrue for that collection of data. It is also possible for a functional dependency to exist in the data because it is a coincident. Semantically, it is allowed to be violated. However, none of the data populating the table at that time violates it.

A DEGENERATE *case exists when a column contains only one value (a constant or a NULL). In this case, it initially appears to be in a functional dependency relationship with all other columns. However, if the rule is applied that eliminates any unnecessary LHS columns, the LHS becomes empty. This means that you can determine the value of the column without the help of any other column.*

The most common reason for constant columns is that they have never had data put into them: they are not used. Systems often get changed during implementation, and columns remain in the data structure but are not used. This is analogous to "dead code" in programming. Constant-valued columns should not be used in dependency analysis because they produce results that are not useful.

Keys

Keys are a significant part of the structure definition of data. They identify rows within tables and they connect tables to other tables. Figure 9.2 is an example of keys that are described in this section.

Functional dependencies are the key to understanding the primary keys in a table, denormalized column sets embedded in a table, and derived columns within a table. If you knew all the functional dependencies, you would be able to determine all of these. In addition to keys defined through functional dependencies, there exists another key type, the foreign key, which is also important in structure analysis.

PRIMARY KEY

A primary key is a set of columns that uniquely defines each row of a table. A primary key has a functional dependency in which the LHS columns and the RHS columns include all of the columns in the table. The LHS is the primary key.

ORDER_NO	DATE_CREATED	CUSTOMER_ID

Functional dependency: ORDER_NO $\longrightarrow$ ORDER_NO, CUSTOMER_ID
Primary key = ORDER_NO
Foreign key = CUSTOMER_ID

ORDER_NO	ITEM_NO	PRODUCT_ID	DESCRIPTION	QTY	UNIT_PRICE	PRICE

Functional dependency:
ORDER_NO, ITEM_NO $\longrightarrow$ PRODUCT_ID, DESCRIPTION, QTY, UNIT_PRICE, PRICE
Primary key = ORDER_NO, ITEM_NO
Foreign key = ORDER_NO
Foreign key = PRODUCT_ID
Functional dependency: PRODUCT_ID $\longrightarrow$ DESCRIPTION
Denormalized key = PRODUCT_ID
Functional dependency: PRICE $\longrightarrow$ QTY, UNIT_PRICE
Derived attribute = PRICE, RULE: PRICE = QTY * UNIT_PRICE

PRODUCT_ID	DESCRIPTION

Functional dependency: PRODUCT_ID $\longrightarrow$ DESCRIPTION
Primary key = PRODUCT_ID

FIGURE 9.2 Keys.

A table can have more than one consolidated functional dependency that satisfies the definition of a primary key. A fact often overlooked in data analysis is that many tables have two primary keys: a token key and a natural key.

The token key is usually columns that have been assigned system identifiers to uniquely define each row. The key may consist of multiple token columns. A natural key is a combination of values from the real world that uniquely identifies a row.

For example, in a personnel database the natural key would be some combination of the employee's name, home address, and birth date. You would allow two or more employees with the same name. They may even live at the same address (as, for example, in a father and son who share the same name but do not use Jr. and Sr. to distinguish themselves). However, once you put birth date into the natural key, you get uniqueness guaranteed. However, you would not want to use this primary key for processing: it is too long and contains personal information.

The SOCIAL_SECURITY_NUMBER is also a primary key candidate and is a single column. It is much better for system use. However, this is also personal information employees would not want to have used for identifying them on reports going around the corporation. Therefore, you generate a third primary key, the PERSON_ID, which is a unique number assigned to each employee when hired. This is a token key because it comes from the system and not from the real world.

RELATIONAL *theory defines only one primary key. Tables in third-normal form should only have one primary key. However, database designers generally define more than one for conserving space in keys, for increasing performance for queries, and for security reasons. If a column needs to be protected from some of the users of the table for security reasons, it should not be part of a primary key.*

Relational theory also requires that all tables have a primary key, meaning that every row is unique. However, virtually all relational systems allow a table to be defined that includes no primary key and, in fact, allow two rows to be completely identical. All rows can be tagged with a unique identifier, which means that it is possible to create a primary key for any table. However, if identifying individual rows has no semantic value to the database designer, appending a primary key merely adds space to the disk that is not needed.

The theory of relational data calls for all tables to be in third-normal form. This means that for each table all columns are dependent on the KEY, all of the KEY, and nothing but the KEY. In practice, these rules are frequently violated for operational reasons.

This example shows three separate functional dependencies that satisfy the definition of a primary key for the same table. Only one would be specified as the primary key for data management purposes. However, as we will see later, the others have an analytical value in finding inaccurate data values.

A primary key may require all columns in the table to define each unique entry. For example, a table that describes an employee's college degrees may consist of columns for PERSON_ID, UNIVERSITY_NAME, DEGREE, and MAJOR. Because an employee may have multiple degrees from the same university, and may have multiple B.A. degrees from the same university, it takes all four to define each row uniquely. There is one functional dependency in the table that has no RHS. The term *primary key* is often referred to as the key to the table. That convention is used in this chapter.

DENORMALIZED KEY

When a consolidated functional dependency exists that does not include all columns in the table on both sides, it represents a denormalized key. It determines the values of some of the other columns but not all of them. All of the columns, including the LHS columns, may or may not also be part of another dependency that describes a true primary key candidate for the table.

In relational theory these should not exist. However, in practice they exist all the time.

An example is shown in Figure 9.2. The functional dependency where PRODUCT_ID determines the DESCRIPTION is a denormalized case. The DESCRIPTION could just as easily have been obtained by looking it up in the PRODUCT table. However, the database designer copies it to the ORDER_DETAIL table when orders are created in order to improve performance when processing queries against the order database.

DERIVED COLUMNS

Derived columns are those that exist as the RHS of a functional dependency and whose value can be determined from a rule on the values of the LHS. For example, if COLUMN_C = COLUMN_A + COLUMN_B, then COLUMN_C is a derived column and the functional dependency is COLUMN_A, COLUMN_B → COLUMN_C.

The rule may be a mathematical formula (such as UNIT_PRICE * QUANTITY = PRICE) or a business rule (such as that all customers in Chicago get a 10% discount and all others get only a 5% discount). The functional dependency that defines a derived column may include all attributes in the table (making it a key to the table) or subset (making it a denormalized key). What makes it a derived column is that you can compute the RHS by knowing the rule or formula and the values on the LHS. Derived columns are a special case of the other types of functional dependencies.

FOREIGN KEY

A foreign key is one or more columns in one table (the dependent table) that identifies a row in another table, the parent table. It is usually only one column but is sometimes more than one column. It is almost never the primary key of the dependent table. It is just another column in the row. For example, a DEPARTMENT table may have a column that identifies the department manager, such as DEPT_MANAGER_ID. Instead of having the manager's name and other information about the manager, it just includes a foreign key reference to the personnel database where this information is held. The foreign key DEPT_MANAGER_ID references the PERSON_ID column of the PERSONNEL table.

In this example, it may be that the PERSON_ID is also a primary key of the DEPARTMENT table. This would be true if every department had a manager and no two departments had the same manager. This would technically be a second key candidate for the table (in addition to DEPARTMENT_ID). However, if a person could be manager of two departments at the same time, it would not be a primary key.

The foreign key in a dependent table is a primary key in the parent table. Both tables may be the same table. For a single row, the foreign key will generally identify a different row of the same table. This must be true because it must identify a single row of the other table.

Foreign keys are used for multiple purposes. One is to connect the subtables of a single business object in the database. A functional dependency within the object may have multiple occurrences for each key to the primary object. The columns that do not have multiple occurrences are placed in a parent table with the key to the object. The columns within the functional dependency that can repeat are placed in a dependent table, where each row is one occurrence. The rows of the dependent table are connected to rows of the parent table through the foreign key column. For example, the ORDER_NUMBER is used to connect ORDER_HEADER information to ORDER_LINE_ITEM information.

THE *PERSON_ID example demonstrates another principle at work here. The columns in the department table do not have a semantic affinity to the department manager but rather have a semantic affinity to the department number. The department manager PERSON_ID is a key only because* it is unique within the table. In pure relational theory, it is not a key at all for that table because the other columns (although invariant for each PERSON_ID value) have no natural meaning relative to who is the manager. These are important distinctions when trying to analyze key candidates.

The second use of foreign keys is to connect different business objects. An example is an ORDER_NUMBER used to connect to an INVOICE table. Orders and invoices are different business objects but have a relationship reflected in the ORDER_NUMBER foreign key.

Normal Forms of Data

Data has a natural structure that shows how columns relate to each other. Database theory defines several forms of data organization to guide a data designer to get to a proper structure. These are called normal forms. Theorists have defined six levels of normal forms. Each form is a more restrictive version of the previous form.

In practice, most data exists in first-, second-, or third-normal form. Although there is some theoretical interest in higher levels of normal forms, they add little value to operational handling of data. The goal of structure analysis is to determine the current form of data sources at the level of no normal-form first, second, or third level. Figure 9.3 shows an example of data in first-normal form and in third-normal form.

FIRST-NORMAL FORM

To be in first-normal form, a table must have the same columns for every row. Each column contains only a single value. The meaning of the values in the column are the same for all rows. A fact is represented in only one column. This means that you cannot have multiple columns for multiple occurrences of the same fact. Repeating groups are not allowed.

If the data in a table has REDEFINE definitions over one or more columns, if some columns are missing from some of the rows, or if columns are overloaded (as defined in Chapter 8), they are not in any normal form.

SECOND-NORMAL FORM

A table in second-normal form must satisfy the requirements of first-normal form. In addition, it must have a key. Each column in the table must depend only on all of the columns in the key, not a subset of the columns.

For example, in Figure 9.3, the initial parent table has a key of PRODUCT and PART. Each row identifies a single part used in the manufacturing of the product. However, the column DESCRIPTION is dependent on only the PART column and not the entire key. To get to second-normal form, you remove this situation by creating a second table of PART and DESCRIPTION. At this point the parent table is better off, because everything depends on the key. It still has a problem that keeps it from being in third-normal form.

A first-normal form relation

PRODUCT	PART	DESCRIPTION	QTY	DRAWING_CODE	CODE_TYPE

KEY is PRODUCT, PART
Functional dependencies are:
PRODUCT, PART ———▸ DESCRIPTION, QTY, DRAWING_CODE, CODE_TYPE
PART ———————▸ DESCRIPTION
DRAWING_CODE ———▸ CODE_TYPE

Second-normal form representation

PRODUCT	PART	QTY	DRAWING_CODE	CODE_TYPE

PART	DESCRIPTION

Third-normal form representation

PRODUCT	PART	QTY	DRAWING_CODE

PART	DESCRIPTION

DRAWING_CODE	CODE_TYPE

FIGURE 9.3 Example of data in normal forms.

THIRD-NORMAL FORM

Data is in third-normal form if it satisfies first- and second-normal form rules
and no column is dependent on any nonkey column. In the example shown in
Figure 9.3, the column DRAWING_CODE references where a part is used in
a blueprint drawing of the product. The CODE_TYPE column shows what
type of reference it is. Each drawing code only has one code type. This means
that the CODE_TYPE needs to be broken out to get the parent table to third-
normal form. This is shown in the figure as the three-table set. All three tables
are in third-normal form.

DENORMALIZED FORM

A table is denormalized if it is not in third-normal form. This means that it
contains one or more denormalized functional dependencies.

Denormalization is very common in database systems. There are a number of distinct cases of denormalization that can be used to describe the concept, as well as the motivations for having each of them.

The first case is the situation in which all data is included in a table. For example, a single table contains a subset of columns that includes one or more columns that are dependent on a denormalized key. The example shown in Figure 9.4 shows the situation in which ZIP_CODE determines CITY and STATE and is therefore denormalized in the table. It could be broken out into a separate table with ZIP_CODE as the key and CITY and STATE as the dependent columns. However, because these fields are always used together, they are merely embedded in the primary table and no such normalized table is created. This type of denormalization is common.

The second case shown in Figure 9.4 is the situation in which data is repeated in a table from another table. In this example, PRODUCT_ DESCRIPTION is carried in the ORDER_LINE_ITEM table, along with the PRODUCT_ID. The description column is clearly redundant to the same information in the INVENTORY table. It is copied into the ORDER_ITEM table to improve performance on queries by not having to perform a JOIN.

The third case shows the situation in which a single table contains all fields of two tables. This is shown in Figure 9.3 for the first-normal form example. In this example, there are two denormalized functional dependency sets within the same table, causing a great deal of redundancy of data. The reason for doing this is again performance on query.

Denormalized tables always cause data to be repeated within the set of tables. This leaves open the possibility of inconsistencies arising between the various duplicates, due to inaccurate data entry or updating some but not all of the occurrences of the data. The possibility of inaccurate data rises, and the detection of it becomes more difficult.

Case 1: Embedded dependency

PERSON_ID	NAME	STREET	CITY	STATE	ZIP

ZIP ⟶ CITY
ZIP ⟶ STATE

Case 2: Duplicate data

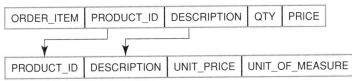

FIGURE 9.4 Examples of denormalized tables.

SPLIT TABLE FORM

A split table occurs when two tables have the same primary key but all other columns are different. In this case, the two tables could be combined into one. The database designer has divided the columns between the two tables for some purpose. It may be to improve performance by putting the highly referenced columns in one table and the less frequently referenced columns in the other. Another reason for splitting a table is to aid in managing the security of information by putting more sensitive information into one table and less sensitive information in another table. Some data architects consider this a violation of third-normal form because all columns that are dependent on the key are not in the same table.

Tables may be split into more than two tables. This practice can easily lead to additional denormalization by adding redundancy to avoid multiway JOINs in order to access all of the data needed by each client.

Synonyms

Two columns are synonyms of each other if they contain the same business fact. They may be using it for different reasons, but the content in each column of the synonym has the same business meaning. For example, a column called DEPARTMENT_NUMBER in the department's master database, a column called DEP_NO in the personnel database, and a column called DEPT_ NUM in the project's database would all be synonyms of each other. They would constitute a synonym column set.

Having the same values does not qualify two columns as being synonyms for that reason alone. For example, a column of EMPLOYEE_HIRE_DATE would not be a synonym of the column ORDER_CREATED_DATE, even though they are both dates and both identify the date a business object was created. They are not synonyms because they represent the date of creation of different types of business objects. The values may be drawn from a common date domain. However, the fact that they come from a common physical domain does not make them synonyms. Both columns of a synonym pair can exist in the same table.

Synonym analysis is an important part of structure analysis because it identifies and validates foreign keys, identifies redundant data, and identifies representation inconsistencies between columns that record the same facts.

There are four distinct types of synonyms. This is shown in Figure 9.5. Each type has unique characteristics and, as will be shown later, has different analytical techniques for discovery and verification testing.

Primary key/foreign key synonyms

DEPARTMENT table

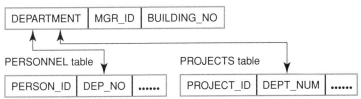

PERSONNEL table   PROJECTS table

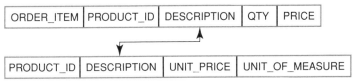

Redundant data synonyms

Domain synonyms

CUSTOMER_ID | ADDRESS | CITY | ......

EMPLOYEE_ID | ADDRESS | CITY | ......

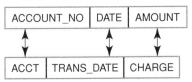

Merge synonyms

ACCOUNT_NO | DATE | AMOUNT

ACCT | TRANS_DATE | CHARGE

FIGURE 9.5 Synonym types.

PRIMARY/FOREIGN KEY SYNONYMS

Primary key/foreign key pairs are synonyms. They are used to relate data between tables. This is a very common relationship in which one of the columns in the pair is a primary key of a table. It identifies the specific business object. The table containing the other column references the business object. In Figure 9.5, this is shown for the DEPARTMENT_ID column.

A single column that identifies an important business object, such as a department, can be used in numerous tables to provide a reference to department information. For example, the department identifier may appear in a PROJECT table, a PERSONNEL table, in financial tables for expenses and expense accounts, in BENEFIT tables, and many more. It is not uncommon for a single column in a master table to be the primary key component of hundreds of synonym pairs. In many corporations, the commonly used columns of DEPARTMENT_ID, PERSON_ID, and PRODUCT_ID typically connect hundreds of tables through individual synonym pairs.

REDUNDANT DATA SYNONYMS

Redundant data exists when a column is a synonym of another column in a different table. In one table, the column is dependent on the key. In the other table, the column is dependent on the corresponding foreign key. This is shown in Figure 9.5 for the PRODUCT_DESCRIPTION column. The two PRODUCT_DESCRIPTION columns are synonyms of each other. Neither is a key in its respective table, but both are dependent on the PRODUCT_ID columns in each table. The connection between individual values is indirectly made through the surrogate primary key/foreign key synonym. In this case, one of them could be eliminated without any loss of information. However, it would require adding a JOIN to query statements against the dependent table.

Redundant column synonyms always have a functional dependency for each column where the RHS is the synonym column and the LHS is part of a primary/foreign key synonym.

DOMAIN SYNONYMS

A third category of synonyms is where the pair has no structural relationship, unlike the previous two types. They are just the same business fact. Figure 9.5 shows this for the CITY columns. Each of these contains the same business fact: the name of a CITY. The occurrences have no relationship to each other.

It is important to distinguish domain commonality at the business level, not at the physical data type level. The previous example of date fields demonstrates a physical domain equivalence. Similarly, two columns containing integers such as QUANTITY_ORDERED and QUANTITY_ON_HAND share only a physical data type domain. These are of no interest whatever because they represent different business facts. They should not be considered synonyms. However, domains that identify specific business entities are valid domain synonyms. Examples of this are CITIES, STATES, UNIT_OF_MEASURE, and COLOR.

These synonyms have no structural value. They are worth identifying in order to study the representation of values in each column to determine if they are consistent. Identifying them is also useful in helping users of data connect data in queries. For example, if the CITY column is used in both the ORDER table and the SUPPLIER table, a user may want to see if there are any suppliers in the same city that have a large number of orders. To make that query work, the representation of city values must be consistent across the CITY column pairs.

Domain synonyms exist across the foreign key columns of multiple primary key/foreign key synonyms that share the same primary key column. For example, as shown in the first part of Figure 9.5, the two columns for DEPT_MGR and PROJECT_MEMBER are domain synonyms. They represent the same business fact (an employee) but have no structural meaning. These types of synonyms have no value because validation and representation consistency is accomplished through the associated primary key/foreign key synonyms.

MERGE SYNONYMS

Synonyms are also used to match columns across different data sources when trying to consolidate data. This is very common in projects designed to consolidate databases of corporations that have merged or to eliminate multiple departmental applications in favor of a single central application. In this case, every column in each source needs to be synonymed with columns in the other sources.

9.2 Understanding the Structures Being Profiled

The data profiling process works best when looking at data from a table perspective. If the data is in other forms, it is generally extracted into a table form. The process of extraction can be helpful or harmful for structure analysis.

For example, if the source data is in IMS, extraction can simply extract each segment into a separate table. This requires that keys be generated for each row of each table from the logic of the IMS hierarchy and embedded in the rows of the extracted table. Special attention needs to be paid to cases where IMS is sensitive to the order of segments within siblings. In these cases, a sequencing column needs to be generated in the extracted table to designate the required order. Often the extraction designer is not aware of this condition and fails to generate the required column. This makes the extracted table less accurate than the IMS segment.

Many extraction routines combine multiple segments into single rows of an output table. This is acceptable, provided the parent/child relationship is always one-to-one. If the relationship supports multiple occurrences of a child segment for each parent segment, the resulting table repeats the parent columns for each output row. This distorts data profiling and other analytical processes because it gives wrong cardinalities over computations off these columns. Unfortunately, this is done all too often.

Another common source of structural flaws occurs when extracting data from structures that support REDEFINE and OCCURS structures. The extraction designer needs to understand the semantic meaning of these structures in order to extract properly. For example, the REDEFINE must be understood to be a remapping of either the same fact or different facts, depending on the value of some other column. Similarly, the OCCURS structure must be understood to be either the same fact with multiple occurrences or multiple different facts. Failure to understand the meaning of these constructs will often lead to extraction files that are structurally different from the data source.

Structure errors made in extraction will lead to wrong answers in data profiling. The step of extraction is generally not given enough attention in the process and often leads to generating inaccurate data from accurate data.

Extraction routines are generally not created exclusively for data profiling. Almost all new uses of data result in an extraction step that prepares the data for the target or for other software that begins the steps of transforming the data to the target form. It is best if the extraction formats used in data profiling are the same as those that begin the journey when the data itself is eventually moved. This means that the extraction step is not a step designed only for data profiling.

Most shops do a hurried job of extraction and pay little attention to the details that often cause problems. A proper job includes careful design and documentation of the source data structures, the extraction logic, and extraction formats. These should be reviewed by business analysts in conjunction with the data handlers to ensure that semantic issues are properly addressed.

9.3 The Process for Structure Analysis

The process for analyzing structure is the same as that for examining column properties. This is shown in Figure 9.6. The source of information is different and the analysis tools used are very different, but the overall process of collecting available metadata, looking at the data to fix inaccurate or missing metadata, and using the accurate definition of the metadata to expose inaccuracies is the same.

One of the key differences is that when inaccuracies are flushed out, the specific values that are inaccurate are not determined. This is true because all structure rules relate either multiple values in a column or values in multiple columns. This means that any rule violation only shows you the narrowed set of data within which the inaccuracy exists, not which of the values in the set are inaccurate.

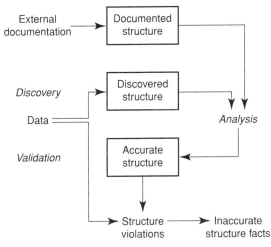

FIGURE 9.6   Structure analysis process.

Gathering Information

Structure information can be acquired in a variety of ways: from existing documentation, from metadata repositories, from data models such as entity-relation diagrams, and from database definitions, or by commonsense examination of data columns. The information from these sources can and often is inaccurate and incomplete. Some of this information can be believed, and others can only be considered proposed structure.

METADATA REPOSITORIES

Metadata repositories will tell you some things about structure. They usually identify primary keys and foreign keys. The basic affinities of columns are defined to the table level. A good source of information will not only itemize tables, segments, or records (and the columns that fall within them) but will include information on the business meaning of the business objects themselves. This information is generally lacking in detail.

DATA MODELS

Formal data models may exist that describe the data structures in great detail. Modeling tools became popular in the mid- to late 1980s, and many organizations started using them to develop data structure designs. If those models are still around, they can describe the entities that should end up in profiling tables and the relationships that connect entities. These will identify the primary key of each table, foreign keys, and rules surrounding the connections.

Many of these models will be out of date. A common practice was to use them to get started. However, as the data models were tuned for implementation and performance, the new information was never put back into the models. This is particularly true where denormalization for performance reasons was a common practice. It is also likely that these models do not address natural keys, derived columns, or synonyms.

Information should be taken from them to use as a starting point for the data profiling process. The process will validate the information or drive modifications to show how the data really behaves.

DATABASE DEFINITIONS

Most applications have information available in the form of program source files or database definitions that describe structure. For simple file systems such as VSAM data, the pervasive COBOL copybook provides insights into record layouts, key definitions, REDEFINE, and OCCURS structure information. For IMS, the PSB control block provides valuable information. For relational databases, the SYSTEM catalog or directory gives much information. You should mine these data sources and construct as much information as you can from them to use as the starting point for structure analysis.

Many of these can be believed because the database system enforces them for you. For example, a primary key defined to DB2 will certainly be a key, and the key values will be UNIQUE. This is also true of primary key/foreign key relationships. However, this is not to say that other functional dependencies or foreign keys may exist in the data that are not defined to DB2.

It may be helpful at this point to compare the information gathered from external sources (such as data repositories and data models) to the database implementation. This is where some of the differences show up. If a data model shows a primary key/foreign key relationship that is not defined to the database system, it may be because the implementors did not want the processing overhead of enforcement. If that is true, there are probably several violations of the rule due to inaccurate data.

Another example is discovering that a table was split in implementation although defined as a single table in the metadata. When this occurs and the database system does not relate the primary keys of the two tables as a primary key/foreign key pair, there will probably be instances in which there is a record in one table with no corresponding record in the other table. This again points to inaccuracies in the database.

COMMONSENSE SPECULATION

Many of the structure elements are intuitively obvious to a student of database architecture. If there is a serious lack of information on structure, the analyst can speculate about structure components by merely looking at column definitions.

For example, a column called PRODUCT_IDENTIFIER in an INVENTORY table is probably a primary key. The same column in an ORDER table is almost certainly a foreign key.

Most of the documentation you have usually calls out only a single primary key of a table and only foreign keys that are enforced. Documentation rarely covers such things as derived columns, embedded denormalization, or unenforced foreign keys.

It is helpful to speculate on all structural possibilities so that the data profiling process can confirm them or demonstrate their nonconformance in the data. The analyst should develop a data model that describes how they think the data is structured. This will be very helpful in the data profiling process.

Discovery from Data

The process shown in Figure 9.6 shows a step for discovery of structural information from the data. This sounds good but is particularly difficult without special software. You are not likely going to write a program to dig out all functional dependencies in the data programmatically.

There are two approaches to accomplishing this step. The first is to use special software that will discover all functional dependencies in the data and find all column pairs that appear to be synonyms. The second method is to test the structural rules you believe to be true against the data and find the degree of conformance between them.

Discovery of functional dependencies and common column pairs is clearly preferable because you can discover things you would not think to test. It is more efficient to say "These are the dependencies that are true in the data and these are those the available metadata seems to indicate are true" and then analyze the difference.

However, without special software, the best you can do is to test against the data. This requires that you do a thorough job of collecting and speculating on what may be true. The problem with this approach is that you leave open the possibility of missing a structure relationship that exists in the data but that you are not aware of. The missing relationships are often those that cause problems when mapping data to other structures, loading data to target systems, and reporting on data.

THE *reason special software is needed to find all functional dependencies programmatically is that the number of potential functional dependencies that can exist in a table where the LHS has only one column is* n * (n − 1), *where* n *is the number of columns in the table. For two columns in the LHS, this becomes* (n * (n − 1) * (n − 2))/2 *potential dependencies.*

If you wanted to evaluate all potential dependencies in a 300-column table, the number of tests for single LHS dependencies would be 98,700, the number of additional tests required for finding all two-column LHS dependencies would be 13,455,000, and for more than two-column LHS dependencies the number gets out of sight. You have to do this no matter how many rows of data you have. However, the number of rows makes the testing only longer to execute. If you are testing this over 100 million rows of data, this would run forever, even if you could construct the test queries.

Finding all functional dependencies within a table with any significant number of columns or rows requires software capable of efficiently cutting through these numbers to complete in a reasonable period of time.

It may be necessary to employ the testing method against the data even when structure discovery software is used. This is because a structural component may not show up in the results of discovery if a sufficient amount of inaccurate data exists that masks the condition. This is not uncommon when examining data that does not have the benefit of database management system enforcement. This again supports the need to develop a complete list of dependencies you think may be true before you begin analysis.

Verification of Results

Mapping the results of discovery to the gathered metadata can be started by the data profiling analyst. A straightforward physical analysis that shows which keys are supported in the data and which column pairs have strong data overlap are easy to do.

However, verification needs to be done with business analysts and subject matter experts. Structural issues always boil down to the basic business definition of data structures. Tables need to correlate to real-world objects, and relationships between tables need to make clear business sense. Most business analysts are not educated on data architecture issues and terminology and therefore will have trouble following the discussions unless the data profiling analyst translates structure into terms that make sense to the audience. This may require building diagrams that show the functional structure groupings and relationships between them.

Too often the data profiling analyst believes that structure issues do not require semantic interpretation and leaves the business experts out of the process. This is a big mistake and can lead to serious problems later on.

A RECENT *structure analysis data profiling action resulted in a verification meeting with the business analysts and some of the users. After a discussion about an unexpected discovery of an embedded denormalized functional dependency set, the businesspeople realized that this was the root of a* *nagging problem they had been investigating unsuccessfully concerning aggregation totals on a decision support report. Because denormalization often results in redundant information as well as unnecessary rows, aggregation reports can easily be distorted.*

9.4   The Rules for Structure

This section demonstrates some of the techniques you can use to analyze the structure of data. The goal is to find the correct structural definition of the data as well as to find violations that point to inaccurate data. This is not intended to be a description of an implementation of the methods, just a survey of the techniques that can be implemented for structure analysis.

The techniques described vary widely. Each technique looks at a single aspect of structure.

As in the case of values, structure analysis cannot be done by running a single program to get the results. All along the way it requires semantic interpretation of results to determine the relevance of structure discovered and the impact of inaccurate data.

Finding Functional Dependencies

Finding functional dependencies in each table of source data is the starting point. This leads to discovery of primary keys, embedded denormalized key sets, and derived columns. This information is vital to other data profiling activities. As described earlier, there are two approaches to digging out functional dependencies: using discovery software or validating proposed dependencies.

DETERMINING CANDIDATE DEPENDENCIES

Speculation about what might be a functional dependency is the first thing to do. These should be recorded in the data profiling repository as candidate dependencies. This should always be done first. You would normally have a collection of candidate dependencies to start with that were gathered from various external metadata sources. The process of speculation is designed to add to this list dependencies that would not normally be documented. Of course, the available metadata may have very little to offer in terms of candidate dependencies requiring you to invent candidates for everything.

The best way to create a list of candidate dependencies is to start by classifying columns. The goal is to identify those column sets that are possibly LHS components of functional dependencies. Some columns are obvious candidates for keys, and others are obviously not candidates for keys.

Columns that have only one value should be excluded from analysis. Likewise, columns with a significant percentage of nulls, whether actual nulls or blanks, would also normally be excluded from LHS consideration. This is not always true, but is true so often that they should be considered excluded unless the semantic of the column suggests otherwise.

Most other columns should be classified as identifiers, descriptors, quantifiers, dates, or free-form text fields. These classifications are purely semantic. This is why a thorough value analysis needs to be performed before coming to structure analysis. The actual business meaning and content characterizations of columns are key to successful classification.

Identifier columns are those that by their nature identify one object within a table. Some of them are clear: ORDER_NUMBER, PRODUCT_ID, DEPARTMENT_NUMBER, CLASS_ID, and CUSTOMER_NO. These columns are clearly encoded identifiers, and their presence in a table indicates that they are components of keys, whether primary keys, denormalized keys, or foreign keys. If you know what business object each row of the table represents, you can easily guess which ones are primary key candidates and which are foreign key candidates.

Sometimes these identifier columns require additional columns to identify unique rows of the table. This is true when the table is not the primary table for the business object but is a sub-table. For example, in the EMPLOYEE table the EMPLOYEE_ID is probably the primary key. However, in the EMPLOYEE_EDUCATION table, additional columns need to be combined with EMPLOYEE_ID to get unique records. This is because each employee may very well have multiple educational achievements recorded. The additional columns can usually be determined easily from the semantic meaning of the table and of the columns in the table. If you guess wrong, you can find the correct combination in later steps of structure analysis.

Natural key identifier candidates require some knowledge of the object the table represents. Columns with titles such as NAME, EMPLOYEE_ NAME, and PRODUCT_NAME are all clearly candidates for natural keys. These often require additional columns to uniquely identify an object in the table. For example, CUSTOMER_NAME may require ADDRESS or PHONE_NUMBER to achieve uniqueness when you support having multiple customers with the same NAME.

Again, speculation about the column sets required to achieve uniqueness can be done, generating multiple candidate keys. These will all be sorted out later, in the testing phase of the process.

Descriptor columns provide a value that helps describe a single characteristic of the table. Examples are CUSTOMER_TYPE, ZIP_CODE, COLOR, MODEL_YEAR, UNIT_OF_MEASURE, PRODUCT_DESCRIPTION, REGIONAL_OFFICE, and COUNTRY_CODE. Some tables have a very large number of descriptor columns. These columns are very popular for drilling down in decision support products and producing important business reports.

Descriptor columns are generally RHS candidates. Each of them should be looked at with regard to each of the key candidates listed from identifier columns. They should be associated as potential RHS candidates. Sometimes a descriptor column will be an LHS component, but rarely are LHSs made up entirely of descriptors.

Quantifier columns are those that define a numeric value that indicates a quantity associated with a row. Examples are PRICE, QUANTITY, ON_HAND, ON_ORDER, ACCOUNT_BALANCE, GRADE, and PERFORMANCE_RATING. Note that some of these are not numeric, such as GRADE. It still has the same effect as quantifying something about the object. In this case, it quantifies how well a student did in a course relative to the course standard.

These columns are generally not LHS candidates. They should be associated with LHS keys as RHS candidates by considering the semantic meaning of each.

Quantifier columns are generally strong candidates for participation in derived columns. The way to look at these is to speculate on which of them could be computed from the others. Looking for columns with names such as TOTAL, PRICE, NET_PRICE, and QUANTITY_AVAILABLE_FOR_ ORDER will produce a list of likely candidates for RHS of derived dependencies. This can then be used to construct a likely LHS list of columns the result may be computed from. The actual formula is not required to test for functional dependence, just the list of candidate columns. Deducing the actual formula or rule is outside the scope of this book.

Many tables have *date* columns because they describe when significant events occurred for the business object. Some tables have many date columns. Examples are DATE_OF_ORDER, DATE_CREATED, BIRTH_DATE, SHIP_DATE, DATE_LAST_UPDATED, and HIRE_DATE. These columns are also rarely LHS candidates. They are very similar to descriptor columns in the role they play. However, they need to be looked at separately and associated with key candidates.

The last type of column is the *free-form text field*. These columns, which are not easily queried, contain text that consists of multiple-word components. Examples are SHIPPING_INSTRUCTIONS, AUDITOR_COMMENTS, REVIEWER_NOTES, and INSPECTION_VIOLATIONS. They contain free-form information that enhances the other information on the row. They clearly do not identify the rows. These columns are never LHS candidates. Almost always they are RHS-associated columns that belong only to primary keys. It is not likely that any two of these will be identical.

At this point, you have a list of candidate functional dependencies. You will then need to have some method of verifying this against the actual data source in order to prove that they are dependencies or whether they have inaccurate data that prevents them from being true all of the time.

DISCOVERING DEPENDENCIES

The best way to test dependencies is to discover them. This is a process that finds all functional dependencies within a table. The dependencies produced will be true over all of the data used in the test. You will probably not use all of the data, because for very large data sources the processing time will be prohibitive. You will want to create samples of the data to use for discovery. You may want to create multiple samples, using different criteria, and then compare the outputs to see how similar they are.

One very important characteristic to understand when using discovery software is that all true dependencies are true in all samples. This means that you do not need to worry about finding true dependencies when using samples: you will find them all. The side effect of using a sample is that you get false positives (dependencies that are true in the sample but not true in the larger population). These can generally be weeded out by semantic review or testing against the larger population to determine if they are really true.

If the discovery process returns far too many dependencies, it generally indicates the presence of a large number of false positives. The sample size is probably too small, or the sample is biased in some way. When you see this, you want to resample and rerun to reduce the number of dependencies you need to examine.

If you profile multiple samples separately, you can compare the result sets by leaving for consideration only those dependencies that are found in both sample sets. Again, for a dependency to be true in the entire table it must be true in all samples. However, the dependency may be hiding out as a different dependency because in some samples it may not need all LHS columns to be true. For example, if ORDER_NUMBER and ITEM_NUMBER determine

QTY in the full table, some samples may show ORDER_NUMBER determining QTY if the sample only has one item per order. However, this functional dependency would also be true if ITEM_NUMBER were added to the LHS. The analyst must look for cases such as this where manipulation of the LHS column list is needed to show the functional dependency needed for the full table.

Once you have the list of discovered dependencies, you need to compare this to the list of candidate dependencies in your data profiling repository. You will probably discover some you did not expect. You need to make a judgment as to whether these are semantically interesting or not. An uninteresting dependency is one that is clearly a false positive (makes no business sense).

You should mark each dependency as confirmed through discovery, not confirmed through discovery, or uncovered through discovery (those that were true but you did not expect). Of course, these last are only those you felt were semantically meaningful.

THE *following are examples of dependencies you would throw away:*

- *Often a NAME field shows up as a primary key in discovery with all other columns appearing as being dependent on it. If this occurs in a table where you know from a business perspective that two different entries may be allowed to have the same name but that the sample used for discovery had all unique names, you would discard this dependency.*

- *Another example of a dependency you would not keep is where CODE determines DESCRIPTION and DESCRIPTION determines CODE. You would keep one, CODE determines DESCRIPTION, but not the other.*

- *Finding out that ZIP_CODE determines CITY, STATE is also generally not interesting. You are not likely to break these out as a separate table.*

A dependency is significant if it defines the basic structure of the object, if the RHS column is likely to also exist in another table (indicating redundancy), or if it is very important that the relationship always be correct.

TESTING DEPENDENCIES

If you do not have software for performing discovery of functional dependencies, you need to construct tests of those you think are true. Even when you do have the ability to discover functional dependencies, you may well want to do this for candidate dependencies that did not show up on the discovered dependency list. Another reason for testing dependencies is to check the larger data source for conformance to dependencies found in discovery when discovery only used a sample of the data. The purpose here is to find out how close they were to being true.

You do not need to test functional dependencies based on a single column defined to a database system as a primary key or that have a UNIQUE constraint if the database system enforces uniqueness. Likewise, if you have determined that the cardinality of the column is the same as the number of rows in the table, you are certain that it is a true key. No further testing is required.

The process of testing is to sort the data source by the key of the dependency (LHS). Then examine the data by determining if the value of the RHS is constant for each combination of values for LHS columns. This is an easy algorithm to implement.

This process can be improved upon by first combining candidate dependencies with overlapping LHS columns and testing all RHS columns that share the same LHS columns. For example, if you think $a \rightarrow b, c, d$ and $ac \rightarrow e$, then a single sort by a, c, b, d, e can test all of the dependencies at one time.

The output of the test is either confirmation that all rows support the dependencies proposed or a list of violations. Each violation consists of an LHS value combination and multiple rows that match it but have different RHS column values.

CLASSIFYING DEPENDENCIES

Once the output has been determined from all of the tests, the analyst can match these to the candidate and discovered dependencies to determine which are true, which are close to being true, and which are so far off they are probably not true dependencies.

EXAMINING *multiple primary key dependencies can be very useful. Tables that depend on an encoded key for uniqueness generally do not look for nor enforce uniqueness on natural keys. This means that violations can easily occur and go undetected. By testing natural keys, you may find duplicates. These duplicates may indicate inaccurate data, or they may indicate that a corporate rule has been violated. Examples of things people have discovered through natural key testing are:*

- *Same person working for company under two different EMPLOYEE_IDs*

- *Same product with two different PRODUCT_NUMBERs*

- *Multiple accounts for same CUSTOMER*

If these conditions are not permitted by corporate business rules, discovering violations is very worthwhile.

The list of functional dependencies would have each marked as being expected, discovered to be true, tested to be true, or violated with the percentage of rows involved in violations. You would also know if each was a primary key candidate or a denormalized key candidate.

It is also valuable to sort through the primary key dependencies and designate one of them as the one to use for database implementation and enforcement. This is important for later uses of the data.

Taking this information to a review by business analysts and subject matter experts is extremely valuable. This group can finish the process by classifying them further as being derived column dependencies or structurally significant dependencies.

Finding Synonym Columns Across Tables

The next step of structure analysis is to find pairs of columns that represent the same business fact and to classify the structural relationship between them. This analysis is done within a table as well as across tables.

The data profiling process will find all the synonyms, determine their type, set their rules, and test the data to find violations that indicate inaccurate data. This step is critically important whenever you are trying to consolidate data from multiple sources, particularly if the sources were created independently from each other.

The process is executed from two different perspectives: a single data source or merged data sources. In a single data source, all tables represent different business object components and you are trying to determine how they connect. In the merged data source, pairs of tables represent the same business object components. The process is oriented toward finding identical business facts at the column level that must be consolidated into a target data source. This step is concerned with finding the pairs that are the same and testing their ability to be consolidated.

DETERMINING CANDIDATE SYNONYMS

As in the case of finding functional dependencies, the process of profiling synonym structures begins with collecting and speculating about what synonyms may exist. Synonyms need to be documented in the data profiling repository.

You can find existing synonym candidates in metadata repositories, data models, database implementations, or through speculation. Metadata repositories, data models, and database implementations will never tell you information about synonyms across diverse data sources. You can only determine them through manually matching columns using the business meaning of each column.

Additional, very helpful information is provided through the results of column property analysis. Thoroughly profiling the properties of each column in a data source provides valuable foundation information for all steps in the synonym profiling process.

Metadata repositories and data models are very helpful in identifying primary/foreign key pairs, the relationship between them, and the rules they are supposed to follow. Do not assume that this documentation is either complete or accurate. Data models often do not identify relationships between columns in one business object and other, different objects.

IN *one example, an ORDER data structure identified the relationship between ORDER_HEADER rows and ORDER_DETAIL rows through a pair of columns labeled ORDER_ NO, as well as the relationship between an order and a customer through a pair of columns labeled CUSTOMER_ NO. However, it failed to document the fact that the SALESMAN_ID identifier in the ORDER_HEADER was actually a synonym of the PERSONNEL_ID in the HR database.*

Profiling the pair of fields revealed a number of orphans (salesperson IDs that did not exist in the personnel data), as well as missing values.

Because this was the only information about who the salesperson was, this was not a reliable source of information for some forms of post-sale analysis. The synonym profiling process allowed the customer to tighten up processing and to provide more reliable data.

Database implementations will generally be helpful in identifying synonym pairs that are involved in primary key/foreign key relationships. Most relational systems allow these to be defined with rules so that they can be enforced whenever data is created, updated, or deleted. This is valuable information that gives you a head start. You need to indicate in the data profiling repository that the appropriate ones have been enforced and therefore do not need to be tested.

Older legacy systems may also provide help. For example, IMS data definitions show the hierarchical relationship between segments. Examination of the keys for each segment will clearly indicate the fields that connect the parts. IMS, however, has shortcomings in some areas. One is that you cannot define cross–business object relationships through the same mechanism or cannot define them at all. You might have a logical relationship defined that is helpful, but then again you may not. Another problem is that not all keys are complete, because some of the relationship may be determined by the hierarchical structure. This just says that the IMS definitions may be helpful but could very well be incomplete.

The final source of candidates is speculation. You can look for the obvious synonyms through examination of the business purpose of each table, looking for the columns that are probably used to associate the multiple parts of the object. Additionally, perusing the columns of each table looking for columns that are encoded identifiers will generally yield synonym candidates.

Looking for candidate-redundant columns is best done by examining denormalized dependency sets. The LHS is probably a primary key/foreign key candidate. Columns on the RHS are candidates for being pure redundant data from columns in the table the LHS connects to.

When you are trying to consolidate data from more than one source, you are looking for synonyms for all columns. This process is much more complex. The basics are to start by looking for homonyms (column pairs that share the same or very nearly the same name). A match can be deceiving, but it at least provides a good starting point. Beyond that, matching must be done on a semantic basis using the results of column property analysis. Speculation should include not only pair names but also the relationship rules.

All of our discussion to this point has involved synonyms that were pairs of single columns. However, in some primary key/foreign key relationships, the synonym can be multiple columns on each side. Figure 9.7 shows how this might work. The PROJECT table has a primary key/foreign key relationship

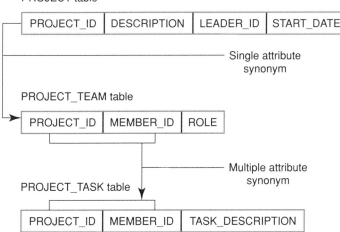

FIGURE 9.7 Multiple-column synonym example.

to the PROJECT_TEAM table through the PROJECT_ID column. However, each team member can have multiple tasks assigned against multiple projects. To show this, a third table (the PROJECT_TASK table) connects to the PROJECT_TEAM table using a combined key of PROJECT_ID and MEMBER_ID.

Where they exist, they must be treated as a single concatenated value, because the full value combinations must match between the tables. Having matching values on the individual columns within the synonym is not sufficient.

CLASSIFYING SYNONYMS

Synonyms need to be classified across multiple dimensions. These classifications need to be in place before testing and verification against the data can be done. Information about the data can be helpful in setting the classifications. These dimensions are shown in Figure 9.8.

All synonyms should be considered pairs. Synonym chains do exist, but they can all be represented by individual synonym pairs that have common columns across the pairs. There is no need at this point to consider chains.

The *synonym type* has been discussed previously. This shows the probable reason the synonym exists. This is important in terms of which testing method to use.

The *value correspondence* indicates whether the values are encoded the same in both columns of the synonym. If they use different representations for the same facts, a transform needs to be developed to get them into a common

- Synonym type
  - Primary key/foreign key
  - Redundant data
  - Domain
  - Merge
- Value correspondence
  - Same values
  - Transform
- Inclusive relationship
  - Inclusive
  - Bidirectional inclusive
  - Exclusive
  - Mixed
- Degree of overlap
  - One-to-one
  - One-to-many
  - Many-to-many

FIGURE 9.8 Synonym classifications.

representation. Transform correspondence can be true for redundant, domain, or merge synonyms.

The *inclusive relationship* indicates whether all of the values in one are expected to be found in the other (inclusive), all values are expected to be found in both tables (bidirectional inclusive), none of the values in one are expected to be found in the other (exclusive), or some are expected in both and some are not (mixed).

An example of *inclusive* is PRODUCT_NO across INVENTORY and ORDER_DETAIL. All products must not necessarily have been ordered. It is inclusive in only one direction (all products ordered must have an inventory row).

An example of *bidirectional inclusive* is ORDER_NO across ORDER_HEADER and ORDER_DETAIL. This means that every order number must have at least one row in each table. You cannot have order details without an order header, and you cannot have an order header without at least one order detail.

An example of *exclusive* is SOCIAL_SECURITY_NUMBER across two different personnel databases being merged. You would not expect the same person to be working for both companies.

An example of *mixed* is CITY across CUSTOMER and EMPLOYEE tables. Any CITY value could exist either in one alone or in both. The *degree of overlap* specifies whether the expected occurrences of values between the tables are one-to-one, one-to-many, or many-to-many.

DISCOVERING SYNONYMS

Testing can include both discovery or verification, as in dependency analysis. The purpose of discovery is to expose potential synonyms that were overlooked when building the candidate synonym list.

Discovery from the data is the process of looking across all of the columns in the project and finding pairs that have an identical or high degree of data value overlap. The analyst can then look at the pair and determine whether they are true synonym candidates or not. That decision is based purely on the semantic meaning of each column. However, often the user is surprised at the pairings that show up, and by looking at the values you can determine that a synonym really does exist. The example of the SALESMAN_ID previously cited is a perfect example of a synonym pair that would not have been suspected without discovery. Discovery from the data cannot find synonym candidates that are exclusive or that have transform value correspondence.

Another discovery technique that can be used to expose potential synonyms is discovery against the column names. It can look for homonyms that are either identical names or very similar-sounding names. Typical homonym discovery routines consider typical abbreviations for names and discount special characters, numbers, and other qualifier type characters in the names. For example, the columns UNION_CODE and UNIONCD would be suggested homonyms.

Homonym discovery is useful in identifying synonyms that are exclusive or that have transform value correspondence. It is also useful for determining merge synonym pairs.

Discovery can only provide you with candidates for synonyms. They cannot determine programmatically whether the columns in a pair have any real relationship. For example, it may discover that HOURLY_PAY_RATE and UNIT_PRICE have a high degree of value overlap. These are clearly not synonyms of each other.

A good data discovery routine can provide statistical information that is helpful in determining the potential for being a synonym. The percentage of values that overlap, the frequency of occurrence of values in each, and the presence of nulls, blanks, or other empty indicators can all be useful in looking for synonyms and setting the rules.

TESTING FOR SYNONYMS

Testing differs from discovery in that you have a synonym definition established and you want to verify it against the data. If the data does not conform to the expectation, either it is not a synonym or inaccurate data values prevent all of the rule expectations from being true. You focus on one synonym at a time.

The test for a single pair is quite simple. You compare the distinct values and their frequency of occurrence in one of the columns to the distinct values and frequencies in the other column. This tells you the degree of overlap and the presence of orphan values on either side. It also confirms or denies the rules you expect for the pair. You can easily verify one-to-one or one-to-many relationships through the result set. You can easily verify exclusive relationships as well by determining if any common values exist.

This method of testing is used for primary key/foreign key synonyms, domain synonyms, and merge synonyms that have same-value correspondence. It does not work for redundant synonyms or synonyms that have transform-value correspondence.

If the two columns have different ways of expressing the same values (transform-value correspondence), the values in one column need to be transformed before they can be compared to the values in the other column. In this case you need to list the distinct values in both columns and then manually match them. This process is called value mapping. There is no programmatic way of doing this. You need to understand the semantics of each value in both data sources. Once the mapping is done, you can transform the values in one of the columns and then compare the two columns in the same way you did for same-value correspondence.

If the pair are redundant column synonyms, the testing is more complex. You need to build a list for each column that concatenates the LHS columns of their respective functional dependencies and then compare these values. To be redundant, it is not sufficient that the synonym values match; they must also have the same parent key value. For example, if DISCOUNT RATE in the CUSTOMER_ MASTER table and DISCOUNT in the ORDER_HEADER table are redundant synonyms, the discounts for each CUSTOMER_ID must be the same.

When testing domain synonyms, you need to find the values that do appear in only one of the columns. These need to be visually examined to determine if they are caused by inconsistent representation.

DETERMINING THE CHARACTERISTICS OF EACH SYNONYM

After all of the computations have been done, it is easy to validate the rule sets of the candidate synonyms. The discovered pairs need to be confirmed as being synonyms or discarded as a mere coincidence-of-value overlap.

Careful attention needs to be used to classify two columns as a redundant synonym. Sometimes they appear to be redundant, but in fact one is capturing the values of the other at a point in time, and an update of the primary source would not be reflected in the other column. This can happen, for example, in columns such as DISCOUNT_RATE or UNIT_PRICE. The reason for copying the data from one table to the other is to capture the value at the time the row is created in the second table.

Determining the classification of synonyms and the rules for them should be done in conference with business analysts and subject matter experts. Interpretation of differences as being semantically acceptable versus errors can be safely done only by those who know the applications.

As in the case of functional dependencies, you need to translate the synonym information to language understandable by the audience. You should not expect the business analysts and subject matter experts to understand all terminology and concepts of data structure.

ANALYZING SYNONYMS IN THE SAME TABLE

Synonyms can exist where both columns are in the same table. This is a common occurrence. In some cases the synonym pair is a primary key/foreign key pair. An example is having a PART_NUMBER column as the key to the

INVENTORY table and having another column in the same table for ALTERNATE_PART_NUMBER. This semantically means that the other part can be used in its place. It is referring to another row in the same table.

AN *unusual form of same-table synonyms occurs when the data has not been properly put into first-normal form. This occurs when there are a number of repeating columns that specify multiple occurrences of the same fact. The columns are all synonyms of each other because they contain the same business fact.*

An example that builds on the INVENTORY example is where each part can have up to five alternate part numbers. Instead of breaking these out into a separate table containing two columns PART_NO and ALT_ PART_NO, the data designer just creates five columns in the primary table named ALT_PART_1, ALT_ PART_2, and so on. Synonym discovery will find that six columns contain the same business fact. Five of them are dependent on the single one, PART_NO.

This is a special case of domain synonyms that needs to be identified for what it is. The data is not in first-normal form because a single fact is not recorded in one column but rather is spread over five columns. It does not show up as a denormalized dependency because each is dependent on only the primary key.*

This condition can also occur over multiple column sets. For example, an employee table may contain repeating columns for postsecondary education. Each occurrence is a set of columns for COLLEGE, DEGREE, and YEAR. There would be multiple occurrences of each of these columns. All of them would be dependent on the EMPLOYEE_ID primary key.

A good analyst can spot these situations during synonym discovery. It is very useful to go back and recast the data used for profiling into third-normal form by breaking these out into a separate table, with each occurrence being a separate row. Having these as separate columns makes typical reporting on the data meaningless. Sometimes it is better to note the condition and handle it when moving data.

Another case is where the two columns have only a domain relationship to each other. Additional synonyms involving these two columns exist that are primary key/foreign key pairs pointing to a third column that is the primary key to a different table. A classic example of this is having a PROJECT table that contains a column for PROJECT_MANAGER_ID and another column for PROJECT_RECORDER_ID. Both of these are domain synonyms of each other because they both contain personnel identifiers. Their relationship to each other is purely incidental. Both columns also participate in separate primary key/foreign key synonyms through the PERSONNEL_ID column of the PERSONNEL database.

CLASSIFYING RELATIONSHIPS BETWEEN TABLES

In addition to classifying synonyms of columns, this is the time to classify the nature of relationships between tables. This is done by examining the primary key/foreign key relationships between columns in the two tables, along with an understanding of why multiple tables were involved in the profiling exercise. The types of relationships that are possible are primary/secondary, partitioned data, split tables, and merge pairs.

Two tables are connected in a *primary/secondary relationship* when they are connected by a primary key/foreign key pair. It is possible for more than one such synonym to connect two tables.

In all primary key/foreign key relationships there is a hierarchy. It defines which column (and thus table) contains the values the other column draws from.

Two tables are related in a *partitioning relationship* if all columns of one are synonyms to all columns of the other and the synonym of the two primary keys is exclusive. This means that they both contain the same information but about different instances of the business objects. For example, one table may contain employee data for all employees of one division, and a different table may contain employee data for a different division.

Two tables are considered *merge tables* if they are either partitioned or split, come from different data sources, and your intention is to combine them. Partitioned tables are said to be *vertical merge pairs*, meaning that each row of both tables becomes a separate row in the merged table. They are said to be *horizontal merge pairs* if they have a split table relationship in which each row of the merged data consists of some columns from one of the source tables and the other columns of the other table.

Two tables are connected in a *split table* relationship when the primary key columns of the two tables are synonyms in an inclusive one-to-one relationship and no other columns of one table are synonyms of any columns of the other table. Generally, one of the two tables is considered the dominant one, and the other one split apart from it.

RECORDING INACCURATE DATA FACTS

It is also important to capture all of the instances of structure rule violations. These indicate inaccurate data. Each instance may include a number of values or rows that contain the inaccurate data but do not identify which values are inaccurate. It is also possible that the inaccurate value is not included in the set captured. The inaccurate-fact data comes from primary key violations, denormalized key violations, derived column violations, or primary key/foreign key violations.

Primary key violations include lack of uniqueness in the key itself. This means that you have two or more rows in the data that have the same value for the primary key. The inaccuracy is that all but one of the key values are wrong. It may be that all of them are wrong.

If you are evaluating a natural key, the duplicate values should be investigated carefully to be sure that it really is a natural key. In cases such as a Social Security number, you are pretty safe that it is a real key. In cases such as NAME and ADDRESS data, there is always the outside chance it may be correct to be duplicate.

It is also a violation of a primary key to be NULL or empty. For multicolumn primary keys it is acceptable to have NULL values in some of the columns, but it is never correct to have all of the columns containing NULLs. NULL values in any of the key columns are always suspect and generally are not allowed.

For other dependencies that cover less than an entire row, a rule violation can mean more than just that the LHS is wrong. On denormalized dependencies, duplicate LHS entries are always acceptable. What is not acceptable are variations in values of the RHS columns in a single LHS value set. When this occurs, you can easily spot which column or columns have more than one value across the set. The inaccuracy can come from the LHS value set being wrong where any column in the LHS can have the inaccurate value or the value in the RHS set may contain the error. You cannot tell from the data. All of the values need to be collected in the inaccurate data set.

For derived columns, you have an additional capability. You have a formula or rule that determines precisely what the value in the RHS column should be. You need to test this rule instead of testing the functional dependency. Although the functional dependency test may surface some problems, the rule test may surface more problems because invalid RHS values may pass the dependency test. A violation does not tell you which of the columns contains the error, just that an error exists. You need to retain the values of all of the columns from the rows involved in the violation.

Synonyms offer many opportunities for violations. Most synonyms are not enforced at the database level, allowing ample opportunity for errors to creep in. The errors that occur in synonyms are orphans or degree-of-overlap violations.

Orphans are a case in which a value exists in one of the columns and is supposed to exist in the other but does not. This requirement belongs to all synonyms that have an inclusive relationship. This may occur in primary/

foreign key synonyms, duplicate data, or merge synonyms. When they do not have orphans you can still have violations if the synonym requires a one-to-one correspondence and the data has a one-to-many relationship. This means that you have more than one row, with the same value in one of the columns.

An orphan leaves you with only the row that contains the value that does not have a matching pair. This is the case in which the inaccurate data may not be in the result set. This is because the other table may have a row with an inaccurate data value in the synonym column that, if accurate, would have satisfied the rule. Additionally, the matching row in the primary table may have been deleted without cascading the delete to the secondary table. You still know you have an error, and you have one half of the data that potentially contains the error. You do not have the other half.

Developing a Data Model

After completing structure analysis, you have enough information to construct a third-normal-form data model. This is a very useful thing to do because it helps validate your perception of the business objects involved in the data and reconfirm your discovery of structure components. Even if you have a data model, constructing one from what you learned from the data is helpful in validating the model you have.

BUILDING THE MODEL

The method of construction uses the following logic. First, find the primary key of each table you want to use as the table identifier. Then find all denormalized dependencies that are embedded inside tables. Each of these needs to be spun out into its own table. The new table consists of all columns in the denormalized dependency of the table it is coming from. It also needs to have embedded within it the primary key of the table it comes from. This may be part of the denormalized dependency or not. This will make a new synonym pair that is of type primary key/foreign key. It is also inclusive. Then you would remove all duplicate rows in the new table.

You then look for tables that are part of horizontal merge pairs. These should be combined into a single table retaining only one instance of the primary key columns.

Vertical merge table pairs should be combined into a single table. Because both tables contain the same column set, no new columns need to be created.

The last step is to map all of the other synonym pairs across the table set. Synonyms that are of the type duplicate data can have the column removed from one of the tables. Which one to remove will depend on the semantics of use. It is normally very obvious.

VALIDATING THE MODEL

Once the model is constructed, you need to review the result with the business community. Every table should make sense as part of a discrete business object, and every connection between them should make business sense. If the model is nonsensical, you have missed finding some functional dependencies or synonym pairs, and you need to return to the structure analysis steps to look for more. What to look for is generally pretty clear from the model you have constructed.

As can be seen, this step is a check on the completeness of your analysis of structure. Bypassing this can lead to unexposed problems persisting in the data and potentially inaccurate data that was discoverable not being discovered.

9.5 Mapping with Other Structures

In projects that involve extracting data from one or more sources and moving to a new target data structure, there is an additional task of structure mapping. The last chapter described the process of column-level mapping. Too often that is the only mapping exercise that is done. Failure to consider structure issues can lead to inaccurate results.

Mapping is much easier if the data structures for source and target systems is represented in third-normal form. If you can do that, you can always transform the data to the third-normal form in order to move it correctly.

After you have completed the column mapping as described in the previous chapter, you begin the structure mapping process. Each target table should be traced back to find the various tables data is to come from.

Single-Source Tables

If the data comes from a single table, you need to look at primary keys only. If the primary key of the source table maps to a primary key of the target table, it is a good match. If not, you need to look further.

If the columns in the source table that map to the primary key of the target are not a primary key or constitute only part of a source table primary key, you need to determine if it could be a primary key for the target table. It only need be a primary key in the source over the column set that is being mapped to the target. Thus, if not all of the source table columns are mapped, it is possible that the new, proposed key is a primary key over that subset. You need to execute a test in the source data for this key to determine if it works. If it does, there is no issue; if not, you can see the extent to which the data does not support that combination as a primary key.

If the target key is not fully mapped from the source, a problem may also exist. You need to determine if the columns that are mapped constitute a valid key in the source, as described previously. If so, you can do the move by adding a NULL to the missing columns. If not, you have an issue. Of course, this requires that the target system allows NULL values in multicolumn primary keys.

Multiple-Source Tables

When data lands in the target table from more than one source table, you need to not only verify the primary key compatibility but ensure that the data can be properly aggregated for the target.

If the source tables are vertical or horizontal merge pairs, you already have confidence that a merge can occur. You only need to verify that the merged rows end up with a primary key that is acceptable to the target. This is performed by using the same logic described previously for a single-source table but using it instead on the merged set.

If the target table contains data from more than two source tables, each table should participate in a merge relationship with the other tables. It may be a mixture of horizontal and vertical merges. You need to be able to combine the tables using information from structure analysis to get a single-target-row image. This image is used to validate primary key compatibility, as described previously.

The multiple-merge case can become complex. It is best accomplished by first picking two tables to combine to get an intermediate output image. This image should include only columns matched to target columns. A new image is then created by adding one more table. This process is completed until all tables are in the image. At each step you need to ensure that a proper merge synonym step exists to make the match. This becomes the key to combining data. The merge key must be preserved throughout the matching process.

If the source tables are not in a merge synonym relationship, you may still be able to accomplish the task. The merge relationship may have been missed in structure analysis. If the target uses only some of the source columns, it may exist on that subset even if it does not on the total set of source columns. The subsets of the tables can be analyzed to see if the merge will work.

If the multiple-source tables have a primary/foreign key relationship but are not a merge relationship, you can still move the data, provided primary key tests are positive. You will be creating a denormalized target table. If that is what the target wants, it will work. Target systems frequently denormalize data to achieve better query performance. You only need to satisfy yourself that it can be done.

9.6 Structure-Level Remedies

There are a number of data inaccuracy issues that come out of structure analysis. Some of these are indictments on the data source and should lead to remedies in the source systems. Others are issues that can be handled when moving data.

Fixing Source Systems

Structural issues in source systems generally do not cause problems with their applications. They merely invite inaccurate data to be entered without detection. The remedies that are commonly used are to add data checkers for data entry, update, and delete to ensure that rules are not violated by new data. This is generally easy to do with relational database systems, but more difficult with others.

A COMMON *story involving relational systems is where the original application developers specified use of extensive database functionality to enforce structural constraints only to have the database administrators remove the definitions because of either performance problems in processing transactions or performance problems in performing loads. Additionally, if* *primary key/foreign key synonym chains get too long and involved, they must be turned off for load and have all data checked after the load completes. The check step is often left out. This means that it is not sufficient to specify the constraints. It is also important to ensure that they are used all of the time.*

Most issues that come out of structure analysis violations involve bad original database design. It is very difficult to get an IT department to want to change the structure of a database that is in operation. The cascading effects can be large, creating an expensive project with a high degree of risk. When changes cannot be done, it is doubly important to document the structure of the source systems to help fend off errors in using the data.

You can always add batch checkers to look for rule violations outside transaction processing. Often this is a good compromise between tearing up a running system and doing nothing.

Issues Involved in Moving Data

The most interesting quality issues come up for projects that try to extract the data from source systems and move it to new, different target systems. The mismatches on structure issues can make or break a project. Assuming you identify the source structure properly and map it correctly to target structures, there can still be issues left to deal with.

One issue is structural mismatches between source and target regarding primary keys. It may be that the data just cannot make the trip to the other side. It lacks the structural compatibility to find its proper place at the target. When this occurs you have to consider either scrapping the project or changing the target design. Sometimes you have no choice about going ahead with a project, requiring some creative design to fix the problems. Having the profile of the source system's structure in the level of detail described in this chapter is the perfect input for coming up with a solution.

A last area for remedies is to ferret out and deal with data inaccuracies when moving data. Ideally, you would want to fix the source systems. However, when this is not possible or will take a long time to complete, screening data as it is being moved for structure rule violations will at least keep junk from getting into target systems.

The last value is in designing proper data movement processes. The logic discussed for data model development is the basis for building a proper series of data transformation and merge steps that will result in a correct target. Trying to build a design for data movement without this road map just invites errors.

9.7 Closing Remarks

Structure analysis can uncover rules in the data that are crucial for correct extraction and mapping to other data structures. Overlooking this step in the data profiling process can lead to difficulties in moving data. If denormalized data is moved and remains denormalized in the target, it can lead to inaccurate results when aggregating the data for decision support reports.

Structure rules can be violated in source systems without detection due to inaccurate or incomplete data. If they are not uncovered before using or moving the data, they can result in failures on loading data or in subsequent attempts to use the data.

It is important to complete the structure analysis and document the true structure of the data before proceeding to the next step of data profiling: business object data rule analysis. That step is described in the next chapter. Some of the data rules depend on a correct understanding of the structure as it relates to the association of columns to each other in defining a business object.

RELATIONAL *systems often contain structural issues, even though the relational DBMS provides a great deal of support for structural enforcement. Denormalized tables are common in relational applications. In the 1980s, relational systems were criticized often for slow performance. Data designers were encouraged to use denormalization to solve many of the performance problems by avoiding JOINs. Duplicate data was also commonly used to avoid performance issues as just another form of denormalization. Most of the time, when denormalization was done, it was not documented. The relational directories have no mechanism for telling them that denormalization exists within a table and what the columns involved in the denormalization are.*

Another common shortcoming of relational implementations is a conscious choice not to employ the referential constraints on primary/foreign key pairs. This is often done to alleviate difficulties in loading data or to reduce processing requirements for high-speed transactions. You may have an entity-relationship diagram that shows the RI constraints but not have it implemented within the DBMS. When this is done, you can bet there are orphan rows in the database.

CHAPTER 10

Simple Data Rule Analysis

After fully data profiling column properties and data structure, it is time to deal with data rules. Technically, all testing discussed in the last two chapters involves rules in that they define conditions the data must follow to be considered accurate. However, it is easier to understand and profile column and structure rules if they are cast in traditional database architecture terminology. At this point, however, the remaining rules to consider are general enough in nature that they require an expression language all to themselves.

Data rules are specific statements that define conditions that should be true all of the time. A data rule can involve a single column, multiple columns in the same table, or columns that cross over multiple tables. However, they always involve relationships between multiple values. Rules can also be restricted to the data of a single business object or involve data that encompasses sets of business objects.

This chapter attempts to simplify the analysis process by first considering only data rules that fall within the analysis of a single business object. Dealing with sets of business objects is the topic of the next chapter.

The prior chapters have used data rule expressions to demonstrate many points. You should be fairly familiar with the syntax and intent of these rules by now. This chapter may repeat some of the information already covered. However, it is necessary to provide a thorough coverage of the material in one place to ensure complete treatment of this important data profiling step.

10.1 Definitions

These definitions are not as conventional as are those for column and structure. Different writers use terms differently in this area. The definitions used here are those I prefer to use.

Business Object

The term *business object* describes a single object that data is collected for; for example, an order, an employee, or a single item in inventory. This is analogous to a type definition in programming terminology. The data for a single business object is stored in at least one row of one table. No row of any table should be describing data for more than one business object.

A business object almost always has a table within which a single row identifies the object. This is generally the primary data descriptor for the object. The object is identified within that table by its primary key. Other columns exist that provide additional facts about the object.

The object may also have rows present in other tables. These secondary tables describe additional information about the object that cannot be described in a single fact. For example, if an employee has multiple college degrees, a secondary table is needed to describe them all. In this case, multiple rows may be needed in the secondary table to supply all of the information needed for one employee. If the employee has no college degree, there are no rows in the secondary table.

Some data architects would describe the education rows of the secondary table as independent objects (employee education achievement objects). If you take this line of thought, all business objects are single row entries in tables. However, in the real world, considering the secondary parts of objects as separate objects is not terribly useful. An order is an order. It has a header and multiple items being ordered. Most queries involving the order deal with the order as a single object with all of its parts.

The secondary tables that contain part information for the object are attached to the primary table through the primary key/foreign key columns. These bring together all parts of a single object.

A business object may refer to another business object through a foreign key column. The other object provides additional information to the referencing object. However, it is not part of the object under consideration. For example, a PROJECT object may have a secondary table that identifies each of the project members, along with their role in the project. The identification of each member is done through the EMPLOYEE_ID column. This is used to obtain additional information from the EMPLOYEE database, such as the employee's name, department, phone number, e-mail address, job title, and education level. All of this information may be useful for purposes of the project. However, it would not be useful to consider the employee personnel object as being part of the project object.

Data Rule

As we have said previously, a data rule is an expression of a condition involving multiple vales that must be true over a collection of data for that data to be considered accurate. A data rule may address a single column using values from multiple rows, it may involve values from multiple columns and/or rows of the same table, or it may involve values from multiple tables. A collection of data may have many data rules that must be true. Each data rule deals with a single relationship between columns of the business object.

Data rules examine data in a static state. This means that you look at a database at a point in time when all of the business objects described by that data are expected to conform to the rules. Data rules must be cognizant of state boundaries. Data rules that operate within an application to achieve a stable state are called process rules. Data rules and process rules together are part of what is normally referred to as business rules.

Most people pretty much agree on what is a business rule and what is a process rule. However, there has emerged no specific standard regarding how a data rule is expressed. This is not to say that attempts have not been made.

It is not the purpose of this book to create a standard nor to promote any specific standard. The data rules in this book follow a common approach of expressing the logic of a rule in an SQL-like language in a form that describes what constitutes correct data. This is only used to express the concepts of rules, not to provide a syntax for formal rule specification.

Data rules are negative rules. This means that the expression says what must be true in the data. However, no one is ever interested in seeing the results of what is true, only what is not true. Therefore, the execution of data rules generally involves selecting data that is *not* what the rule says. Some implementations of rule execution engines have the user express the rule according to what is correct and then execute the NOT ( ) of the rule. Others have you merely create a query statement that defines what you want to select, which is usually the data that describes a violation.

All data rules should be recorded in the data profiling repository in two parts. One part is a text description of the rule. It should state very simply the condition that is intended. The rule should be documented in a logic language in the second part. The logic specifications can be very difficult for business analysts to understand. The text description should serve as a basis for validating whether the logic is an accurate specification of the rule.

FOLLOWING *are two examples of data rule syntax:*

Consider a rule that defines the business condition that an employee cannot be part-time and assigned to a research department. The data rule is

IF EMPLOYEE.STATUS='PART_TIME'
   THEN DEPARTMENT NOT = 'RESEARCH'.

- *The selection rule for violations is*

SELECT EMPLOYEE-NUMBER, EMPLOYEE NAME
FROM EMPLOYEE
WHERE EMPLOYEE.STATUS='PART-TIME AND DEPARTMENT
= 'RESEARCH'

- *A truly negative expression that finds the violations would be*

SELECT EMPLOYEE_NUMBER, EMPLOYEE_NAME
FROM EMPLOYEE
WHERE NOT(EMPLOYEE_STATUS='PART_TIME' AND
DEPARTMENT NOT= 'RESEARCH)'

Expressions should be written as simply as possible to express either the condition that must be true or the exceptions you want to see.

Hard Versus Soft Data Rules

Some data rules are absolutely required to be true. Any violation is considered a case of inaccurate data. These are called *hard data rules.* For example, your HIRE_DATE must be later than your BIRTH_DATE. There cannot be an exception to a hard rule.

A *soft data rule* is one that is expected to be true almost all of the time but exceptions can occur. For example, HIRE_DATE must be greater than BIRTH_DATE+18 years. This means that all of your employees are expected to be 18 years old or greater. However, if you hire a super-genius who already has a Ph.D. but is only 16 years old, you have an exception to the data rule. Exceptions normally require a businessperson to approve them.

Soft data rules are difficult to deal with. When a violation occurs, it does not necessarily indicate inaccurate data. However, discarding the rule because of the off chance that an exception may occur will block you from finding many truly inaccurate data conditions. It is only logical that you would include these rules for testing and then research each violation to see if it is an exception. This requires additional research after the violations are found. If you determine that an exception has occurred, you do not want to see that same exception each time you execute the rule. This requires more complex rule execution design.

A WELL-DESIGNED *data structure would have a column in the database that indicates whether an exception to a rule has happened. In the example of the age of an employee when they are hired, a column could have been added that includes a flag value for whenever someone is hired who is younger than* 18. *This would allow a very specific rule to be generated that included the phrase IF HIRE_EXCEPTION FLAG NOT 'E'.*

This type of sophistication in database structures is very rare. However, it ought to be used more often to aid in keeping data accurate.

The tighter you define data rules, the more likely a rule crosses the boundary between a hard data rule and a soft data rule. The looser you define data rules, the more inaccurate data conditions you fail to detect. It is a trade-off that each data profiling analyst needs to deal with.

Appendix A shows an example of a small database situation and data rules that can be constructed from them. Studying this example is probably more instructive in explaining data rules than any text.

Data Rules Versus Process Rules

A process rule is one that takes an action based on the values of one or more columns. It may compute the value of another column, create a row in another table, delete a row, or take other actions. These actions generally result in data changing from one state to another.

For example, a business process rule might be that a CUSTOMER is classified as GOOD if the amount of sales last quarter exceeds $10,000 and the number of late payments last quarter is zero and they have no currently overdue invoices. A customer is classified as BAD if the number of late payments last quarter or currently overdue invoices is greater than two. GOOD customers get a 10% discount. BAD customers are not allowed to enter new orders. Other customers get no discount but can enter new orders.

This is a rather lengthy process rule. It defines multiple actions that result from various data points. It causes a customer classification to be set and applies this to the acceptance of new orders and to the setting of the prices for new orders.

Process rules are not intended to be data validation rules. They are used to set values of data, not to determine if values that have been set are correct. These rules can be turned into data rules to test the state of a database to determine if the rules are being used. Violations may mean that the data is inaccurate or that exceptions are being made to the rules.

An important factor to consider when using such process rules is how and when the computations are made. In this example, the rule could be computed periodically, such as weekly, through a batch process. When this is done, there will be a number of rule violations in the database simply because a number of transactions may have taken place since the last time the program was executed. If the logic is executed every time any change is made to the customer's information, it will be more accurate. However, because overdue payments are not a function of a transaction but rather a function of elapsed time, this can also leave a set of records in noncompliance, waiting for another transaction to occur.

Data Rules Versus Column Properties

Data rules always define relationships between multiple data values. Column properties look at individual values in isolation and determine if they are valid, not correct. Column properties consider whether a value is acceptable for any set of conditions for other values. A data rule can be used to restrict the number of valid values for a single column based on other criteria. In essence, it narrows the acceptable values for a single occurrence based on factors outside that column. For example, the values permitted in a column called CLASS_ID would be all currently active class identifiers for the column properties testing. However, the list can be narrowed based on whether the student is a freshman, graduate student, or postdoctoral student. Each category of students can have its own sublist of acceptable values. To determine which sublist to use for validation, you need the value from the STUDENT_LEVEL column.

The process of examining column properties and subsetting them based on other column values is a common source of data rules. Subsetting can be done on discrete values, a range of values, or on NULL acceptability.

10.2 The Process for Analyzing Simple Data Rules

Figure 10.1 shows the basic model for profiling business rules. This is different from the model for handling column properties and data structures. In those cases, discovery routines could be constructed to suggest rules to augment those that were collected externally. In the case of data rules, there is no such discovery. The potential for data rules is almost infinite from a discovery point of view. It would not be practical or beneficial to try to discover data rules from the data.

Data rules have an enormous semantic component. You need to understand how the data relates to other data in the context of how the business chooses to operate. Semantics are not discoverable by a program.

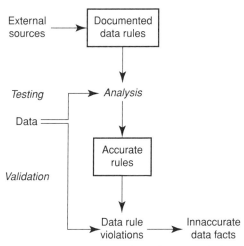

FIGURE 10.1 Process for analyzing simple data rules.

Gathering Data

The first step is to gather the data rules you wish to apply to the data. Most meta-data repositories do not have much in the way of data rules defined in them. There are multiple places to look for rules: source code of the applications that operate over the data, database stored procedures, business procedures surrounding the applications, and speculation using business and data experts.

SOURCE CODE SCAVENGING

Many, many data rules are captured in the thousands of lines of source code that constitute the application software for the data. These applications have code in them that screen for inaccurate data combinations or that set data values based on other values.

Commercial software exists that assists analysts in examining the tons of source code over an application and extracting discrete bits of logic that constitute a specific business rule. Some of these are data rules and some are process rules. An experienced analyst can fabricate testable data rules from them.

Source code scavenging can be very useful in understanding the rules that evolved over time. However, this approach is rarely used. One reason is that the analysts doing the data profiling are not educated in the programming languages used for many legacy systems. Another reason is that the process is very tedious and time consuming. Often there is not enough time to tackle the mountains of source code that surround legacy applications. An additional reason is that the source code may not be available. This is true for packaged applications or for some locally built applications where it just got lost.

THE *existence of source code that enforces a rule or executes a process rule would normally appear to be something that does not need to be tested. However, such is not the case. Violations can still exist in the data for a variety of reasons.*

One reason is that the code you are looking at may not be the only path for the data to enter the database through. In this day of multiple data channels, there may be many different application paths for creating the same data. For example, an order may be placed by a data entry operator using a legacy green-screen application, or it may be placed using a new XML-based Internet application, or still further placed through a pseudo-legacy application built around a 4GL using EDI (Electronic Data Interchange) format as a data source. Each of these paths to the data may apply rules differently. More likely, some would apply a rule and some would not.

Another way for data to get into a violation state is through updates that come through a separate application path. Rules may be enforced on initial entry but not enforced when updates are made.

Another source is ad hoc queries coming from a database administrator or other person who knows how to use SQL to change things. This often gets used to handle emergency problem situations such as failure on load after a reorganization because of a constraint violation.

And yet another source is that the data in question may have been created before the source code was employed. When you look at source code, you are looking at only the code that is executed now, when new data is created. The data in the database may have been created months ago, when the current source code was not in use. If no attempt was made to bring all old data into conformance with a new rule, there may well be many violations of the rule.

Despite all of these difficulties, source code scavenging should always be considered as a step in the process of gathering data rules. If it is not reasonable to do so, fine. At least it should be considered for those cases where it is reasonable to do so.

DATABASE-STORED PROCEDURES

These encompass source code that is added to the database systems to enforce data conditions on data insert, update, or delete. These are sometimes called stored procedures, triggers, editprocs, and other things. This is a common structure in relational database systems and generally not available in older database systems. The concept is to add data qualifying logic to the database engine and have it deny any data entry to the database records that violate it.

Database procedures can be data rules or process rules. For example, an INSERT transaction may trigger the creation of other database records or determine the values of columns through rules or algorithms. A rule may set a CUSTOMER credit worthiness flag to high or low based on values in the INSERT transaction. Database procedures are more likely to hold true over all of the data because it is very difficult to backdoor the database and change things.

Scavenging rules from database-stored procedures is similar to scavenging from application source code. It requires time and an expert in the procedure language. Some of the older database implementations did not preserve the original source language statements for the procedure. The procedure as stored in the database catalog was a compiled pseudo-code of the logic, not the original statements. It is not understandable in that form. In these cases, the logic is embedded in the CREATE TABLE statements and may no longer be available.

You can generally expect to get very little in the way of data rules from this source. Even though the facility is available, the harshness of no violations allowed leads many a database administrator to drop them from the implementation. They can also severely slow down the execution of database calls with subsequent unacceptable response times to transaction applications. This means that they are not used a lot.

One of the problems seen is that an analyst may find a CREATE TABLE script that contains many data rules and assume they are being used, and further assume it is not necessary to test for them. However, the actual database may not have the rules active, because a database administrator may have turned them off. In spite of all of these possibilities, it may be worthwhile to look for them and to convert them into testable data rules.

BUSINESS PROCEDURES

Many data rules are encapsulated in business procedures and not captured in the application logic. Instead, they are instructions to data entry personnel or to business clerks processing various transactions. For example, the assigning of an interest rate to customer loans may be a very distinct business rule, resulting in a potential for a data rule to determine the degree of conformance to the business rule or to find inaccurate data. It may not be executed in any programming language, just a rule for people entering data to follow. The businessperson must determine values externally to the programs and then enter the right value into the database. This leaves plenty of room for inaccurate computations, as well as inaccurate entry of results.

Once a data rule is captured from the business processes, it can be used to test the data for conformance. The fallout can be exceptions to the data rule, incidences of failure to follow the data rule, or inaccurate data entry. The data rule can also be used to automate the process and take much of the error out of operations.

SPECULATION

Another source is to examine the data columns and structure and create data rules using common sense. It can be very helpful to do this to create rules no one would expect to check for. The simple rules that just define common-sense relations between data columns are those that are often not defined and yet yield inaccurate data when tested.

Gathering data rules through speculation is best done in a group setting that includes data structure experts, business analysts, and subject matter experts. Speculation should be done as a last step in the gathering process and should include a review of rules gathered from other sources as well. Examination of the data rules by business analysts and subject matter experts will help improve the completeness and accuracy of the list.

A group setting will yield many rules, probably more than you want to test. The group should prioritize the rules to help sort out which to test.

All of the rules you gather should be recorded in the data profiling repository. These rules are the subject of rule testing. No data rules should be eliminated from the data profiling repository, whether they are used or not.

Testing Simple Data Rules

Once the data rules are gathered, they need to be tested against the profiling data. Testing can be done through a business rule engine, a data quality software product, or by executing query statements against the data. Each data rule should be executed and row identifiers returned for all rows involved in violations. This information should be stored in the data profiling repository so that the analyst investigating the violations can look back through all of the data surrounding each violation.

The reason you want all of this information is that violation of a rule does not reveal inaccurate values. It only reduces the amount of data within which the inaccurate data exists. As long as more than one value is used to test the rule, you cannot tell which value causes the violation. In addition to the values used in the rule execution, surrounding values in the same rows can be used to help research the violation to determine if it is a true violation, if violations are connected to some other factors, or whether it is an exception to the rule.

Because executing data rules against operational systems can be very processing intensive and disruptive, the testing of rules is often done using large samples of data and preferably on separate machines from those used for operational processing. The analyst needs to be able to execute, probe, and poke on the data to find as much information as possible about each data rule. Once the data rules are accepted as valid, they can then be executed against the real data source to find all violations.

Validation of Output Data

After executing the data rules, you need to reconvene the group of reviewers to determine if the output is reasonable. They need to consider whether the data rule formulation was correct, whether the execution was proper, and whether the output represents real violations.

Validation can cause data rules to be changed either because they were formulated wrong or because the output reveals new insights to the business-people. They may have thought a rule was in effect, but the sheer volume of violations leads them to investigate, and they find out that the data rule is not being used or was changed to something else.

It is important to document everything about the output. If data rule exceptions are found instead of inaccurate data, the reason for the exceptions should be documented as well as the number of such exceptions. This may lead to data issues that result in either training for businesspeople or strength-ening of rule conformance processes.

Another important part of this step is to classify rules according to their importance as well as to their value in extracting issues. This is important because rules can be very expensive to execute in operational systems. They consume a lot of processing time and can negatively change the performance characteristics of transactions. Implementors need to make the proper deci-sions about if, where, and when rules are to be executed. They need input from the data profiling process to make these decisions intelligently.

10.3   Profiling Rules for Single Business Objects

This section describes a variety of data rules as examples that can be formu-lated and tested. It classifies rules in order to demonstrate the areas where data rules are normally used. Once you gain a data rule orientation, you will acquire a knack for spotting potential data rules.

Data Rule Execution

Data rule execution can be laborious and expensive. Rule engines may be used to do some of the work. The alternative is to formulate queries over the data for each data rule. This is greatly facilitated if you have put the data into a table form prior to data profiling. Data rule testing against primary data sources that are not in table form and that have not had messy problems resolved, such as column overloading, can be an enormously complex task.

The more data you use, the more machine resources will be burned. However, if you profile over too small a sample, you may not get the results you seek. It is best to use as much of the data as possible for data rule testing.

Data rules do not need to be executed singly. It is possible to combine several rules into a single executable by either using a rule-based engine that can do that for you or formulating complex query statements yourself. If you do this, you can reduce the cost and time of executing data rules, but you have to deal with the problem of separating output by rule (which rule caused which output). Sometimes this is obvious from looking at the data, and other times it is not so obvious.

Types of Data Rules

Searching for data rules begins with a methodical examination of the business meaning of each column in a table. Some very obvious relations between columns surface when you do this. Some of them can be constructed solely on the basis of commonsense logic. Digging out deeper rules requires more extensive knowledge of the business practices of the corporation.

DATES

Columns with a DATE or TIME data type are a good place to start. Some business objects have many dates in them. These dates generally reflect a logical progression of activities regarding the object. For example, an employee has a BIRTH_DATE, HIRE_DATE, LAST_PROMOTION_DATE, RETIREMENT_DATE, and possibly others. A purchase order has an ORDER_DATE, BACK_ORDER_DATE, SHIPPED_DATE, RECEIVED_DATE, INVOICED_DATE, and potential others. These all have an ordering implied in their definitions. Date values that are out of order generally, if not always, indicate that at least one value is inaccurate.

Some objects also include TIME_OF_DAY columns that also can have an implied ordering. For example, START_TIME should always be earlier than STOP_TIME for data-recording repair activities in an auto repair garage, provided the repair activities do not cross over the end of a day.

These fields can be mapped out to determine the expected ordering and then one or more data rules formulated to test for conformance. If all of the dates are in the same row of the table, one query can find all violations. It is generally very easy to spot the violation by examining the output. Examples of validation rules are

SHIPPING_DATE IS NOT EARLIER THAN ORDER_DATE
RECEIVED_DATE IS NOT EARLIER THAN ORDER_DATE
RENEWAL_DATE IS 1 YEAR AFTER CONTRACT_DATE

Other dates that are important in rules are the CURRENT_DATE and a milestone date. Many date fields are not allowed to be later than the CURRENT_DATE. For example, an ORDER_DATE cannot be forward dated. A milestone date is one that sets a boundary for objects. For example, the date a company was founded would be a milestone date for ensuring that no employee had a start date that preceded it. These types of rules are generally not included in this section because they can usually be part of the column value definition, as described in Chapter 8. They generally involve only a single column.

DURATIONS

A time duration is the computation of time between a pair of date and/or time columns. For example, the function YEARS(HIRE_DATE – BIRTHDATE) will determine how old you were when you were hired.

Some durations have boundaries set by the company. For example, a rule may exist that all orders sent to suppliers must be filled in 60 days or be automatically cancelled. A duration of more than 60 days would mean that either the rule was violated on purpose or one of the dates was wrong. Violations of duration rules generally indicate inaccurate data. One of the dates is wrong, causing the duration to be unreasonable. Examples of duration rules are

DAYS(SHIPPING_DATE – ORDER_DATE) LESS THAN 60
YEARS(HIRE_DATE – BIRTHDATE) GREATER THAN OR
  EQUAL TO 18

Duration rules can also check for order of values as discussed earlier. Negative duration values would indicate that values are not in the proper order.

OBJECT SUBGROUPING COLUMNS

Another place to look for simple data rules is to seek columns that divide the object type into subtypes. For example, GENDER divides employees into MALE and FEMALE, MARITAL_STATUS divides employees into MARRIED and NOT_MARRIED, ACCOUNT_TYPE may divide customers into RETAIL and COMMERCIAL, and INVENTORY_TYPE may divide inventory into NORMAL, TIME_SENSITIVE, RADIOACTIVE, and TEMPERATURE CONTROLLED.

This division of the objects into subgroups probably has an impact on the acceptable values in other columns. Some of the columns may be used only for one subtype. In this case they must be NOT_NULL or not blank for that subgroup, and NULL or blank for others. They may also restrict the permitted values in some columns based on the subgroup. Examples of object subgrouping columns rules are

> SPOUSE_NAME IS 'BLANK' IF MARRIED _FLAG IS NOT YES
> DATE_OF_LAST_BIRTH IS NULL IF GENDER IS 'MALE'
> IF EMPLOYEE_TYPE IS 'PART_TIME' THEN PAY_TYPE IS
>   'NONEXEMPT'

Violations of rules such as these are almost always the result of inaccurate data entry. These types of errors can have large impacts on decision support routines that tend to use the subgrouping columns to define comparison groups.

SUBGROUPING *rules are particularly useful in finding sloppy data in large databases involving health or health insurance information. Errors generally have little to do with getting claims paid. However, they have a large impact on any attempts to mine information from aggregations over the data.*

Common errors found are misentering GENDER or AGE (BIRTH_DATE). Simple checks generally yield a number of men having babies or other female-only procedures and children having diseases only possible in adults or the other way around.

These types of inaccuracies are easy to get into the database because these columns are rarely part of a key. In addition, the columns that depend on them are often specified as being NULL_ALLOWED because some of the time they require NULL and other times they do not. The database systems do not have the capability of enforcing conditional NULL rules. This means that there is no database support for catching problems at entry. It requires data rule formulation and execution to discover inaccuracies.

WORK FLOW

A similar type of rule involves data objects that record multiple steps in a process. As each step is completed, more data is added to the object. Each of the points in the process defines a "state" the data can be in. Each state generally involves some columns that are applicable only to that state. This means that if the step has not completed yet for a state, the columns with affinity to that state should be NULL. If the step has completed, they should be NOT NULL.

Work flow rules are a subset of process rules. Data rules can be constructed from them to determine the correctness of values within each valid state.

As in the previous section, the database systems are not functionally sufficient to enforce this conditional NULL rule. A data rule is needed to ensure that all columns conform to the requirements of the current state.

The state may not affect only whether other columns are empty or not. It may also restrict the content of another column to a subset of the values permitted in value analysis.

Examples of work flow data objects are ORDERS (placed, shipped, received, returned, cancelled), LOAN_APPLICATION (requested, reviewed, accepted or rejected, made), and EMPLOYMENT_APPLICATION (received, reviewed, interviewed, background check, offered/rejected, employed). Examples of data rules for work flow process rules are

IF APPLICATION_STATUS IS "REVIEWED" THEN
　INTEREST_RATE IS NULL
IF APPLICATION_STATUS IS "ACCEPTED" THEN
　INTEREST_RATE IS NOT NULL

DERIVED-VALUE RULES

Sometimes a column is determined by consideration of values from other columns through a business procedure or policy. Setting a customer rating or a risk factor on a security investment are examples. If the rules for setting these values are deterministic enough, they can be converted into data rules to test against the data. An example is

IF INVENTORY_USAGE_LAST6MONTHS IS 0 AND ONHAND IS
　GREATER THAN 0 THEN SALVAGE_FLAG=YES

Sometimes the business rule is vague, allowing discretion on a businessperson, and thus cannot be conveniently encoded as a data rule. However, a subset of the business rule may be absolute and can be encoded as a valid test. For example, a rule that defines a BAD customer as opposed to a GOOD customer may be very complex and allow some leeway. However, within the rule it may be an absolute that a customer with an OVERDUE amount in excess of $100,000 that is overdue by more than 90 days is a BAD customer. Even though some of the criteria for a BAD customer is open to discretion, this part of the rating process is not. The part that is an absolute can be converted into a data rule and tested.

RULES INVOLVING MULTIPLE ROWS OF SAME COLUMN

The rules shown so far involve values contained in a single row. Sometimes an object has multiple rows for parts of the data object. For example, an ORDER has line item detail rows; a project has multiple people working on it. Rules can apply to these that involve looking at more than one row at a time but still within the boundaries of the single data object.

An example is testing for uniqueness across the PRODUCT_ID column of ORDER_LINE_ITEMS. This is a column that is not unique across the entire table but is expected to be unique across the rows of each order. In this example, it appears that only one column was being used. However, there were actually three columns used: PRODUCT_ID, ORDER_NUMBER, and LINE_ITEM_NUMBER. Another example of this is a data rule that says that multiple entries for the same employee for emergency contact cannot have the same telephone number.

OTHER DATA RULES

Of course, additional data rules can be created that are not included in the samples shown. Many are more complex than those shown here. These are generally data rules dealing with business policies. Many times these rules are soft rules that are allowed to be violated at times. Examples are

> EXPENSE LINE ITEMS FOR A SINGLE EXPENSE REPORT CAN-NOT INCLUDE DATES FOR MORE THAN ONE WEEK WHERE A WEEK IS DEFINED AS SUNDAY THROUGH SATURDAY

> AN ORDER CANNOT INCLUDE ITEMS THAT REQUIRE DIFFERENT SHIPPING MODES

10.4 Mapping with Other Applications

For projects that involve more than just data quality assessment, there remains a step for matching data rules from source systems to target systems. This is an important step that is often overlooked, only to cause problems after the data has been moved to the new environment. Mapping analysis varies by type of project, although the comparison process is the same.

Migrating to a New Application

When replacing an existing application with a new one (often a packaged application), you need to consider the business and data rules of the new system. It does not much matter if a rule required of the old system is not enforced by the new system. The important point is to ensure that the data in the old system will support the rules of the new system. If they do not, it may be difficult to move the data from the old to the new. If the data is movable, you will end up with some of the data being in violation of new system rules.

If possible, identify the data rules of the new system and use them in profiling the data from the old system. This means restating them relative to the column names and structure of the old system. In this way, you can see the violations that exist in the old data before it is moved.

The best way to profile is to profile both the rules of the old system and the rules of the new system. Ignoring old system rules leaves open the possibility of not finding inaccurate data in the old system. This is useful whether it causes data migration problems in the new system or not.

When you are done, you need to look at all of the rules. If a rule exists in the old system and not the new system, you need to consider whether the new system ought to have the rule. If the rule expresses a business policy, you may have uncovered a difference in behavior of the new system that the conversion team needs to consider. If a rule exists in the new system and not the old system, you need to consider whether it is necessary in the new system. If it is valid in both systems, you do not have to be concerned.

Incompatible rules become issues the conversion team needs to resolve. Often they can change the customizing parameters of the new system to make it behave more like the old system and more like the corporation wants it to behave. If data is incompatible, the team has to craft a transformation method to allow the old data to populate the new system.

Consolidating Systems

Projects that combine data from more than one system have to consider how rules play against each other in the various systems. These projects are generally spawned by mergers and acquisitions where the source systems were built and maintained without any knowledge of the other systems. The probability that all data structure and rules will line up is next to zero.

As in the previous section, you need to profile all of the rules of each system against their respective data in order to dig out inaccurate data. You will then know which rules are applicable to each system. You then need to identify the rules of the target system and profile those rules against the data in each of the source systems to determine which data will cause problems in the consolidation. This is identical to the process defined in the previous section.

In consolidations, you may be pushing all data to a new target system or picking one of the existing source systems and using that as the target. In any case, the analysis of data rules and their compatibility with the data can influence the decisions made on which system to use as the target or in how to modify the target system to be more accommodating of the data.

Extracting into Decision Support Systems

Data rules are generally not of particular concern in databases built from operational systems and used for reporting or decision support. The important point of these databases is that they contain accurate data. The only reason the data import functions would execute a data rule would be to check for inaccurate data. This means that there is really no matching of rules to be done. Carrying forward rule checks to the load process may be indicated by the amount of violations detected in data profiling. A better solution would be to add the checkers to the operational systems and get the data clean long before it is moved to the decision support data stores.

10.5 Simple Data Rule Remedies

The analysis of data rules generally involves creating several new data rules that are not implemented anywhere in the operational systems. Violations indicate the presence of inaccurate data or of excessive exceptions to rules. Because most system developers are not rule oriented, this presents a large amount of new material that can be incorporated into their operational systems or company procedures to prevent errors from getting into databases or to improve the design of the systems themselves.

System developers are becoming more and more aware of rule approaches to building better systems. This encompasses not only data rules but process rules. This leads to a better documentation of rules, standardization on how and where rules are executed in operational systems, and using rules for feedback.

The data profiling process will identify a number of data rules, along with test results from applying them to real data. The logical process to follow at this point is to evaluate the usefulness of the rules and to determine how they can play a role in improving operational systems. Not all rules can be handled the same way. Some are more suitable for direct monitoring of transactions and some are not. It is the job of the analyst to determine what is the best disposition of each rule.

Data Rule Evaluation

Not all data rules are equal. Some have important business implications if not followed, and others do not.

Some rules have no violations. This is often because checks exist somewhere in the data acquisition process that enforce the rule, thus making it impossible for violations to exist after the data is entered. For example, if screen specifications for entering orders and subsequent steps always use the CURRENT DATE to fill in date fields for ORDER_DATE, SHIPPING_ DATE, and RECEIVED_DATE, these columns will always have correct values and the ordering rules will not turn up violations.

It is always important to test rules in the data profiling process regardless of whether you think they are enforced in operational systems or not. You are sometimes fooled into thinking they cannot be violated only to discover that there is an alternative way for data to enter that causes problems. However, after profiling the data, you have a better idea of which rules expose most of the problems.

You cannot put all data rules into operational settings. They will consume too much system resource and slow down the systems. If you attempt to, some database administrator or other steward of the operational systems will take them out to achieve the performance goals of the applications.

RULES THAT CAN BE CHECKED DURING DATA ENTRY

These are rules that can be checked during data entry and that would not incur significant overhead in processing. The checking logic can be placed in code at the data entry station (usually a personal computer) and requires no system time to execute. These data rules generally only involve interaction between values in the transaction. They do not generally involve reading data at the server side.

RULES THAT SHOULD BE CHECKED DURING TRANSACTION PROCESSING

These data rules are important enough to spend valuable server-side processing time to check in order to avoid improper data from entering a database. They are done at the server end because they require access to data that is not in the transaction. They usually execute within the context of the transaction, sending rejection or confirmation information back to the data entry station within the context of the transaction.

RULES THAT SHOULD BE DEFERRED FOR EXECUTION

These are rules that are more complex and require extensive machine resources to execute. They show few violations in the data. The checking for these rules can be deferred until a periodic sweep of the database can be done.

RULES THAT DO NOT NEED TO BE CHECKED

These are rules that do not show violations. Analysis of operational systems assures you that the rule will not be violated on data entering the database.

You may be willing to accept some others that do not have any significant amount of violations and for which the consequences of a violation are not important. This choice would be made to avoid overloading operational systems.

You may want to reexecute these rules in the data profiling venue periodically to ensure that they continue to have little operational value. Systems change a lot, and so do people executing data acquisition processes. A rule may move up in importance if a change starts causing more inaccuracies.

Data Rule Checkers for Transactions

Checkers in transaction code can be implemented for rules in the second category previously mentioned. These can be implemented as screen logic, application server programs, database procedures, or by the insertion of a rule engine for processing. When this remedy is used, the data profiling repository should keep track of where the rule is executing.

Note that almost all rules for individual business objects can be checked this way. Because only the data of a single object is involved, it never takes much resource to perform the check.

The point in the data flow process where a rule is executed can be influenced by what data is available at each point in the process. If the data entry screens contain all of the columns in the rule, the checking can be done right on the screen and the transaction stopped before it enters the transaction path. If it requires fetching some of the data that is not on the screen but already in the database, processing may be deferred until later in the process.

Data Rule Checkers for Periodic Checks

Batch programs can be written that sweep the database periodically and look for rule violations. This should be done for rules that are not appropriate for transaction checking. Almost none of the single business object rules fall into this category.

Improving Business Procedures

Analysis of the results of data rule execution may uncover the need to alter business policies and practices. This can occur in either direction. A rule often violated may indicate that the corporation is really not following the rule. Evaluation of the business process may uncover the fact that the rule is no longer applicable and should be discarded.

Similarly, the frequent violation of a rule that is deemed to be important may lead to changes in business practices that ensure that the rule is honored either all of the time or that acceptable exceptions are made. Analysis of results may also indicate the opportunity to provide feedback to people generating the data. They may not be aware of the mistakes they are making or the existence of a rule.

Maintaining a Data Rule Repository

If you have gone through the process of generating a library of data rules, tested the rules against the data, and then used the output to generate issues for system improvements, it only makes sense that you would want to preserve all of this information for future use. It is extremely important to either capture the data rule in the data profiling repository or move it to a rule engine repository or an enterprise repository at the end of data profiling. You will want to use these rules to check improvements, ensure data continues to conform, and as the basis for system change decisions in the future.

10.6 Closing Remarks

Data rule execution is different from the data profiling described in the last two chapters. For columns and structure, you are looking for inaccurate data. Any violations point to wrong data. For data rules, you may be looking at inaccurate data, or you may be looking at correct data that results from the business activity violating one of its business rules. The responsibility of the data is to record the truth. If an exception to a rule is made in the business, the data should reflect this.

Data rule analysis can lead to paralysis through analysis. An overly zealous analyst can dream up countless rules that can be tested. Some of these will prove to be worthwhile, and some will not. A good data profiling analyst can reach a balance between too many rules and not enough rules.

Data rule analysis is an area that is ignored too often. The problem is that data quality assessment is sometimes considered the role of business analysts. To be effective at rule definition, execution, and interpretation, you need to be an expert at SQL or some other rule language. These tend to be very programming oriented. Many business analysts do not have the education or experience to be effective at doing this. They try, it becomes too much of a challenge, and they give up.

The opposite is also true. Rules are, by their very nature, semantically based. This means that the business analyst is the only realistic expert in identifying and expressing them. The technical person who is adept at SQL in all likelihood does not understand the business side. If they are left alone, they will formulate some very obvious and not too important rules.

To make this work, you need a strong working partnership between multiple people who together possess all of the skills needed. Without it, not much rule testing will be done.

Failure to take this step seriously leaves a number of problems undiscovered. By now it should be apparent that each data profiling topic discovers different problems in the data. Leaving out a step will just reduce the effectiveness of the assessment.

The next chapter stays on the topic of data rules. It talks about types of rules that apply to sets of business objects instead of single business objects. These two topics were separated merely to make it easier to describe. Everything said in this chapter about data rules applies equally to the next chapter.

CHAPTER 11

Complex Data Rule Analysis

This chapter is a continuation of the last chapter. This one deals with data rules that require a set of business objects to test over instead of looking inside just one business object at a time. Most of the information of the previous chapter applies equally to this chapter.

This is just another part of the process of trying to find as many data rules as possible that can be used to find evidence of inaccurate data. Data can look correct completely within all business objects, satisfying value, structure, and data rule tests but incompatible in the context of data in other business objects. Because these data rules involve multiple objects, finding incompatibilities does not identify the offending data, it simply narrows the amount of data within which the wrong data exists.

11.1 Definitions

The terms *business object* and *data rule* were defined in the previous chapter. What remains is a definition of a set of business objects.

Business Object Set

This is a collection of business object instances that can be isolated in terms of columns of the objects. Each object instance remains a discrete entity within the set. The set can include multiple instances of the same business object type; for example, all inventory rows for each discrete part type. They can also include rows from multiple different business object types; for example, supplier information combined with orders sent to each supplier. A business object set may include all of the data in a table. The set is everything.

A business object set requires a definition of how to select multiple instances or how to join rows between tables. These definitions divide the rows of tables in groups of business object instances data rules can be applied to. Examples of selection criteria are each REGION, each DIVISION, each TYPE_CODE, and LAST MONTH.

The set may consist of all of the data in one database combined with the data in another database. This would be considered when data is partitioned across multiple databases or when data is being profiled in anticipation of consolidation.

Data Rules

Data rules are the same for sets as for individual objects. However, they have at least one component that is new. They must define the set.

Another structure you see in data rules concerning sets of objects you do not see with data rules for individual objects is aggregation functions. The rule may involve a test against a COUNT, SUM, AVERAGE, or STANDARD DEVIATION.

Hard Versus Soft Rules

Data rules for sets of objects can be hard rules or soft rules, just as in the case of single-object data rules.

Data Rules Versus Process Rules

Most of the rules in this category are the result of process rules. They can be very complex. You probably will not find them in business procedures because they do not represent transactional activity. You will probably not find them documented at all.

11.2 The Process for Profiling Complex Data Rules

Figure 11.1 shows the process model for profiling data rules over sets of business objects. It is substantially the same as in the case of single-object data rules. The complexity of these rules and the semantic nature of them makes them not amenable to discovery. There is no step for the discovery of complex data rules.

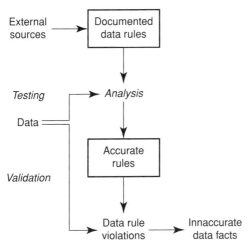

FIGURE 11.1   Process for profiling complex data rules.

Gathering Data

You can use the same sources you did with simple data rules. However, there are some differences in these rules, described in the sections that follow.

SOURCE CODE SCAVENGING

These types of rules are rarely scavenged from source code. Most rules embedded in code are rules that can be applied to a single transaction. Rarely does source code perform checks that involve extensive checking of an entire database before it allows a transaction to execute.

Some of these rules require that a period of time elapse before all data is present to process the rule. These types of rules cannot be executed on a transaction basis but must be executed whenever it is thought that the collection is complete. This means that if you intend to look for rules in source code, look for programs that run against the database at the end of a week, month, quarter, or some time interval.

DATABASE-STORED PROCEDURES

Complex data rules are almost never embedded in database procedure logic. Database-stored procedure logic generally involves only the data of a single transaction or only one instance of a business object. Data rules over sets of business objects normally do not fit this model.

BUSINESS PROCEDURES

Business procedures will also generally be lacking because they concern themselves mostly with processing a single transaction. Sometimes they come into play when considering objects that have a characteristic that cannot invade the space of another object. This is discussed later.

SPECULATION

The most fruitful source of rules is again speculation: sitting down with the business analysts and subject matter experts and building data rules that should hold true over a collection of data.

Testing Data Rules

Data rules are crafted and then executed against the data to find violations. This is not anything new. What is new is that you are looking at sets of business objects and not individual objects. This requires that the data you use to test against must contain all relevant data. Taking samples may result in violations that are not true violations. In addition, extracting the data for data profiling at the wrong time can also result in the data being incomplete relative to the grouping function. For example, if the grouping function is MONTHLY, you cannot take the data for only part of a month; you have to wait for the month to end and get it all.

Validation of Output Data

As before, the results need to be examined by the same team of analysts and business experts to determine if the data rule is correct and to determine the meaning of violations. Accepted data rules need to be recorded in the data profiling repository. Data violations need to be converted to data issues if they warrant it.

11.3 Profiling Complex Data Rules

The data profiling process is not dissimilar to that for the previous section. You formulate a process for each data rule and execute it against the data. The difference is that you need to ensure that the data used is complete, and the execution time required can be much higher.

Data Rule Execution

Multiple-object rules tend to be much more complicated in their processing logic. Often it is not possible to formulate them as an SQL query. It may require a special program or script of SQL statements to be written by an application developer to test a data rule.

Formulation of the process is very important. They must not only accurately reflect the data rule but be optimized. Some of the data rules will require comparing every record in a table to every other record in the table. If not carefully crafted, this type of process can run for a very long time. Because these rules can require complex logic to execute, it is also possible that the logic is flawed. This means that you should run tests on the data rule logic before you run it against the real database.

Some rules may require access to data from more than one database at the same time. This may involve a scheduling or access issue. If the data is extracted and staged for profiling, it is important that the data from all sources conform to the same time-boundary requirements.

Note how this step often requires collaboration and cooperation with application programmers and database administrators. Everything runs much more smoothly if these folks are involved in the process early and are excited about what they are being asked to do.

Types of Complex Data Rules

Data rules for multiple business objects can take a large variety of forms. This section presents some of the more common forms to provide examples of what to look for. There are two broad categories of complex data rules: data rules that deal with column values and data rules dealing with aggregation.

DATES AND TIME

One category of multiple business object data rules is where multiple instances of the same object type cannot share the same space at the same time. The obvious example of this is date-and-time space.

An example of this is rental records for equipment. The data rule is that a single piece of equipment cannot be rented out at the same time to more than one client. If the records show an overlap, an error exists in the data. The test is to group all records by equipment type. Then for each record you need to check all other records. The testing logic (assuming all records have start date/times earlier than end date/times) is as follows:

```
IF RECORD2.END_DATE&TIME IS EARLIER THAN
    RECORD1.START_DATE&TIME THEN OK
ELSE IF RECORD2.START_DATE&TIME IS LATER THAN
    RECORD1.END_DATE&TIME THEN OK
ELSE ERROR;
```

Sorting the records by OBJECT_IDENTIFIER and START_DATE& TIME makes execution more efficient. This example is true of anything that requires serial usage. For example, checking books out of a library, scheduling of conference rooms, billable-time consulting hours, billable time for lawyer charges, flying records for corporate jets, or expense records for executives or salesmen can all be checked for overlap inconsistencies using this logic.

This testing can go one step further for objects that should have a record for all or most time periods to compute the time period durations between any rental or checkout. If these are unexpectedly long, it may indicate either inaccurate dates in some of the records or missing records. Durations of checkout time periods can also be looked at to determine if they are too short to be reasonable.

AN *interesting application that demonstrates these principles is genealogy. Records that define a person in a family tree must satisfy a number of date and time relationships with others in the tree. For example, someone listed as a father of a person must have a reasonable duration of time between his birth date and the birth date of the child. The duration of each person's life must be reasonable. A child cannot be born after a parent is dead. In addition to these checks, it begs for checks for multiple fathers or mothers listed for the same person, as well as other relationships that make no sense.*

LOCATION

Time may not be the only factor that causes two objects to be incompatible. Location may be as well. For example, consider an inventory database that has a column for storage location down to the bin number. If you discovered two or more discrete items with the same physical location, this would indicate that an inaccuracy exists.

OTHER TYPES OF EXCLUSIVITY

There may be other columns that have an exclusion relationship across the rows of a database. For example, consider the SPOUSE column of a personnel record. You would not expect two employees to share the same spouse.

The way this error happens is that one employee gets a divorce and the spouse marries someone else in the same company. The first person fails to update personnel records to show the change in marital status. When the second person updates his record, the database has an incompatibility. This is an example of data decay that is surfaced through analysis of the SPOUSE column using a data rule.

Anytime you have the requirement that the value of one column cannot be shared with other objects and the column is not a structural column that would be enforced through database key processing, you probably have errors that have gone undetected. Profiling these columns will determine the extent of errors in the column and lead you to determining if corrective actions are needed or not.

AGGREGATIONS

Aggregations are tests not on individual column values but rather on a computation over a group of objects. The types of aggregation values that can be the subject of the rule are COUNT, SUM, AVERAGE, MEDIAN, STANDARD DEVIATION, or anything else that makes sense.

These are good rules for checking for completeness. For example, you may know that the number of trips taken by a truck should be greater than 10 per month. This is the minimum any truck would take. The rule might be

GROUPBY TRUCK, MONTH
IF OUT-OF-SERVICE NOT YES
THEN NUMBER_TRIPS GREATER THAN 10

Sometimes computations are made and checked against data from a different source. For example, accounting records may be required to cross-reference against data maintained at the departmental level.

LOOKUP

Another way of identifying the existence of inaccurate data is to check the data in a database with corresponding data in another database that should be the same. The simplest form of correlation is lookup. You have a column in the subject database that must contain only values that are in another file or database column. This is another form of verifying that the value is in the set of acceptable values. Reasons this would not be considered a column property (list of acceptable values) may be that the list is too long to encapsulate in metadata or that the list changes over time.

The next step up is a case in which the value in the subject database has a key and the key can be used to look up the corresponding value in another database. For example, an employee Social Security number on a 401K record can be correlated against the employee Social Security number in the HR database. In this case, there are two columns involved, employee number (or name) and Social Security number. If they do not correlate, the error may be in either (or both) columns.

Correlations can get more complicated. For example, in name and address error checking, you can use a database supplied by the U.S. Postal Service that identifies all valid combinations of street name and number, city, state, and Zip code. Name and address correlation is best done with specialized software designed exclusively for that purpose. This is so complicated and important that entire companies have emerged that provide this software.

The other source can either be more trusted or less trusted. If trusted, the lookup source is considered correct when they differ. Less trusted sources can also be used. If they deliver a difference and you have found an inaccurate data situation, you just do not know which one is wrong. In addition, remember that when verifying with less trusted sources you may get correlation while both values are wrong.

You need to be careful when establishing a correlation test. Sometimes the test is not valid but appears to be so. For example, an ORDER_DETAIL record may contain a UNIT_PRICE field, as does the INVENTORY record. What appears to be duplicate data may be tempting to use for accuracy correlation. However, the UNIT_PRICE in the order detail may be different for two reasons: it reflects the unit price on the date the order was placed, not on the current date, or the customer was given a special unit price just for that order. This underscores the need to understand your data thoroughly.

11.4 Mapping with Other Applications

As in the other steps of data profiling, you need to map complex data rules from source systems to target systems when migrating applications and consolidating data sources. The types of data rules described in this section are likely to be very important to the target system because they represent business policy.

Decision support systems would rarely have code to check data rules of these types. They assume that the data coming to them is accurate and that any checking has occurred either in the operational systems or in the transformation process.

11.5 Multiple-Object Data Rule Remedies

All of the discussion of rule remedies in the previous chapter apply to these as well. The difference is that remedies for these types of rules are more likely to result in programs that check the data on a periodic basis rather than being inserted into transactional processing. Database management system procedures are generally not appropriate for these types of data rules.

As in the previous chapter, rules need to be evaluated as to whether they need to be included in remedies or not, based on their proclivity to find inaccurate data. Because they are expensive to create, maintain, and operate, this becomes more important. If several violations occur, it may be valuable to review the business procedures surrounding these rules and to consider changing them.

11.6 Closing Remarks

This concludes the description of using data rules to find evidence of inaccurate data. This step is not easy and requires staff that is very good at formulating correct and efficient queries. And yet, the content is mostly business oriented. It again calls for a team effort between good technical staff and good business staff.

At this point in data profiling you have completed all of the testing that defines explicit data rules. If you have done everything as described, you have done a lot of work and have a very solid handle on the accuracy of your metadata and the accuracy of your data. The next chapter describes how to use other types of computations to indicate the presence of inaccurate data. They are not rules in that they do not specify what the data should say. They are computations that will alert you to problems if their results are too far from being reasonable.

CHAPTER 12

Value Rule Analysis

The previous four chapters discussed column properties, data structures, and data rules that provide a specific definition of what is valid and what is invalid. For "soft" data rules, the rule is very specific about what constitutes correct, whereas a violation may have been caused by someone making an exception to the rule. However, the data rule itself is a clear definition of what the data ought to be.

There are additional tests you can construct that point to the presence of inaccurate data that are not as precise in establishing a clear boundary between right and wrong. These are called value rules. You compute a value or values from the data and then use visual inspection to determine if the output is reasonable or not. You can easily distinguish between the extremes of reasonable and unreasonable but cannot be sure about the center, fuzzy area.

This type of analysis will surface gross cases of data inaccuracies. Surprisingly, this is possible even when all of the column values are valid values and there is no external reason to suspect a problem.

12.1 Definitions

There are only a couple of definitions that apply here. These are common-sense definitions that will help to understand this chapter.

Value Rules

A value rule is the computation of one or more values from real data. It can mean anything that is computed from either selection of data values, summaries of values, or computations over the values. The results can be put in a file, on a report, in a spreadsheet, or anywhere that facilitates review. They can also be recorded in the data profiling repository for a permanent record of results.

Visual Inspection

This is the process of reviewing the results of a value test to determine whether the result matches your expectations. Because value tests are not hard-rule tests, the expectations will be very broad in nature. You are looking for surprises.

12.2 Process for Value Rule Analysis

The process is shown in Figure 12.1. It is a simple process of creating the tests, executing them, and reviewing results. You generally do not have these defined before you perform data profiling, because these are not normally considered part of the metadata for an application.

Gathering Value Rules

You need to gather value rules from the user community. Those who understand the application and work with the data every day can provide valuable input. This includes business analysts and subject matter experts. The data

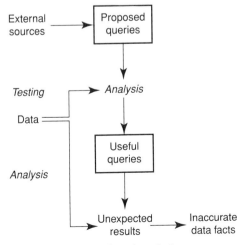

FIGURE 12.1 Value rule analysis process.

profiling analyst may want to suggest some value tests that seem obvious from the nature of the data. Others will not be obvious.

These types of tests are just quick checks of the data to see if it conforms to some very broad indicators of completeness and correctness. It is not intended to be an extensive processing of the data, producing complex reports that require many hours to review. Accountants commonly produce such reports to check the reasonableness of data before doing their normal cycle of reports and audits. This is analogous to that.

You need to create an expectation of results before you execute them. This expectation should have been part of the reason for creating the test in the first place. Expectations should be documented. Often this is done as a range of possible outputs. For example, you may expect the percentage of BLUE gadgets in the INVENTORY database to be between 5 and 10%. You are setting the boundaries for judging whether the output is reasonable or not.

The generated tests and expectations need to be documented in the data profiling repository. If they prove to be useful for data profiling, they may be useful for periodic use in the operational setting.

Executing Value Rules

Because value rules often deal with aggregation values, it is important that all of the data be used. This means that attention must be paid to time period boundaries such as WEEK, MONTH, or QUARTER. Ensuring that all of the data for the period is included is necessary for some of the tests to have any meaning.

Using samples may produce alarming results even though the data may be accurate. The reason for this is that samples may include only some of the data within each discrete set. If sampling is used, complete sets of business objects need to be samples, not just randomly selected rows from the tables representing the business objects.

Evaluating Results

The results need to be verified in a group setting with the data profiling analyst and the business experts. You are looking for large deviations from normal. If the results are close to normal, they may be hiding some data inaccuracies. However, it is not worth the time to validate every value produced.

The results should be compared to the expectations. You should always have expectations in advance. If the result is outside the boundary of the expectation, you need to investigate the cause. It may be that the data is either incomplete or inaccurate, or it may be that the test was implemented inaccurately or possibly that the expectations were inaccurate.

After the first time through, you can tune the test and the expectations. Sometimes the expectations were set through a false understanding of the data. Investigation of deviations hopefully will educate the team on the nature of the data and allow them to set the expectations correctly.

Another useful activity is to compare the expectations to those produced in a prior execution of the test. Once you are comfortable with the test, you can repeat the test periodically and compare output sets. This may reveal trends within acceptable levels of values that may further extend your understanding of the data.

You may also decide to discard a test after seeing the results. It may be that the variability of the data is high enough to prevent setting expectations narrowly enough to be helpful. Either you are always investigating differences only to find no issues, or you are never investigating differences because the boundaries are set too far apart to catch anything. It is a perfectly valid response to discard a value test.

There may be data quality issues that result from this evaluation. Some of the issues will have very specific identification of inaccurate data, and others will have only the outward manifestation without being able to identify specific wrong values.

12.3 Types of Value Rules

Value rules can take on a large variety of forms. The data itself will suggest rules that make sense. Most of them, however, have to do with computations over the data.

Cardinality

A simple computation of the cardinality of a column along with a count of the number of rows can reveal disparities. If the column is expected to consist mostly but not always of separate values, a larger than expected disparity may indicate that there are excessive duplicates. A check of the cardinality against the number of rows can indicate if the values are reasonably varied over the data.

A higher than expected cardinality may indicate a number of things. It may indicate that you have more values than you expect. It may indicate that some data values are represented in multiple ways. It may also indicate misspellings of values.

For example, a corporation may expect that it does business in only 10 states. The database has many duplicates. However, if the cardinality of the column is determined to be 25, an investigation is needed. It may be that the state column values are inconsistently recorded, some of the state codes are mistyped, or you do business in more states than you thought. It is possible that all three things are going on in the data. The cardinality test just alerts you to dig deeper into the data.

Frequency Distributions

Another, deeper check is to select all of the distinct values in a column along with the frequency with which they occur. This list can then be sorted to generate a list by frequency of occurrence. You can compute cardinality at the same time.

This is a very useful tool. There are a number of inaccurate data situations that pop out when it is done.

A report from this can list all of the values. If the value list is too long to reasonably view, it can show the fringes: values that have the highest number of occurrences and those that have the lowest number of occurrences. A graphical chart showing the frequencies can also make it easier to spot potential problems.

This list should show all of the NULL and blank values and the frequency with which they occur within the column. These are very valuable numbers to have. The types of expectations that can be set are

- the number of distinct values

- the maximum frequency expected from any one value

- the frequency expectation of all values for small value sets

- the percentage of values expected to be NULL or blank

THIS *particular test was the one used to find the large number of misspellings of the color BEIGE found in an auto insurance claim database. It not only* *indicated far too many values but was small enough of a list to actually spot all of the wrong values.*

You can also spot cases in which an encoded value is not used at all. The expectation is that a value should exist for at least some number but, in fact, does not. It would be clever in this case to merge the expected value list in the metadata and include both in the result set. A frequency of zero would indicate that they were not present.

The list can be spell-checked. If the list contains words that are not in a dictionary, this can be a useful exercise.

This type of test is very useful in finding data entry problems. In addition to misspelling and alternative ways of expressing the same value, it can spot cases in which data entry people make up values when they do not know the correct value. People tend to use the same wrong value when they do this. Of course, this only applies to cases in which a single data entry person enters a lot of data. These inaccurate values show up as values with higher than expected frequencies.

In Internet applications that collect data that people do not consider the collector's business, this will spot the famous Donald Duck *and* Mickey Mouse *entries in the NAME field. Even though each person enters only one form, these made-up values tend to be used by many people. A look at only duplicates beyond some number will show a variety of popular names used as aliases for people.*

You may be surprised at even valid names that appear with an unusual number of occurrences. For example, *if you looked at the high-frequency first names of people, you would expect to see a lot of JOHN values. If the most popular name to appear is GAVIN, you might have a problem.*

You cannot set expectations on individual names, but you can look at the fringe lists on frequency and spot some very interesting facts. Once you have done this, you can set goals to eliminate bad data entry and check for this particular list of offending names in the future.

Extreme Values

A continuation of this theme is to look at extreme values. Extreme values are values that contain particular characters that are not expected. Extreme characters may be punctuation marks and numerics or other special characters (such as line enders).

Extreme values may be difficult to spot on a value/frequency list if the characters are embedded within the value and are not leading characters. If they are leading characters, they may turn up on the fringe of a value/ frequency list. If they are embedded, they will not.

For example, any list that contains names, company names, product descriptions, and the like would not be expected to have most special characters and numbers embedded. You might expect dashes and dots, but you would not expect characters such as *&^%#@?).

You can be fooled. For example, there is a company named I2. This means that you cannot make a hard rule to exclude numbers. However, you can extract all values and their frequencies that have unexpected characters embedded within them. This should be a short list that can be visually inspected to determine if errors exist or not.

Extreme values on numbers and dates would normally be determined through the column properties' definitions by setting boundaries. However, an area where this can apply is in the computation of durations of time between two dates. Extremely short or extremely long durations may indicate a problem. In essence you can produce a value/frequency list on durations between two date columns. These could be graphed in a chart for easy spotting of high and low occurrences.

Sometimes, highest and lowest values for numbers, dates, and durations are valid values by column property definitions but are not expected in significant numbers. You would expect only a small number of purchases of office supplies to exceed $5,000. If you have a large number of these, you may need to investigate to find out why.

Group Comparisons

In the last chapter we saw rules being set for group aggregations such as COUNT, SUM, AVERAGE, and so on. Sometimes you need to just compute the values and look at them to determine if they are reasonable or not. Sometimes it is not possible to set the values precisely enough to create a rule, but you can eyeball results from a list and then decide if they require more investigation.

12.4 Remedies for Value Rule Violations

Issues resulting from value tests can take the same path as those of other data profiling activities if they uncover data inaccuracies as the cause of output deviations. However, they lend themselves to additional remedies through adding the value tests as part of the operational environment to help data stewards monitor data over time.

This is useful for catching changes that are negatively affecting the quality of data, for capturing metrics on the impact of improvements made, or to catch one-time problems such as the loss of a batch of data or trying to push data to a summary store before all detail data is collected.

Transaction Checkers

Most value tests do not apply to executing transactions because they deal with values over a group of data. However, it is possible to perform continuous monitoring of transactions by caching the last *n* transactions and then periodically, such as every minute or 10 minutes, executing the value test against the cached set. The cache would be designed to kick out the oldest transaction data every time a new one is entered. This is a circular cache.

Although this does little to validate a single transaction, it can catch hot spots where the data accuracy is making a rapid turn for the worse. Profiles of value distributions are particularly appropriate for this type of monitoring. You would not use it for most value tests.

Periodic Checkers

Value tests are particularly suited for execution on a periodic basis: daily, weekly, monthly, or quarterly. They are also useful when performing extractions for moving data to decision support stores. In fact, every extraction should include some tests on the data to ensure that it is a reasonable set of data to push forward. It is much more difficult to back out data after the fact than to catch errors before they are loaded.

Value tests are also very useful to execute on batches of data imported to your corporation from external sources. For example, you may be getting data feeds from marketing companies, from divisions of your own company, and so on. It only makes sense that you would provide some basic tests on the data as part of the acceptance process.

Periodic checks suggest that the steward of the data be able to modify the expectations on a periodic basis as well. Each value rule can have a data profiling repository entry that includes documentation for the test, expectations, and result sets. This facilitates comparing results from one period to another and tracking the changes to expectations.

ONE *of the benefits a data quality assurance group can provide to the business side is to help them formulate a set of quick tests that can be applied to a collection of data to determine its relative health. A concentration on how inaccurate data can distort computations is helpful in building such a suite.*

What is nice about this is that it is fairly easy to do, and execution of the suite is generally very nondisruptive. It can provide valuable visibility to the data quality assurance group and return value quite early in the process of reviewing older systems.

12.5 Closing Remarks

Value tests can be a powerful tool for discovery of inaccurate data. On the surface you would not expect to find much. However, many examples exist of analysts finding severe problems in the data that went unnoticed through normal rule checking.

This is the last step of data profiling. If you have executed all of the steps, you have done a lot of work. You should have a very detailed understanding of the data, an accurate data profiling repository, much additional adjunct information in that repository, a lot of data on inaccurate groups, and a bunch of issues for corrective actions to take to the implementers.

Although the task of data profiling is large, it is generally very rewarding. The returns for just the short-term value of identifying and correcting small problems generally more than offsets the cost and time of performing data profiling.

Data profiling can generally be done with a small team of data profiling analysts, bolstered by part-time team members from the business and data management communities. Compared to other approaches for data quality assessment, it is a low-cost and quick process if the analyst is armed with adequate tools and expertise at performing data profiling. It generally does not take long to gain experience. Most of the process is common sense and follows a natural path through developing and testing rules.

CHAPTER 13

Summary

The intention of this book is to promote the use of analytical techniques in pursuit of better accuracy of data in corporate databases. It has focused on the concept of accurate data and techniques that are particularly suited for finding inaccurate data. It outlines a complete process for formulating metadata rules and using them to efficiently evaluate data and to improve the completeness and accuracy of the metadata.

The book has several specific messages that together make a story. A summary of that story follows.

13.1 Data Quality Is a Major Issue for Corporations

➤ *Corporate databases are plagued with poor-quality data.* The quality has become an ever-increasing problem.

Can anyone doubt that this is true? The evidence is everywhere. The problem of poor data quality is pervasive, affecting all organizations with significant information systems activity. Corporate executives no longer deny data quality problems. Data quality is getting on more radars all the time.

➤ *The cost to corporations for poor data quality is high.* Corporations generally do not know the cost.

Quality improvement programs routinely disclose a sufficient number of issues to demonstrate the high cost of poor data quality. The number is always higher than anticipated. Day-to-day operational costs due to bad data are estimated as high as 20% of operating profit.

➤ *The cost of poor data quality is increasing.* The quality of data is decreasing.

As corporations get more complex through product line expansions, mergers, and acquisitions, requirements to comply with increasingly complex government regulations, and many other factors, the demands on data go up. As corporations move data up the food chain to play increasing roles in corporate decision making, the cost of poor-quality data is magnified. The increasing use of the Internet as a data source and the acquisition of data from outside the corporation are causing a decrease in the quality of data.

➤ *Poor-quality data and poor-quality metadata frustrates implementation of new business models.*

This statement is true for many corporations. The enormous evidence of failed projects, projects that last years, and projects that finish but fall far short of expectations all point to a lack of understanding of the data beforehand and a lack of appreciation of the quality of the data.

➤ *Poor data quality is a pervasive issue that impacts all corporations and organizations with significant information systems.*

The reasons for poor data quality are the rapid growth in technology, along with the rapid implementation of information systems to use that technology. The change rate of corporate systems has been relentlessly high. As a result, few corporations have been able to avoid data quality problems.

13.2 Moving to a Position of High Data Quality Requires an Explicit Effort

➤ *Data quality deserves an explicit quality assurance function that is fully supported by management.* It is an ongoing requirement.

Getting to a position of high data quality and maintaining it are complex tasks that require dedicated professionals who are armed with appropriate methodologies and tools. It takes a lot of work to fix quality problems and to prevent them from recurring in new ways.

➤ *Data quality must become a part of everyone's job.* The education and inspiration must come from the data quality assurance group.

The data quality assurance group must have the cooperation and effort of many different people to be effective. They need business analysts, subject matter experts, data architects, database administrators, data entry personnel, and others to cooperate and contribute. If they operate entirely within themselves, they cannot succeed.

➤ *The most effective way to organize a data quality assurance function is to work with the data first to find inaccuracies, research them to create issues, and then monitor the progress of issue resolution.*

Many data quality issues lurk in the data without obvious external manifestations. These can often be dug out and used to build a case for making system improvements. Even when issues come from the outside, they need to be investigated in the data to find the extent of the problem and to find related problems that are not as obvious. The data will tell you a lot about itself if you only listen.

➤ *A large return on investment can be realized through helping new initiatives improve the quality of the data they are working with and avoid making new data quality problems through inappropriate transformation or use of data.*

Pure data quality assessment projects have difficulty in gaining approval because of the low promise of return and the disruption it brings to operational environments. Having a data quality assurance team work with funded projects that are trying to change or extend a system can generally return more value to the project than the cost of assessment. In addition, they can improve the quality of the data at the same time. This is a win-win strategy for everyone.

13.3 Data Accuracy Is the Cornerstone for Data Quality Assurance

➤ *Data accuracy is the most fundamental dimension of data quality.*

Although data quality has many dimensions, data accuracy is the foundation dimension. If the data does not represent the true facts, all other dimensions are less important.

➤ *Data profiling technology is the best way to find most data inaccuracy problems.*

Using the inside-out approach by performing extensive analysis over the data is a fast and efficient way to dig out a lot of data inaccuracy issues. It cannot find all issues because it is always possible that data satisfies all rules and is still wrong. However, the majority of bad practices in entering data result in telltale conditions in the data that can be exposed through application of rules.

➤ *Data profiling technology produces accurate and complete metadata as a by-product of the process.*

In addition to finding a lot of inaccurate data, the data profiling process described in this book will also produce an accurate metadata description of the data. This description will generally be more complete and more accurate than any descriptions previously held.

➤ *Data profiling provides a foundation of information for crafting remedies for the problems uncovered.*

The information produced through data profiling technology often provides the clues to the right solutions for improving and monitoring systems.

This is not a definitive book on data quality. It focuses on an aspect that has not been given much coverage but promises to provide major value to corporations. The focus on data accuracy and data profiling technology as a means of improving it is a powerful message to those wanting to do something about poor data quality.

The time has come for corporations to move their interest in the quality of data to a new level. You can expect most corporations to invest in new initiatives aimed at this topic. A failure to do so can mean your competitors will leave you behind.

The big gains are not in the small improvements to your environment, wherein you eliminate shipping the wrong product occasionally, avoid losing a customer from time to time, or get too low a discount from a supplier. The big gains come from being able to respond to business opportunities faster with systems that are resilient and flexible. To be flexible, your systems have to be well documented, and well understood, and the data must be as squeaky clean as possible.

The corporation that implements a new technology or business model in one year will be better off than one that takes three to four years. A corporation that can consolidate data from a merger or acquisition in nine months will beat the competitor who takes three years.

You can achieve high performance in implementing new business models if you make significant improvements in the accuracy of your data and in the metadata that supports it. If nothing is taken from this book other than one fact, it should be this:

➤ *The primary value of a data quality assurance program is to position a corporation to quickly and efficiently respond to new business demands.*

Examples of Column Properties, Data Structure, Data Rules, and Value Rules

This appendix demonstrates definitions of column properties, data structure, data rules, and value rules over a sample database. The information shown is not intended to be exhaustive, just representative. This is not a real database definition; it was invented to demonstrate principles in this book.

A.1 Business Objects

The business objects in this example include INVENTORY data, SUPPLIER data, and PURCHASE_ORDER data. The inventory business object records the current state of parts in the corporation's warehouses. These are parts needed for manufacturing, as well as parts needed for operation of the business. Each part in the inventory has current status information, as well as history information.

The supplier business object describes companies from which parts are acquired. This includes the subject corporation as well: parts that are manufactured internally. It includes information about the supplier, as well as ordering and invoicing information.

The purchase order business object records each order of parts from a supplier. It tracks the order from inception through delivery to the inventory warehouse.

A.2 Tables

The following table definitions exist for these business objects. Figure A.1 shows a diagram of the integration points between them.

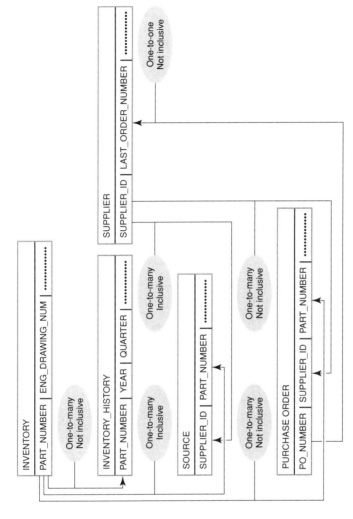

F I G U R E   A . I   Table diagram.

Each part in inventory has a master inventory row in the INVENTORY table and one row in the INVENTORY_HISTORY table for every calendar quarter the part has been carried in inventory.

INVENTORY	
PART_NUMBER	CHARACTER(8)
DESCRIPTION	CHARACTER(20)
TYPE	CHARACTER(1)
UNIT_OF_MEASURE	CHARACTER(3)
QUANTITY_ONHAND	INTEGER
QUANTITY_ONORDER	INTEGER
ENG_DRAWING_NUM	NUMBER(9)
INVENTORY_PRICE	MONEY
LAST_PURCHASE_PRICE	MONEY
DATE_LAST_RECEIVED	DATE
LAST_PURCHASE_ORDER	NUMBER(8)
DO_NOT_ORDER_FLAG	CHARACTER(1)

INVENTORY_HISTORY	
PART_NUMBER	CHARACTER(8)
YEAR	SMALL INTEGER
QUARTER	SMALL INTEGER
QUANTITY_SOLD	INTEGER
QUANTITY_ORDERED	INTEGER
QUANTITY_RECEIVED	INTEGER
NUM_ORDERS_PLACED	INTEGER

Each supplier of parts has one row in the SUPPLIER table and as many rows in the SOURCE table as parts that respective supplier is a source for. A part may be supplied by many suppliers.

SUPPLIER	
SUPPLIER_ID	INTEGER(6)
COMPANY_NAME	CHARACTER(20)
COMPANY_ADDRESS	CHARACTER(20)
CITY	CHARACTER(20)
STATE	CHARACTER(2)
ZIP	CHARACTER(10)
PHONE	CHARACTER(10)
CONTACT_NAME	CHARACTER(20)
DATE_ESTABLISHED	DATE
DATE_LAST_ORDER	DATE
LAST_ORDER_NUMBER	NUMBER(9)

SOURCE	
SUPPLIER_ID	CHARACTER(6)
PART_NUMBER	CHARACTER(8)
SUPPLIER_PART_NUM	CHARACTER(10)
PRIORITY	SMALLINTEGER
MINIMUM_QUANTITY	INTEGER
ORDER_MODE	CHARACTER(1)
ORDER_ADDRESS	CHARACTER(20)
ORDER_EMAIL	CHARACTER(20)
ORDER_EDI_ADDRESS	CHARACTER(20)
BILL_TO_ADDRESS	CHARACTER(20)

Each order for a part causes a single row to be created in the PURCHASE_ORDER table. An order can only order one part.

PURCHASE_ORDER	
PO_NUMBER	NUMBER(9)
DATE_OF _ORDER	DATE
SUPPLIER_ID	INTEGER(6)
PART_NUMBER	CHARACTER(8)
DESCRIPTION	CHARACTER(20)
SUPPLIER_PART_NUM	CHARACTER(10)
QUANTITY	INTEGER
UNIT_OF_MEASURE	CHARACTER(3)
UNIT_PRICE	MONEY
DATE_SHIPPED	DATE
QUANTITY_SHIPPED	INTEGER
DATE RECEVIED	DATE
QUANTITY_RECEIVED	INTEGER
RECEIVED_BY	PERSON_ID
RECEIVED_BY_EXT	CHARACTER(4)
QUANTITY_RETURNED	INTEGER
DATE_RETURNED	DATE
STATUS	CHARACTER(1)
REASON	VARIABLE CHARACTER(200)

A.3 Column Properties

The following is not an exhaustive list of column properties. The following column properties are described to demonstrate concepts.

Domain:	PART_NUMBER
Business Name:	Inventory Part Number
Business Meaning:	Internally generated value to uniquely identify each part maintained in inventory. Numbers are assigned through a single program that is part of the inventory application (NEW_PART_NUMBER). Once assigned, a part number never changes.
Data Type:	CHARACTER
Length Boundaries:	Minimum and maximum are both 8.
Value Rules:	Character pattern requires that the first character identify the business area that owns responsibility for the part number. This must be the uppercase letter A, B, C, D, or E. The remaining seven digits are numerals from 0 to 9. All zeros are permitted.

Storage Name:	INVENTORY.PART_NUMBER
Business Meaning:	Primary key for this table
Domain Name:	PART_NUMBER
Property Rules:	UNIQUE

Storage Name:	INVENTORY_HISTORY.PART_NUMBER
Business Meaning:	Part of primary key for this table
Domain Name:	PART_NUMBER
Property Rules:	NOT NULL

Storage Name:	INVENTORY.TYPE
Business Meaning:	Identifies the type of part. The types that are described are critical manufacturing, general manufacturing, and business general operations.
Domain Name:	None
Business Name:	Inventory Type
Data Type:	CHARACTER
Length Boundaries:	1
Value Rules:	Must come from list of C, G, or O
Property Rules:	NOT NULL

Storage Name:	INVENTORY.UNIT_OF_MEASURE
Business Meaning:	Identifies unit of measure of a part in inventory. This determines the measurement of a minimum unit of the part used for ordering and supplying the part.
Domain Name:	None
Business Name:	Inventory Unit of Measure
Data Type:	CHARACTER
Length Boundaries:	1 to 3 characters
Value Rules:	Must come from list of approved unit of measures. This list is maintained in a separate table called APPROVED_UNIT_OF_MEASURES.
Property Rules:	NOT NULL

Storage Name:	INVENTORY.QUANTITY_ONHAND
Business Meaning:	The amount of a part that is currently on the shelf in the warehouse. The amount available to supply a requisition.
Domain Name:	None
Business Name:	Inventory Quantity Available
Data Type:	INTEGER
Length Boundaries:	Integer restrictions
Value Rules:	Must be in the range 0 to 100000
Property Rules:	NOT NULL

Storage Name:	INVENTORY.DO_NOT_ORDER_FLAG
Business Meaning:	This part number should not be reordered. It has been either discontinued or replaced by another part. Any inventory remaining can be requisitioned until it goes to zero.
Domain Name:	None
Business Name:	Inventory Do Not Order Flag
Data Type:	CHARACTER
Length Boundaries:	1 byte
Discrete Values:	D for do not order; blank for normal
Property Rules:	NOT NULL

Storage Name:	PURCHASE_ORDER.STATUS
Business Meaning:	Defines the current state of the order. It can be either in a state of placed, shipped, received, cancelled, or returned. Cancelled can only be used if not shipped. Returned means the product received was returned. Returns must be for all quantities received.
Domain Name:	None
Business Name:	Purchase Order Status
Data Type:	CHARACTER
Length Boundaries:	1 byte
Discrete Values:	P for placed, S for shipped, R for received, C for cancelled, and X for returned
Property Rules:	NOT NULL and not blank

Storage Name:	PURCHASE_ORDER.REASON
Business Meaning:	A text field that gives a short reason for cancelling an order or returning the parts received
Domain Name:	None
Business Name:	Purchase Order Cancel or Return Explanation
Data Type:	VARIABLE CHARACTER
Length Boundaries:	More than 5 bytes if present
Values:	Any text
Property Rules:	NULLS OK

A.4 Structure Rules

There are a lot of primary key, primary key/foreign key pair, and duplicate data examples in this set of tables. It shows how quickly these can get complex and interrelated.

Primary Keys

Table:	INVENTORY
Key:	PART_NUMBER
Rules:	Unique, not null, and not blank

Table:	INVENTORY
Natural Key:	DESCRIPTION, TYPE
Rules:	Unique, not null, and not blank

Table:	INVENTORY_HISTORY
Key:	PART_NUMBER,YEAR,QUARTER
Rules:	Unique, not null, and not blank

Table:	SUPPLIER
Key:	SUPPLIER_ID
Rules:	Unique, not null, and not blank

Table:	SUPPLIER
Natural Key:	COMPANY_NAME,COMPANY_ADDRESS,CITY,STATE
Rules:	Unique, not null, and not blank

Table:	SOURCE
Key:	PART_NUMBER,SUPPLIER_ID
Rules:	Unique, not null, and not blank

Table:	PURCHASE_ORDER
Key:	PO_NUMBER
Rules:	Unique, not null, and not blank

Primary Key / Foreign Key Pairs

Primary Table:	INVENTORY
Column:	PART_NUMBER
Secondary Table:	INVENTORY_HISTORY
Column:	PART_NUMBER
Characteristic:	ONE-TO-MANY NOT INCLUSIVE
Note:	There may be no history records if the part is new in the current quarter.

Primary Table:	ENGINEERING_DRAWINGS
Column:	ENG_DRAWING_NUMBER
Secondary Table:	INVENTORY
Column:	ENG_DRAWING_NUMBER
Characteristic:	ONE-TO-ONE NOT INCLUSIVE
Note:	This value may be blank in the INVENTORY table. It is used only if the part has a drawing number. All inventory rows of type I for internal must have a drawing number.

Primary Table:	INVENTORY
Column:	PART_NUMBER
Secondary Table:	SOURCE
Column:	PART_NUMBER
Characteristic:	ONE-TO-MANY INCLUSIVE
Note:	All inventory parts must have at least one source. They may have many supplier sources.

Primary Table:	INVENTORY
Column:	PART_NUMBER
Secondary Table:	PURCHASE_ORDER
Column:	PART_NUMBER
Characteristic:	ONE-TO-MANY NOT INCLUSIVE
Note:	A part may not have any orders for it. This is not unusual for a part that is new in inventory.

Primary Table:	SUPPLIER
Column:	SUPPLIER_ID
Secondary Table:	SOURCE
Column:	SUPPLIER_ID
Characteristic:	ONE-TO-MANY INCLUSIVE
Note:	All suppliers must supply at least one part. They may supply many parts.

Primary Table:	SUPPLIER
Column:	SUPPLIER_ID
Secondary Table:	PURCHASE_ORDER
Column:	SUPPLIER_ID
Characteristic:	ONE-TO-MANY NOT INCLUSIVE
Note:	A supplier may have no orders. This would be true for a newly established supplier or one who is a low-priority source for a part.

Primary Table:	PURCHASE_ORDER
Column:	PO_NUMBER
Secondary Table:	SUPPLIER
Column:	LAST_ORDER_NUMBER
Characteristic:	ONE-TO-MANY NOT INCLUSIVE
Note:	A supplier may have no orders.

Duplicate Data

There are three duplicate columns in the set of tables. All of them occur in the PURCHASE_ORDER table. Duplication is done for the purpose of making access to the purchase order information of higher performance without requiring joining information from the other tables.

Primary Table:	INVENTORY
Column:	DESCRIPTION
Secondary Table:	PURCHASE_ORDER
Column:	DESCRIPTION

Primary Table:	INVENTORY
Column:	UNIT_OF_MEASURE
Secondary Table:	PURCHASE_ORDER
Column:	UNIT_OF_MEASURE

Primary Table:	SOURCE
Column:	SUPPLIER_PART_NUMBER
Secondary Table:	PURCHASE_ORDER
Column:	SUPPLIER_PART_NUMBER

A.5 Simple Data Rules

The following are examples of rules that apply to a single business object and often only to a single row of data.

Table:	INVENTORY
Description:	Quantity on order cannot be less than minimum-order quantity.
Rule Logic:	MIN_QUANTITY_ORDER <= QUANTITY_ONORDER

Table:	INVENTORY_HISTORY
Description:	If number of orders placed is zero, the quantity ordered must also be zero.
Rule Logic:	IF NUM_ORDERS_PLACED = 0 THEN QUANTITY_ORDERED = 0

Table:	SUPPLIERS
Description:	The date a supplier is established must not be later than the last order placed with this supplier. Both dates must not be later than the current date.
Rule Logic:	DATE_ESTABLISHED <= DATE_LAST_ORDER AND DATE_ESTABLISHED <= CURRENT_DATE AND DATE_LAST_ORDER <= CURRENT_DATE
Note:	Essentially three rules are put here. One is an object rule and the other two are column rules. It is often easier to put all date-ordering rules into one rule for ease of review and efficiency of execution.

Table:	SOURCE
Description:	The order mode must match the ordering information. If the mode is M for mail, an order address must be provided. If the mode is I for Internet, an e-mail address must be provided. If the mode is E for EDI transactions, the EDI communication address must be provided.
Rule Logic:	IF ORDER_MODE = 'M' THEN ORDER_ADDRESS != BLANK OR IF ORDER_MODE = 'I' THEN ORDER_EMAIL != BLANK OR IF ORDER_MODE = 'E' THEN EDI_ADDRESS != BLANK
Note:	This rule does not require that columns that do not apply to the mode be blank. Tolerating them is certainly not a quality problem, and keeping them around in case a mode is changed in the future may be helpful. It is up to the business analyst to determine whether they should be blanked out if not appropriate to the mode.

Table:	PURCHASE_ORDER
Description:	Various fields have affinities to states. Date shipped and quantity shipped require a status code of shipped, received, or returned. Date received, quantity received, received by, and received by text require a status code of received or returned. Date and quantity returned require a status code of returned. Reason code requires a status code of returned or cancelled.
Rule Logic:	IF STATUS = 'P' THEN (DATE_SHIPPED = NULL AND QUANTITY_SHIPPED=0); IF (STATUS = 'P' OR STATUS = 'S' OR STATUS='C') THEN (DATE_RECEIVED = NULL AND DATE_RECEIVED= 0 AND RECEIVED_BY = BLANK AND RECEIVED_BY_TEXT = BLANK); IF (STATUS != 'R' AND STATUS !='X') THEN REASON = BLANK;
Note:	This is an example of process rules that govern when data is placed in an object.

A.6 Complex Data Rules

Table:	SOURCE
Description:	Source rows for a single part number cannot have two with the same priority.
Rule Logic:	(PART_NUMBER : PRIORITY) IS UNIQUE

Tables:	SOURCE, PURCHASE_ORDER
Description:	The quantity on a purchase order cannot be less than the minimum order quantity for the part.
Rule Logic:	PURCHASE_ORDER.QUANTITY >= SOURCE.MINIMUM_QUANTITY AND PURCHASE_ORDER.PART_NUMBER = SOURCE.PART_NUMBER

Tables:	PURCHASE_ORDER, INVENTORY
Description:	There should be no outstanding orders for parts that are marked *Do not order.*
Rule Logic:	(INVENTORY.PART_NUMBER = PURCHASE_ORDER.PART_NUMBER) AND (INVENTORY.DO_NOT_ORDER_FLAG = 'D') AND (PURCHASE_ORDER.STATUS = 'P' OR PUCHASE_ORDER.STATUS != 'S')
Note:	I wrote this rule as a negative: it selects offenders. It is much easier to express it this way than to express it as a positive state.

A.7 Value Rules

Table:	PURCHASE_ORDER
Description:	Compute the number of orders for the same part in each month period and show all part numbers and the number of orders where the number is greater than three.

Rule Logic:	SELECT	PART_NUMBER, MONTH(DATE_OF_ORDER), YEAR(DATE_OF_ORDER), COUNT (*)
	GROUP BY	PART_NUMBER, MONTH(DATE_OF_ORDER), YEAR(DATE_OF_ORDER)
	WHERE	COUNT(*) > 3

Expectation:	Expect none on the list. The inventory reordering algorithm should be ordering enough quantity not to have to reorder more than once a month. Multiple orders may be acceptable, but only under special circumstances.

Table:	PURCHASE_ORDER
Description:	Compute the total value of all purchase orders for a month by each category of inventory. Then compute the percentage of the total orders placed that each category provided. Compare this with historical distribution of orders.

Rule Logic:	SELECT	INVENTORY.TYPE, SUM(PURCHASE_ORDER.QUANTITY * PURCHASE_ORDER.UNIT_PRICE) MONTH(DATE_OF_ORDER), YEAR(DATE_OF_ORDER), COUNT (*)
	FROM	PURCHASE_ORDER. INVENTORY
	GROUP BY	INVENTORY.TYPE MONTH(DATE_OF_ORDER), YEAR(DATE_OF_ORDER)
	WHERE	INVENTORY.PART_NUMBER = PURCHASE_ORDER.PART_NUMBER

Expectation:	The percentage of the value of orders placed for each category should not vary from month to month by more than 10%.

Content of a Data Profiling Repository

This appendix lists information that can be included in a data profiling repository. This demonstrates the information that needs to be collected and maintained in order to record and demonstrate everything you need to know about a data source. This information is invaluable for use on application modifications or intended new uses. A specific organization may find additional information that can be added to this list to make it even more comprehensive.

Some of this information could be transferred to a formal metadata repository for permanent storage. However, be aware that formal repositories do not have constructs for all of the information listed in this appendix.

B.1 Schema Definition

- Identification of the collection of data that is profiled together

- Business description

- Data steward

- Business analysts with knowledge of objects

B.2 Business Objects

- Name

- Business description

- Tables used to store object data

- Data model of business object

B.3 Domains

- Name

- Description

- Data type

- Length boundaries

- Numeric precision

- Value properties
  - Discrete value list
    - Encoded value meanings
  - Range of values permitted
    - Skip-over rule
  - Character patterns required
  - Character set
  - Character exclusions
  - Text field restrictions

B.4 Data Source

- Type IMS/VSAM/ORACLE/...

- Physical location

- Application name

- Application description

- Database administrator name

- Key dates
  - First deployment date
  - Major change dates

- Extraction information
  - Data conversions needed
  - Overloaded field definitions

- Tables that result from extraction

- Extraction executions
  - Date of extraction
  - Type full or sample

B.5 Table Definitions

- Name

- Descriptive name

- Business meaning

- Columns
  - Name
  - Longer descriptive name
  - Business definition
  - Confidence indicators
    - Trusted
    - Susceptibility to decay
    - Enforcement processes
  - Domain names if inherited
  - Data type
    - Data type discovered
  - Length boundaries
    - Maximum length discovered
    - Minimum length discovered
    - Length distributions discovered
  - Numeric precision
    - Maximum precision discovered
  - Value properties
    - Discrete value list
      - Values discovered
      - Inaccurate values
      - Values not used
      - Value frequency pair list discovered
      - Encoded value meanings

- Range of values permitted
  - Range of values discovered
  - Skip-over rule
    - Skip-over rule violations
- Character patterns required
  - Patterns discovered
- Character set
- Character exclusions
- Text field restrictions
  - Keywords discovered
  - Text constructs discovered (embedded blanks, special characters)
  - Upper/lowercase conventions discovered
  - Leading/trailing blanks discovered
- Property rules
  - Unique rule
    - Uniqueness percentage discovered
  - Consecutive rule
    - Consecutive rule discovered
  - Null rule
    - Null indications
      - Null indications discovered
      - Blank or zero rule
  - Inconsistency points
    - Date of change
    - Description of change
- Functional dependencies
  - LHS columns
  - RHS columns
  - Type
    - Primary key
      - Token
      - Natural

- Denormalized key
- Derived column
  - Rule or formula
- Discovered percentage true
  - Violation values

B.6 Synonyms

- Primary table and columns
- Secondary table and columns
- Type
  - Primary key/foreign key
  - Redundant
  - Domain
  - Merge
- Value correspondence
  - Same
  - Transform
- Inclusivity
  - Inclusive
  - Bidirectional inclusive
  - Exclusive
  - Mixed
- Degree of overlap
  - One-to-one
  - One-to-many
  - Many-to-many
- Value lists
- Violation data

B.7 Data Rules

- Name of rule
- Description of business meaning
- Table names and column names used
- Execution logic
  - Rule logic expression or program or procedure name
- Execution results
  - Date executed
  - Number of rows
  - RowID list of violations with data
- Remedy implementation
  - Date/time implemented
  - Type of implementation
    - Data entry
    - Transaction program
    - Database-stored procedure
    - Periodic checker execution
    - Business process procedure

B.8 Value Rules

- Name of rule
- Description of business meaning
- Table names and column names used
- Execution logic
  - Rule logic expression or program or procedure name
- Result expectations
- Execution results
  - Date executed
  - Number of rows
  - RowID list of violations with data

- Remedy implementation
  - Date/time implemented
  - Type of implementation
    - Data entry
    - Transaction program
    - Database-stored procedure
    - Periodic checker execution
    - Business process procedure

B.9 Issues

- Date/time created
- Description of problem
- Supporting evidence
  - Column properties violations
  - Structure analysis violations
  - Data rule violations
  - Value rule violations
- Remedies recommended
- Remedies accepted
- Remedies implemented
- Evidence supporting improvements
  - Reduction in violations

REFERENCES

Books on Data Quality Issues

Aiken, Peter H., *Data Reverse Engineering*. New York: McGraw-Hill, 1996.

Brackett, Michael H., *Data Resource Quality: Turning Bad Habits into Good Practices*. Englewood Cliffs, NJ: Addison Wesley Longman, 2000.

Brackett, Michael H., *The Data Warehousing Challenge, Taming Data Chaos*. New York: John Wiley & Sons, 1996.

Chen, Jie, and Arjun K. Gupta, *Parametrical Statistical Change Point Analysis*. Boston: Birkhauser (Architectural), 2000.

English, Larry P., *Improving Data Warehouse and Business Information Quality*. New York: John Wiley & Sons, 1999.

Huang, Kuan-Tsae, Yang W. Lee, and Richard Y. Wang, *Quality Information and Knowledge*. Englewood Cliffs, NJ: Prentice Hall, 1999.

Loshin, David, *Enterprise Knowledge Management: The Data Quality Approach*. San Francisco: Morgan Kaufmann, 2001.

Redman, Thomas C., *Data Quality for the Information Age*. Norwood, MA: Artech House, 1996.

Redman, Thomas C., *Data Quality: The Field Guide*. Boston: Digital Press, 2001.

Wang, Richard Y., Mostapha Ziad, and Yang W. Lee, *Data Quality*. Norwell, MA: Kluwer Academic Publishers, 2001.

Books on Data Quality Technologies

Agosta, Lou, *The Essential Guide to Data Warehousing*. Englewood Cliffs, NJ: Prentice Hall, 2000.

Aiken, Peter H., *Building Corporate Portals with XML*. New York: McGraw-Hill Professional, 1999.

Brackett, Michael, *Data Sharing Using a Common Data Architecture*. New York: John Wiley & Sons, 1994.

Brackett, Michael, J. A. Berry, and Gordon S. Linoff, *Mastering Data Mining*. New York: John Wiley & Sons, 2000.

Date, C. J., *What Not How: The Business Rule Approach to Application Development*. Englewood Cliffs, NJ: Addison-Wesley, 2000.

Elmagarmid, Ahmad, Marek Rusinkiewicz, and Amit Sheth (eds.), *Management of Heterogeneous and Autonomous Database Systems*. San Francisco: Morgan Kaufmann, 1999.

Hammer, Michael, *Beyond Reengineering*. New York: HarperCollins Publishers, 1996.

Hammer, Michael, and James Champy, *Reengineering the Corporation*. New York: HarperCollins Publishers, 1993.

Hammer, Michael, and Steven A. Stanton, *The Reengineering Revolution*. New York: HarperCollins Publishers, 1995.

Marco, David, *Building and Maintaining the Meta Data Repository*. New York: Wiley Computer Publishing, 2000.

Miller, Howard W., *Reengineering Legacy Software Systems*. Boston: Digital Press, 1998.

Pyle, Dorian, *Data Preparation for Data Mining*. San Francisco: Morgan Kaufmann Publishers, 1999.

Reingruber, M., and W. Gregory, *The Data Modeling Handbook: A Best Practice Approach to Building Quality Data Models*. New York: John Wiley & Sons, 1994.

Ross, Ronald R., *Business Rule Concepts*. Houston, TX: Business Rule Solutions, 1998.

Ross, Ronald R., *The Business Rule Book,* 2d ed. Houston, TX: Business Rule Solutions, 1997.

Tannenbaum, Adrian, *Metadata Solutions*. New York: Addison Wesley Longman, 2001.

Articles

Abate, Marcey L., Kathleen V. Diegert, and Heather W. Allen, "A Hierarchical Approach to Improving Data Quality," *Data Quality Journal*, vol. 4, no. 1, September 1998.

Aiken, Peter, Victoria Y. Yoon, and Tor Guimaraes, "Managing Organizational Data Resources: Quality Dimensions," *Information Resources Management Journal*, vol. 13, no. 3, July/September 2000.

Betts, Mitch, "Dirty Data, Inaccurate Data Can Ruin Supply Chain Projects," *Computerworld*, December 2001.

Bowen, Paul L., David A. Fuhrer, and Frank M. Guess, "Continuously Improving Data Quality in Persistent Databases," *Data Quality Journal*, vol. 4, no. 1, September 1998.

Disabatino, Jennifer, "Unregulated Databases Hold Personal Data," *Computerworld*, January 2002.

Eckerson, Wayne W., "Data Quality and the Bottom Line," Report of the Data Warehousing Institute, January 2002.

Kimbal, Ralph, "Is Your Data Correct?," *Intelligent Enterprise*, December 2000.

Olson, Jack, "Building a Database Topology Strategy," *Database Programming and Design*, vol. 8, no. 6, June 1995, pp. 52–61.

Olson, Jack, "Database Replication," *Data Management Review*, vol. 7, no. 8, September 1997, pp. 36–40.

Olson, Jack, "Data Profiling: The First Step in Creating a Data Warehouse," *Enterprise Systems Journal*, vol. 14, no. 5, May 1999, pp. 34–36.

Olson, Jack, "Data Profiling: The Key to Success in Integration Projects," *EAI Journal*, vol. 4, no. 2, February 2002, pp. 22–26.

Olson, Jack, "How Accurate Is Data," *Communications News Online Edition*, June 2002.

Stackpole, Beth, "Dirty Data Is the Dirty Little Secret That Can Jeopardize Your CRM Effort," *CIO Magazine*, February 2001, pp. 101–114.

Willshire, Mary Jane, and Donna Meyen, "A Process for Improving Data Quality," *Data Quality Journal*, vol. 3, no. 1, September 1997.

INDEX

A

accuracy, 24–25
accurate data. *See* data accuracy
aggregation correlation analysis, 38–39
    defined, 38
    use of, 39
"analysis paralysis," 142
analytical methods (data profiling), 136–140
    assertion testing, 137
    discovery, 136
    iterations and backtracking, 139
    metadata verification, 139
    software support, 139–140
    visual inspection, 138
analytical techniques, 37–40, 42
    aggregation correlation, 38
    element analysis, 37
    imperfections, 36
    structural analysis, 38
    value correlation, 38
    value inspection, 39
    See also inaccurate data; reverification
applications, migrating to, 230–231
assertion testing, 137
awareness, 9, 10–12

B

backtracking, 139
batch checkers, 212
best practices, 77, 99
bottom-up approach, 131
business case, 103–118
    building, 108–117
    for the corporation, 115–117
    costs of slow responses, 106–107
    for data quality assessment project, 110–112
    defined, 105
    general model, 109
    implementation projects, 110
    for project services, 114

    for services to another project, 113–115
    summary, 118
    for teach and preach, 115
    typical costs, 106
    wasted costs, 106
business meaning, 155–157
    defined, 155
    establishing, 157
    example, 156
    mapping and, 168
    See also column properties
business objects, 132, 133
    data profiling repository, 272
    defined, 216–217
    example, 260
    profiling rules, 225–230
    referring to other business objects, 216–217
    rows, 216
    set, 237–238
business procedures
    complex data rule analysis, 240
    improving, 234–235
    simple data rule analysis, 223–224

C

cardinality, 249–250
causes investigation, 87–94
    approaches, 88
    connecting, with foreign keys, 181
    data events analysis, 89–94
    error clustering analysis, 88–89
    not possible, 88
    requirements, 88
checkers
    batch, 212
    building, 170
    data rule, 234
    defensive, 96
    periodic, 253
    transaction, 252–253

classifying
    columns, 202–203
    functional dependencies, 198–199
    table relationships, 207
COBOL copybooks, 54
column names, 149–151
    defined, 149
    descriptive, 150–151
    overdependence on, 149–150
    prefixed/postfixed, 150
column properties
    business meaning, 155–157, 168
    confidence, 165–166
    data rules vs., 220
    defined, 143
    discrete value list, 160–161
    empty condition rules, 165
    example, 263–265
    length, 159
    multiple conflicting rules, 164
    names, 149–151
    patterns, 164
    physical data type, 157–159
    precision, 159–160
    profiling, 155–167
    range of values, 161
    skip-over rules, 162
    special domains, 164–165
    storage, 157–160, 168
    text column rules, 162–163
    time-related consistency, 166–167
    typical, 149
    valid value, 160–165, 168
    violations of, 132
    See also property lists
column property analysis, 132, 143–172
    data validation, 155
    defined, 143
    discovery from data, 153–154
    goals, 152
    information gathering, 153
    process, 152–155
    results verification, 154–155
    summary, 171–172
    value-level remedies, 169–171
columns, 132, 144–145
    breaking overloaded fields into, 127
    candidate-redundant, 201
    classifying, 194, 202–203
    constant, 176
    date, 195–196
    defined, 121, 144
    defining with structure rules, 133
    derived, 179
    descriptor, 195
    discovering, 203–204
    documentation, 144–145
    duplicate, 268
    free-form text field, 196
    identifier, 194–195

    mapping, 167–169
    object subgrouping, 227–228
    with one value, 156, 194
    quantifier, 195
    redundant, 133
    synonyms, 133, 184–187
    text, 162–163
    unused, 156
    values, 144, 148
    See also column properties; data profiling
completeness, 26
complex data rule analysis, 135, 237–245
    data gathering, 239–240
    definitions, 237–238
    mapping with other applications, 244
    output validation, 240
    process, 238–240
    process illustration, 239
    summary, 245
    testing, 240
    See also data rule analysis; simple data rule
      analysis
complex data rules
    aggregations, 243
    dates and time, 241–242
    example, 270
    exclusivity, 242–243
    execution, 241
    location, 242
    lookup, 243–244
    remedies, 245
    types of, 241–244
    See also data rules; simple data rules
confidence, 165–166
    defined, 165
    examples, 165–166
    scorekeeping, 166
    See also column properties
consistency, 29–30
    as accuracy part, 29–30
    time-related, 166–167
    See also inconsistencies
consolidations, 53, 231–232
consultants, 17
continuous monitoring, 100–101
    elements, 101
    with issues tracking, 101
corporations
    business case for, 115–117
    data sources, importance to, 111
    decisions, 115–117
correct information
    not given, 47–48
    not known, 47
correlation, 21–22
    aggregation, 38
    complex data rules, 244
    value, 38
costs
    of achieving accurate data, 108

of conducting assessment, 112
hidden, 111
identified, 111
new system implementation, 13
poor-quality data, 255–256
of slow response, 106–107
transaction rework, 13
typical, 106
wasted, 106
cross-company systems, 7
customer relationship management (CRM), 6, 14
concept, 107
implementations, 16
initiatives, 107
customer-centric model, 16

D

data
breakdown, 33
consolidation, 53
as data profile input, 126–129
decay, 92
delivery delays, 13
discovery from, 153–154
duplicate, 268
extracting, 58–59, 126–129
flattening, 59
integration, 7, 62
loading, 61
matching, 56–57
moving/restructuring, 52–62
normal forms of, 181–184
as precious resource, 3–5
qualifying, 82–83
rejection, 11
replication, 6–7
standardized representation, 170
using, 62–63
data accuracy
air quality analogy, 34
business case for, 103–118
characteristics, 29
consistency, 29–30
content, 29
costs, 108
as data quality assurance cornerstone,
257–259
decay, 50–51
defined, 29–32
form, 29
as fundamental requirement, 3, 23
improvement effects, 40
lack of, 3
object-level, 31–32
percentages, 34
problems, occurrence of, 67
summary, 41–42

total, 34–35
value of, 103–107
data capture processes, 89–92
auto-assist in recording process, 91–92
distance between event and recording, 90
error checking in recording process, 92
evaluation factors, 90
fact availability at recording, 90
feedback to recorder, 91
information verification at recording, 91
motivation of person doing recording, 91
number of handoffs after recording, 90
remedies, 95
skill of person doing recording, 91
time between event and recording, 90
data cleansing, 59–60
adding, 96–97
defined, 59
leaving out rows and, 60
problems, 59
routines, 59, 60
as short-term remedy, 97
tools, 21–22, 53
uses, 96–97
as value-level remedy, 171
data elements
analysis, 37
delay-prone, 50
matching, 56–57
revealing significant variances, 89
use of, 33
value indicators, 46
See also values
data entry
data rules checked during, 233
deliberate errors, 47–48
flawed processes, 44–46
forms, 45
as inaccuracy source, 44–49
mistakes, 44
null problem, 46
processes, 45
system problems, 48–49
windows, 45
data events analysis, 89–94
conversion to information products, 93–94
data capture processes, 89–92
data decay, 92
data movement/restructuring processes,
92–93
points of examination, 89
data gathering (complex data rules), 239–240
business procedures, 240
database-stored procedures, 239
source code scavenging, 239
speculation, 240
See also complex data rule analysis
data gathering (simple data rules), 221–224
business procedures, 223–224

data gathering (simple data rules) (*continued*)
    database-stored procedures, 222–223
    source code scavenging, 221–222
    speculation, 224
    See also simple data rule analysis
data management
    lack of, 1
    team training, 15
    technology, 1
data marts, 61
data models, 189–190
    building, 209
    developing, 209–210
    for primary/foreign key pairs identification, 200
    validating, 210
data monitoring, 20 21
    adding, 96
    continuous checking, 100–101
    database, 21
    defined, 20
    post-implementation, 99–101
    transaction, 20–21
    validation, 100
data profiling, 20
    "analysis paralysis," 142
    analysts, 123, 127, 134
    analytical methods, 136–140
    approaches, 20
    assertion testing, 137
    bottom-up approach, 131
    column property analysis, 132, 143–172
    complex data rules, 240–244
    conclusion, 83
    as core competency technology, 142
    data rule analysis, 134–135, 215–245
    data type and, 159
    defined, 20, 53, 119
    discovery, 136
    emergence, 119–120, 141
    errors, 82
    extraction for, 126–129
    as foundation for remedies, 258–259
    general model, 123–130
    goals, 122
    important databases, 140
    inputs, 124–129
    iterations and backtracking, 139
    for knowledge base creation, 122
    metadata verification, 139
    methodology, 130–135
    model illustration, 123
    output, 20
    overview, 121–142
    participants, 123–124
    process, 122
    process steps, 131–132
    products, 53
    of secondary data stores, 140
    software support, 139–140
    steps diagram, 131
    structure analysis, 132–134, 173–214
    technology, 119–120, 122, 258
    text columns, 163
    value rule analysis, 135, 246–254
    visual inspection, 138
    when to use, 140–141
data profiling outputs, 129–130
    facts, 130
    latency, 130
    metadata, 129
data profiling repository
    business objects, 272
    content, 272–278
    data rules, 217, 277
    data source, 273–274
    defined, 121
    domains, 273
    inconsistency points in, 167
    information, 124
    issues, 278
    schema definition, 272
    synonyms, 276
    table definitions, 274–276
    value rules, 277–278
data quality
    awareness, 9, 10–12
    characterization of state, 9
    defined, 24
    definitions, 24–27
    emergence, 70
    as everyone's job, 257
    facts, 130
    high, moving to position of, 256–257
    improvement requirements, 14–15
    issues management, 80–102
    as maintenance function, 104
    as major corporate issue, 255–256
    money spent on, 105
    as universally poor, 10
    visibility, 1
data quality assessment project, 110–112
    age of application, 112
    future costs potential, 111
    hidden costs potential, 111
    identified costs, 111
    importance to corporation, 111
    likelihood of major change, 112
    primary value, 259
    pure, 257
    robustness of implementation, 112
    See also business case
data quality assurance, 67–79
    activities, 75–78
    comparison, 74–75
    data accuracy as cornerstone, 257–259
    department, 69–71
    educational materials, 18
    elements, 16
    experts and consultants, 17

as explicit effort, 256–257
as full-time task, 70
functions, 71
group, 69–71
implementation, 118
initiatives, 23
methodologies, 18
organizing, 257
program components, 71
program goals, 68
program structure, 69–78
project services, 75–77
rationale, 105
software development parallel, 70
software tools, 18–22
stand-alone assessments, 77
summary, 78–79
teach and preach function, 77–78
team, 68, 76, 77
technology, 16–22
data quality assurance methods, 71–75
comparison illustration, 72
inside-out, 72–73
outside-in, 73–74
types of, 71–72
data quality problems, 3–23
fixing requirements, 14–15
hiding, 11
impact, 12–14
liability consequences, 12
reasons for not addressing, 12
scope, 14
data rule analysis, 134–135
complex, 135, 237–245
definitions, 216–220
simple, 134–135, 215–236
data rule checkers, 234
data rule repository, maintaining, 235
data rules
in assertion testing, 137
column properties vs., 220
data profiling repository, 217, 277
dates, 226–227
defined, 134, 215, 217, 238
derived-value, 229
durations, 227
evaluation, 232–234
exceptions, 219
execution, 225–226, 241
hard, 218–219, 238
loose definition, 219
multiple-rows/same column, 230
as negative rules, 217
object subgrouping columns, 227–228
process rules vs., 219–220, 238
relationships, 215
soft, 218–219, 238
sources, 137
syntax examples, 218
tight definition, 219

types of, 226–230, 241–244
work flow, 228–229
See also complex data rules; simple data rules
data source, 273–274
data transformation routines, building, 170–171
data types, 157–159
character, noncharacter data in, 157–158
defined, 157
profiling and, 159
typical, 158
See also column properties
data warehouses, 61
database management systems (DBMSs), 22
correct data, 22
for structural role enforcement, 134
database monitors, 21
database procedures
complex data rule analysis, 239
simple data rules analysis, 222–223
databases, 6
data integration, 7
definitions, 190
demands on, 8
design anticipation, 27–28
errors, 49
factors, 10
flexibility, 28–29
importance, 8
quality, 9
source, 54, 56–57, 59, 169–170, 212
target, 56–57
date(s)
columns, 195–196
complex data rules, 241–242
domain, 146
extreme numbers on, 252
simple data rules, 226–227
decay
in cause investigation, 92
problems, 92
decay-prone elements, 50–52
accuracy, over time, 51
characteristics, 50
decay rate, 52
handling, 51–52
decision-making efficiency, 41
decisions
based on hard facts, 115–116
based on intuition, 116–117
based on probable value, 116
defensive checkers, 96
deliberate errors, 47–48
correct information not given, 47–48
correct information not known, 47
falsifying for benefit, 48
See also errors
denormalization, 59
cases of, 182–183
use of, 59

denormalized form, 182–183
denormalized keys, 179
denormalized tables, 182, 183
    data repetition, 183
    in relational applications, 214
derived columns, 179
derived-value rules, 229
descriptor columns, 195
discovery, 136
    of column properties, 153–154
    of functional dependencies, 191, 196–197
    homonym, 204
    in structure analysis, 191–192
    of synonyms, 203–204
discrete value list, 160–161
domains, 145–148
    concept, 145
    data profiling repository, 273
    date, 146
    defined, 145
    external standards, 147
    macro-issues, 148
    metadata repository, 145
    micro-issues, 148
    special, 164–165
    unit of measure, 147–148
    zip code, 147
domain synonyms, 186–187
    defined, 186
    existence, 187
    structural value and, 186
    testing for, 205
    See also synonyms
duplicate data, 268
durations, 227

education, 77–78
educational materials, 18
element analysis, 37
    defined, 37
    use of, 39
empty condition rules, 165
error clustering analysis, 88–89
    data elements, 89
    definition of, 88
    See also causes investigation
errors
    data profiling, 82
    deliberate, 47–48
    extraction, 127
    finding, 21
    fixing, 21
    structure, 188
ETL (extract, transform, and load)
    processes, 52
    products, 53

experts, 17
extraction, 58–59, 126–129
    for data profiles, 126–129
    into decision support systems, 232
    defined, 58
    denormalization and, 59
    errors, 127
    failure, 128
    flattening and, 59
    issues, too many, 129
    logic verification, 127
    REDEFINE and OCCURS clauses, 59, 127
    routines, 59, 127
    structure analysis and, 187–188
extreme values, 251–252

falsification, 48
field overloading, 152
first-normal form, 181
fixed source systems, 212
foreign keys, 180–181
    defined, 180
    in dependent tables, 180
    uses, 180–181
    See also keys
free-form text fields, 196
frequency distributions, 250–251
functional dependencies, 174–176
    candidate, determining, 193–196
    classifying, 198–199
    defined, 174
    denormalized, 182
    discovering, 191, 196–197
    finding, 192, 193–199
    illustrated, 175
    LHS of, 174
    marking, 197
    as meta definition of structure, 176
    primary key, 176, 199
    speculation, 193–194
    testing, 197–198
    See also structure analysis

group comparisons, 252
hard data rules, 218, 238
hidden costs, 111
homonym discovery, 204

identified costs, 111
identifier columns, 194–195

impacts
    already happening, 86
    assessing, 85–87
    documenting, 87
    not yet happening, 87
    See also issues
inaccurate data
    acceptance of, 8–9
    blame for, 9–10
    cause investigation, 87–94
    clustering of, 35
    cost, 9, 15
    distribution of, 32–34
    facts, recording, 207–209
    finding, 35–40
    impact, 12–14
    impact assessment, 85–87
    increase in, 8
    reasons for, 34
    remedy development, 94–99
    tolerance levels, 40–41
inaccurate data sources, 43–64
    areas, 43
    data accuracy decay, 50–52
    initial data entry, 44–49
    moving/restructuring data, 52–62
    problem scope, 63
    using data, 62–63
inclusive relationship, 203
inconsistencies
    actual point, finding, 167
    change-induced, 30
    finding with programmatic methods, 167
    object-level, 32
    reasons for, 167
information gathering (column property
        analysis), 153
information gathering (structure analysis),
        189–191
    commonsense speculation, 191
    data models, 189–190
    database definitions, 190
    metadata repositories, 189
information products, conversion to, 93–94
information systems
    complexity, 7
    continuous evolution of, 5–8
    importance, 105
information technology
    evolution, 10
    management, 11
inside-out method, 72–73
    analysis, 72
    defined, 72
    inaccurate data evidence, 73
    outside-in method comparison, 74–75
    problem catching, 74
    rule set, 72
    See also data quality assurance methods

integration, 7, 62
intended use decisions, 169
investigations, 80, 81
    cause, 87–94
    facts, 81
    outside-in, 86
issue collection, 81–85
    metrics, 82–85
    output, 85
issue management, 80–102
    cause investigation, 87–94
    impact assessment, 85–87
    phases, 81
    post-implementation monitoring, 99–101
    remedy development, 94–99
    remedy implementation, 99
    summary, 101–102
issues
    crystallizing, 87
    data profiling repository, 278
    defined, 85
    impact assessment of, 85–87
    life-span, 101
    recording, 85
    tracking, 101

K–L

keys, 176–181
    defined, 176
    denormalized, 179
    foreign, 180–181
    illustrated, 177
    natural, 208
    primary, 176–179
    token, 178
    See also structure analysis
length property, 159
loading, 61
location, 242
lookup, 243–244

M

matching data elements, 56–57
    defined, 56
    problems, 56–57
    structural, 57
    See also data elements
merge synonyms, 187
merge tables, 207
    horizontal, 209
    multiple, 211
    vertical, 209
    See also tables
metadata
    as data profiling input, 124–126
    as data profiling output, 129

metadata (*continued*)
    judging, 154
    matching, to discovered properties, 154
    on column-level layout, 125
    verification, 139
metadata repositories, 19
    domains, 145
    failures, 19
    as new frontier, 64
    poor quality data in, 54
    in primary/foreign key pairs identification, 200
    in structure analysis, 189
    synonym candidates in, 199
methodologies, 18
metrics, 82–85
    benefits, 82 83
    comparing, 83
    drawbacks, 83–85
    examples, 82
    for qualification, 82–83
    as shock factor, 84–85
    uses, 82–83
moving/restructuring data, 52–62
    in cause investigation, 92–93
    data cleansing, 59–60
    with ETL processes, 52
    extraction, 58–59
    integration, 62
    loading, 61
    matching, 56–57
    overloaded fields and, 55–56
    problems, 53
    projects requiring, 54
    reasons, 52–53
    steps, 62
    tools, 52
    transforms, 60
    See also inaccurate data sources
multiple conflicting rules, 164
multiple-source tables, 211

N

normal forms, 181–184
    denormalized, 182–183
    example, 182
    first-, 181
    second-, 181
    split table, 184
    third-, 182
normalization, 128
null, 151
    defined, 151
    indications, 165
    problem, 46

O

object-level accuracy, 31–32
object-level inconsistencies, 32
orphans, 208–209
outside-in method, 73–74
    defined, 73
    facts, 73
    inside-out method comparison, 74–75
    problem catching, 74
    result, 74
    See also data quality assurance methods
overloaded fields, 55–56
    broken into columns, 127
    defined, 55, 152
    examples, 55
    separation need, 128

P

partitioned tables, 207
patterns, 164
periodic checkers, 253
PL/1 INCLUDE file, 125, 144
poor-quality data
    cost, 255–256
    new business models and, 256
    problem, 255
    See also inaccurate data
poor-quality data impact, 12–14
    areas, 12–13
    data delivery delays, 13
    lost customers, 14
    lost production, 14
    new system implementation costs, 13
    transaction rework costs, 13
    See also data quality problem; inaccurate data
post-change monitoring, 99–101
precision property, 159–160
primary keys, 176–179
    defined, 176
    example, 178–179, 266
    functional dependency, 176, 199
    as key to the table, 179
    NULL, 208
    violations, 208
    See also keys
primary/foreign key synonyms, 185–186
    analyzing, 205–206
    example, 267–268
    testing for, 204
primary/secondary table relationship, 207
process rules
    data rules vs., 219–220, 238
    defined, 219
    use of, 219

projects
    case for providing services to, 113–115
    justification, 113
    services, 75–77, 114
property lists, 148–149
    defined, 148
    domain definition, 155
    illustrated, 149
    as output, 155
    See also column properties

Q–R

qualification, 82–83
quality assurance group, 110
quality team, 108
quantifier columns, 195
range of values, 161
redundant data synonyms, 186
reengineering applications, 97
relational systems, 63
    denormalized tables in, 214
    short/long text, 145
    shortcomings, 214
    structural issues, 214
relevance, 25
remedies, 94–99
    as best practices, 99
    data capture processes, 95
    data cleansing, 96–97
    data monitoring, 96
    defensive checkers, 96
    developing, 94–99
    implementing, 99
    multiple-object data rule remedies, 245
    practical vs. impractical, 98–99
    range of, 94
    reengineering applications, 97
    scope of, 94–97
    short-term vs. long-term, 97–98
    structure-level, 212–213
    for value rule violations, 252–253
    value-level, 169–171
replication, 6–7
restructuring data. *See* moving/restructuring data
reverification, 35–37, 42
    drawbacks, 36–37
    error susceptibility, 36
    time, 36
    See also analytical techniques; inaccurate
        data

S

same-table synonyms, 205–207
    with data not in first-normal form, 206
    primary/foreign key, 205–206
    See also synonyms

sampling, 126
schema definition, 272
second-normal form, 181
simple data rule analysis, 134–135, 215–236
    consolidations, 231–232
    data gathering, 221–224
    decision support systems, 232
    definitions, 216–220
    mapping with other applications, 230–232
    migrating to new applications and, 230–231
    output validation, 225
    paralysis, 235
    process, 220–225
    process illustration, 221
    summary, 235–236
    testing, 224–225
    See also complex data rule analysis; data rule
        analysis
simple data rules
    checked during data entry, 233
    checked during transaction processing, 233
    checkers for periodic checks, 234
    checkers for transactions, 234
    dates, 226–227
    deferred for execution, 233
    derived-value, 229
    durations, 227
    evaluation, 232–234
    example, 269–270
    execution, 225
    multiple-row/same column, 230
    no need to be checked, 234
    object subgrouping columns, 227–228
    remedies, 232–235
    types of, 226–230
    work flow, 228–229
single-source tables, 210–211
skip-over rules, 162
soft data rules, 218, 238
software support, 139–140
software tools, 18–22
    data cleansing, 21–22
    data monitoring, 20–21
    data profiling, 20
    DBMS, 22
    emergence of, 18
    metadata repositories, 19
    See also data quality assurance
source code scavenging, 221–222, 239
source databases, 54
    denormalization, 59
    fixed, 212
    improving, 169–170
    matching to target databases, 56–57
special domains, 164–165
    benefit, 164–165
    examples, 164
    See also column properties

speculation
    functional dependencies, 193–194
    gathering complex data rules through, 240
    gathering simple data rules through, 224
    in structure analysis, 191
split table
    form, 184
    relationship, 207
stand-alone assessments, 77
storage properties, 157–160
    length, 159
    mapping and, 168
    physical data type, 157–159
    precision, 159–160
structural matching, 57
structure analysis, 38, 132–134, 173–214
    data discovery, 191–192
    defined, 38, 132
    definitions, 173–187
    elements, 133
    extraction and, 187–188
    functional dependencies, 174–176
    information gathering, 189–191
    issues, 173
    keys, 176–181
    normal forms, 181–184
    process, 188–193
    process illustration, 189
    results verification, 192–193
    summary, 213–214
    synonyms, 184–187
    uses, 39, 134
    violations, 134
    See also data profiling
structure rules, 173, 193–210
    consequences, 173
    example, 266–268
structure-level remedies, 212–213
subgrouping rules, 227–228
subsetting, 220
substitution correction, 21
synonyms, 184–187
    analysis, 184
    analyzing, in same table, 205–207
    candidate, determining, 199–202
    characteristics, determining, 205
    data profiling repository, 276
    defined, 184
    degree of overlap, 203
    domain, 186–187
    finding, 199–209
    inclusive relationship, 203
    merge, 187
    multiple-column example, 201
    primary/foreign key, 185–186
    redundant data, 186, 205
    same-table, 205–206
    testing for, 204–205
    types of, 184–185, 202

value correspondence, 220–223
    violations, 208
system problems, 48–49

T

tables, 132
    business object, 133
    classifying relationships between, 207
    defined, 121
    definitions in data profiling repository,
        274–276
    denormalized, 182, 183
    dependent, 180
    diagram, 261
    example, 260–263
    key to, 179
    merge, 207
    metadefinition of structure in, 176
    multiple-source, 211
    parent, 180
    partitioning relationship, 207
    primary/secondary relationship, 207
    single-source, 210–211
    split relationship, 207
    splitting, 184
    See also data profiling
target databases
    forcing data into, 57
    matching source databases to, 56–57
    metadata repositories matching, 76
teach and preach, 77–78
    business case for, 115
    preach, 78
    teach, 77–78
testing
    complex data rules, 240
    functional dependencies, 197–198
    simple data rules, 224–225
    for synonyms, 204–205
text columns
    generic, 163
    profiling, 163
    rules, 162–163
    types of, 163
    See also column properties
third-normal form, 182
timeliness, 25
time-related consistency, 166–167
tolerance levels, 40–41
    above, 40
    step function influence on, 41
    See also inaccurate data
top-down approach, 131
transaction(s)
    checkers, 252–253
    monitors, 20–21
    processing, 233

transforms, 60
trust, 26–27
typical costs, 106

U

understanding, 26
unintended uses
    principle of, 27–29
    proliferation, 27
    reasons for, 27
    requirements for addressing, 27–29
unit of measure domain, 147–148
using data, 62–63
    data information and, 63
    quality levels and, 63
    See also inaccurate data sources

V

validation
    changes, 100
    column property analysis, 155
    complex data rule output, 240
    data model, 210
    data monitoring, 100
    range of values, 161
    simple data rule output, 225
valid value properties, 160–165
    discrete value list, 160–161
    list of, 160
    mapping and, 168
    multiple conflicting rules, 164
    patterns, 164
    range of values, 161
    skip-over rules, 162
    special domains, 164–165
    text column rules, 162–163
    See also column properties
value correlation analysis, 38–39
    defined, 38
    use of, 39
value-level remedies, 169–171
    data checkers, 170
    data cleansing, 171
    intended use decisions, 169
    source systems improvement, 169–170
    standardized data representation, 170

transformations for moving data, 170–171
    See also column property analysis
value mapping, 204–205
value rule analysis, 135, 246–254
    definitions, 246–249
    evaluation step, 248–249
    execution step, 248
    gathering step, 247
    process, 247–249
    process illustration, 247
    summary, 253–254
value rules
    cardinality, 249–250
    data profiling repository, 277–278
    defined, 246–247
    evaluating, 248–249
    example, 271
    executing, 248
    extreme values, 251–252
    frequency distributions, 250–251
    gathering, 247
    group comparisons, 252
    types of, 249–252
values
    column, 144, 148
    consistency and, 29–30
    distribution of, 39
    extreme, 251–252
    inaccurate, finding, 35–40
    indicators, 46
    inspection, 39
    missing, 30–31
    range of, 161
    valid, 30
    See also data elements
verification
    column property analysis results, 154–155
    data capture information, 91
    metadata, 139
    structure analysis results, 192–193
visual inspection, 138, 247
VSAM data source, 125

W–Z

wasted costs, 106
work flow rules, 228–229
zip code domain, 147

ABOUT THE AUTHOR

Jack Olson has spent the last 36 years developing commercial software. His career includes several years at IBM, BMC Software, Peregrine Systems, and Evoke Software. His jobs included programmer, programming team leader, development manager, product architect, corporate architect, vice president of development, and chief technology officer. Most of the projects he worked on included data management systems or tools. He is considered an expert in the field of database management systems. At Evoke Software he created the concept of data profiling and has evolved concepts for building understanding of databases at the content, structure, and quality levels. He has a B.S. degree from the Illinois Institute of Technology and an M.B.A. from Northwestern University.